nebraska symposium on motivation
1971

Nebraska Symposium on Motivation, 1971, is Volume XIX in the series on Current Theory and Research In Motivation

nebraska symposium on motivation
1971

James K. Cole, Editor

David Elkind

Professor of Psychology
University of Rochester

Langdon E. Longstreth

Professor of Psychology
University of Southern California

Margaret Donaldson

Professor of Psychology
University of Edinburgh

Albert Mehrabian

Professor of Psychology
University of California, Los Angeles

Ralph Exline

Professor of Psychology
University of Delaware

Paul Ekman

Professor of Psychology
University of California, San Francisco

university of nebraska press
lincoln
1971

Publishers on the Plains

UNP

Copyright © 1972 by the University of Nebraska Press
International Standard Book Number 0–8032–0613–5
Library of Congress Catalog Card Number 53–11655
Manufactured in the United States of America

Contents

Introduction

In the 1967 volume of the *Nebraska Symposium on Motivation*, an attempt was made to invite speakers who were working on similar problems instead of a series of generally unrelated papers as had been the practice in prior years. Subsequent volumes continued to be organized according to themes, with each volume containing two themes representing the two sessions held each year. The current volume continues this procedure, with one section devoted to developmental psychology or, more specifically, cognitive theories of development, and a second section on nonverbal communication.

We are planning to develop the thematic approach further next year by devoting the entire volume (both sessions during the year) to one theme: aggression. Furthermore we plan to have a general paper by a discussant in addition to the six regularly scheduled papers. I will continue to serve as general editor, but we will also have Professor Don Jensen, who will serve in the capacity of organizing the content of the symposium, and he will participate directly in the sessions as author of the discussion paper.

In the present volume Professors David Elkind, Margaret Donaldson, and Langdon Longstreth are the contributors to the section on developmental psychology, and Professors Albert Mehrabian, Ralph Exline, and Paul Ekman are the contributors to the nonverbal communication section.

Professor Elkind's paper is concerned with the hypothesis that cognitive growth involves characteristic growth cycles. In the process of development, cognitive abilities pass through phases which include stimulus seeking in which stimuli become nutriments for further cognitive growth, repetitive behavior, stimulus gating and storage, and intellectual play. These phases are the major components of cognitive realization cycles and are involved in the development of simple and complex mental abilities, from rote memory to perception, language, and reasoning. Professor Elkind addresses himself to the task of documenting the evidence for the phases of cognitive realization cycles in the development of these

mental abilities. In reviewing rote memory development, which
develops early in children and terminates in the older child,
Professor Elkind suggests two corollary hypotheses: (a) motivation
inherent in the development of cognitive structures is largely
dissipated once the structures are fully formed, and (b) completed
mental structures require additional, extrinsic motivation for
continued activation and utilization.

After reviewing the evidence for cognitive growth realization in
the development of rote memory, perception, language, and
reasoning abilities, Professor Elkind explores the implications of the
hypotheses on critical periods, accelerated mental growth, and the
role of intrinsic or extrinsic motivation in learning and motivation.
Professor Elkind considers cognitive growth cycles as critical
periods. The possibility of accelerating growth processes depends
upon types of mental abilities, individual characteristics of children,
and the aims of acceleration. With careful consideration of these
factors, training may help maximize the development of mental
abilities. Once cognitive structures are established (primarily
through intrinsic motivation), extrinsic motivation becomes
necessary to ensure their effective utilization. The view that learning
will occur when the child is happy and has the opportunity to learn
may not apply when cognitive structures are established, and
additional extrinsic motivation is necessary to perpetuate their
optimal use.

Professor Donaldson's paper, "Preconditions of Inference,"
discusses the cognitive capacities that appear to be related to the
origins of the ability to engage in inferential thinking. In general
she believes that there is current evidence that basic capacities in
very young children have been underestimated in the recent past.

Professor Donaldson approaches the problem of a theory of reference by analyzing the necessity for inferential activity to handle
relationships of compatibility and incompatibility. Basic questions
relating to this issue involve the capacity to distinguish between
compatible-incompatible relationships, types of specific compatibility judgments, extent of judgments, and dependability of judgments. Evidence for inferential activity can be obtained from two
main sources: (a) tasks designed and controlled by the experimenter, and (b) observation of children in situations not contrived

by the experimenter. The view that young children are exceedingly limited in their inferential ability comes mostly from the former situation. However, there is evidence from the latter situation of complicated inferential behavior in young children. Professor Donaldson then discusses the problem of conditions and constraints that affect the ability to observe inferential behavior in young children.

In addition to general inferential capacity in young children, Professor Donaldson explores capacities of a more specific nature, such as apprehension of central concepts like space, time, or magnitude. She examines the notion that cognitive development proceeds in an orderly, progressive succession of increased capacity. Recent evidence suggests that development proceeds with instances of temporary increase in erroneous or inadequate responding. These data raise the possibility that primitive capacities have not been detected because their operation is obscured at later ages, and the presence of early cognitive skills may be interfered with by other developments.

Professor Longstreth addresses his paper to the concept of secondary reinforcement (S^r) and presents the argument that the S^r concept formulations can be explained better by cognitive analysis. In critically reviewing animal and human studies which are purported to demonstrate S^r effects or which require a secondary reinforcement explanation, Professor Longstreth concludes that the facts supporting the explanation are not evident, and much of the research is methodologically inadequate. Thus the incentive value of "secondary reinforcement" has not been demonstrated. At best the studies on secondary reinforcement illustrate an "associative function" of certain stimuli after certain operations. Much of the data illustrate a frustration effect rather than an S^r effect when a stimulus is paired with a reward and then presented alone.

Professor Longstreth proposes a cognitive interpretation to explain presumed S^r effects and cites evidence to support this view. The cognitive view asserts that a subject reasons about the contingencies between present behavior and future rewards or goals, and his behavior is directed by the implications of his reasoning. Behavior is directed by rational or logical cognitive processes. Subjects process information and develop plans based upon their interpretation of the information to reach a particular outcome. The reinforcing event does not exert an automatic effect; rather, the subject's belief about the event and its relationship to his plan for outcome is the important factor.

In the section on nonverbal communication, Professor Mehrabian focuses on the multidimensional characterization of the referents of nonverbal communication in contrast to approaches which identify discrete nonverbal behaviors and their specific referents. He begins by exploring a semantic space for nonverbal behavior. This approach attempts to identify a general set of categories to characterize communication from a detailed consideration of the referents. Professor Mehrabian reviews the experimental data on facial and vocal expressions, hand gestures, posture and position, and movements and implicit aspects of verbalization, and relates these data to three referential dimensions: evaluation, potency or status, and responsiveness. He believes the three dimensions are aspects of very basic social orientations based upon early developmental and primitive forms of communication, common to both man and animals. Positive-negative affect and evaluation characterize early infancy and are retained in adult life. Potency is particularly important as an aspect of social control and in establishing patterns of social interaction. Responsiveness is a social counterpart of the orienting reflex, the differential responsiveness of humans and animals to aspects of their social environment. All three dimensions represent basic aspects of intelligent or adaptive functioning.

In the remaining portion of his paper, Professor Mehrabian discusses recent experiments on implicit communication cues using factor analyses of verbal and nonverbal cues in social situations; experiments where affiliative behavior is assessed from audio recordings; experiments on complex communications or multichannel communication; an analysis of verbal, vocal, and facial attitudes in terms of a linear equation; the decoding and use of consistent and inconsistent communications; inconsistent communications and psychotherapy; and finally, potential application of the findings of implicit communication in everyday and experimental situations.

Professor Exline's paper is concerned with the relationship between visual interaction between people, and human preference and power. His data suggest that people prefer a moderate amount of visual contact when they are engaged in face-to-face interactions. He explores this interaction in relationship with competition, sex, and need for affiliation. Using eye-contact recordings, Professor Exline found that women engage in more visual interaction than men, and there was significant interaction of affiliation, competitiveness, and sex upon the tendency to engage in mutual glances. Listeners gave more visual attention to another than speakers, and mutual glances were relatively rare in task-oriented discussions. People are more likely to engage in mutual glances when the interaction is perceived as attractive rather than aversive. By creating an experimental situation where certain subjects had power over rewards for the other subjects, Professor Exline found that less powerful subjects looked more at high-power subjects. By measuring subject orientation toward controlling others in their environment, Professor Exline in another study found high-control-oriented subjects looking more at a confederate than low-control-oriented subjects, when both were speaking or listening.

One compelling observation by Professor Exline is the tendency to avoid visual contact. The primate literature suggests that glance behavior is related to threat display and dominance hierarchy. Professor Exline found that human eye contact with the rhesus macaque can serve as a dominance challenge, eliciting attack and threat behavior, and aversion of the gaze will inhibit threat display by the monkey. When the stimulus posture was assumed with eyes closed the monkeys rarely responded with a threat display. Body movement and posture did not seem to be related to threat display.

Professor Ekman's paper, "Universals and Cultural Differences in Facial Expressions," focuses on the question of the relationship between facial expression and emotion, whether or not emotional facial expressions differ between cultures, and whether there are universal facial expressions for various emotions. The relativist (culture-specific) view has traditionally dominated psychology, possibly because of psychology's suspicion or bias regarding the notion of innate causation which is inherent in the universalist position.

Professor Ekman and his coworkers propose a neuro-cultural theory of facial expressions which states that there are universal relationships between facial muscles and specific emotions (fear, anger, happiness, etc.), but cultural differences occur as a result of variability across cultures in learning the elicitors of particular emotions, in learning display rules for controlling emotions in social settings, and in terms of varying cultural consequences of emotional expression. Thus Professor Ekman's theory incorporates both universal (neuro) and relativistic (cultural) determinants of emotion, and facial expression is dependent upon the interaction of both sets of factors.

Professor Ekman's research has focused primarily on isolating and describing in a measurable form the universal determinants as a first step in evaluating the theory. A series of studies have focused on facial expressions and emotion in separate cultures, principally Japan and America, but also South America and two preliterate, isolated cultures in New Guinea. The findings provide strong support for universal facial expressions of emotion across cultures. Thus Professor Ekman believes that we must abandon the idea that facial expressions are languages which vary from culture to culture. An important characteristic of his program of research has been the development of a procedure for measuring facial expression, the Facial Affect Scoring Technique (FAST), which locates and classifies facial expression.

Finally, all of us who have been associated with the Nebraska Symposium on Motivation, including University of Nebraska faculty and students as well as the substantial number of visitors who attended the separate sessions, wish to express our gratitude for the support provided by the National Institute of Mental Health and the University of Nebraska.

James K. Cole
Associate Professor of Psychology

Cognitive Growth Cycles in Mental Development

DAVID ELKIND

University of Rochester

The present paper is concerned with the hypothesis that mental growth, no less than personality growth, involves a press toward structural realization. More exactly, I am suggesting that every mental ability seeks to realize itself in action and to go through a characteristic growth cycle in the process. The major portion of the presentation will be an attempt to adduce evidence in favor of this hypothesis.

Although the differential growth rate of various mental abilities is a well-established psychometric finding (Bloom, 1964; Trembly, 1964), the hypothesis of cognitive growth *cycles* derives from developmental considerations. Accordingly, the present paper will be developmental in perspective and, in the first section, the general characteristics of cognitive growth cycles will be described. Then, in the next section, these general cycles will be illustrated with developmental data regarding the growth of rote memory, perception, language, and reasoning. The final section will deal with some of the issues to which cognitive growth cycles relate, namely, critical periods, mental acceleration, and extrinsic motivation. I have focused the entire discussion upon cognitive growth cycles because of my belief that it is only in the sense of growth forces pressing toward the structuralization of cognitive processes that we can legitimately speak of motivation *and* mental growth.

Cognitive Realization Cycles

A cognitive ability in the process of development shows characteristic phases. In the first phase there is a period of *stimulus seeking* in which the sought-after stimuli become the *nutriments* of further cognitive growth. This stimulus-seeking activity must be distinguished from what has been called "novelty" as a dynamic of action and of "exploratory" or "curiosity" drives. In all of the latter cases it appears to be the stimulus which in part or in whole is the goad to action, and without the appropriate stimuli there is no novelty, exploratory, or curiosity behavior.

In the case of stimulus nutriment seeking, however, the nature of the stimulus plays a more or less insignificant role, at least initially. As far as the developing mental process is concerned there is considerable vicariousness as to environmental stimuli so long as the basic nutritional ingredients are there. A close analogy is the child's ability to use a wide variety of different foods to foster physical growth. Children all over the world grow in roughly the same way despite extremely different diets. Apparently they are able to get the essential nutriments out of many different forms of food. Mental growth, via stimulus nutriment seeking, seems to occur in the same way. It should be said, however, that once a child gets adapted to particular foods, long-range preferences are established. The same probably holds true for the stimuli upon which children nourish their mental abilities.

Stimulus nutriment seeking in the course of mental growth is often observed in *repetitive behavior*. The circular reactions of infancy, wherein the child pulls his mobile, sees it move, then pulls it again, and so on, provide stimulus nutriment for his developing abilities to coordinate perceptual and motor schemata. At a somewhat later age, the proverbial "why" questions of the 3-year-old are probably aimed, in part at least, at providing verbal stimulus nutriment for the child's developing linguistic structures. Again at the elementary school level, the involvement in doing, making, and collecting provides stimulus nutriment for growing structures of practical reasoning.

Another characteristic of mental growth cycles is what might be called stimulus *gating* and *storage*. In order to pursue stimulus nutriment the child must frequently ignore or tune out distracting stimuli. That is what I mean by stimulus gating. Whenever the child has found nutriment for his mental growth and is utilizing it, he tends to be impervious to other intruding stimuli. Here is a nice example taken from Maria Montessori:

I watched the child intently without disturbing her at first, and began to count how many times she repeated the exercise; then, seeing that she was continuing for a long time, I picked up the little arm chair in which she was seated and placed chair and child upon the table; the little creature hastily caught up her case of insets, laid it across the arms of the chair and gathering the cylinders into her lap, set to work again. Then I called upon the children to sing; they sang, but the little girl continued undisturbed, repeating her exercise even after the short song had come to an end. I counted forty-four repetitions; when at last she ceased, it was quite independently of any surrounding stimuli which might have distracted her, and she looked around with a satisfied air, almost as if awakening from a refreshing nap. [Montessori, 1964, pp. 67–68]

In some cases the stimuli gated by the child may not be registered at all, as it apparently was not in the above example. But this is not always the case and occasionally the stimuli may be gated from conscious elaboration but stored unconsciously for later elaboration. This is particularly true when the stimuli may have nutritional value for the child but comes in amounts too big to be digested all at once. One sees this, for example, when young children are taken to the zoo or to the circus. Although the stimuli are valuable to the child, there is too much to be utilized all at once and the child may not begin to talk about or to draw the zoo or circus animals until weeks after the fact of his visit. Obviously, stimulus gating and storage occur after a cognitive ability is established, but the child's competencies in these regards may vary with the kinds of gating and storing activities he engaged in while the ability was in the process of construction.

A final phase in the cycle of cognitive realization is the appearance of intellectual *play*. In the past, play has been described as a preparation for life (Groos, 1914), as the discharge of surplus energy (Spencer, 1896), and as a mechanism of attaining catharsis and mastery (Wälder, 1933; Erikson, 1950). In the case of mental growth, however, play appears to serve a complex of these functions. It is first and foremost an expression of *having attained*[1] mastery, and portrays in action the joy of completion. When an infant has

1. The conception of play as an expression of attained mastery suggests that some play is a reaction *to* relief of tension and is not always, as dynamic theories posit, a mechanism *for* the relief of tension.

attained a sense of permanent objects that exist when no longer present to the senses, then he plays at such games as "peekaboo." Part of the joy of the game derives from the sense of knowing what to expect, of having mastered the situation. Likewise, children who have mastered the distinction between words and things can then engage in word play and in "name calling."

Play has another function in mental growth as well, and this lies in its preparation for further growth. The infant playing at peekaboo is not only enjoying his newfound sense of permanent objects but is also becoming aware of spatial relations that will later suggest new intellectual problems. Likewise, the child who engages in name calling is preparing for an understanding of the metaphorical use and meaning of words. In the context of cognitive realization cycles, therefore, play points backwards to past achievements and forward to new intellectual challenges.

Stimulus nutriment seeking, repetitious practice, stimulus gating and storage, and play are thus the major components of cognitive realization cycles. We need now to look at these cycles in more detail as they apply to the development of mental abilities from the simple to the complex, namely, from rote memory to perception, language, and reasoning.

Rote Memory

In general, rote memory refers to the ability to recall material that was presented more or less outside a context of significant issues and events as regards the individual involved. The digit span test, in which the subject is required to repeat a string of digits after the examiner says them, is the most popular test of this mental ability. From a structural point of view, rote memory ability seems to appear relatively early in life and the structures that mediate it do not seem to change much with age. In recalling digits adults are forced to use the same mechanisms as children (although adults may group more effectively).

Evidence for cognitive growth cycles in the attainment of rote memory ability is anecdotal but so common that its existence is easy to document. Young children memorize materials of all kinds without being told to do so and apparently without any conscious intention of so doing. Most parents have had the experience of reading a book to a preschooler for the third or fourth time, and of then discovering that the child knows the story by heart. Indeed, the child will quickly correct the adult who misreads a word or who skips a page. But the adult, who has heard the story equally often, does not have it memorized. One explanation of this phenomenon is that young children are just in the process of attaining rote memory ability and are, therefore, using any stimuli available upon which to practice their emerging skills.

Gating and storage with respect to rote memory is evident in what Piaget (1951) has called "deferred imitation." He gives many illustrations of children who observe a phenomenon early in the day and imitate it later in the day or on following days. A girl may observe a woman pushing a carriage and will later make believe she is pushing one herself. Likewise, young children will frequently listen to songs which they will not repeat at the time but will sing at some later point. In addition, children who scold their siblings and peers in just the words and tone of voice of their parents ("What am I going to do with you!") are demonstrating deferred imitation, which consists of gating the stimulus before it can precipitate immediate action yet storing it for later utilization.

Psychometric data as well as research studies suggest that rote memory matures relatively early in life and remains relatively constant thereafter until adolescence. With advancing age, immediate memory is among the abilities most subject to deterioration. As it pertains to cognitive growth cycles, the early maturity of rote memory would lead us to expect evidence of rote memory play during the elementary school years. Such evidence can be found. A well-known formalized game of rote memory is the "spelling bee." While the spelling bee originated out of the spontaneous play of children seeing how many words they could spell, it became a highly competitive activity which lost most of its playful, or tension-free, aspect.

Other rote memory games that children used to play have become obsolete by the growth of technology. At one time, many young children took delight in identifying and naming every make and model of car they saw go down the street. Today, however, the variety of models is so great that this game is no longer possible. Likewise, the collections of baseball and football player cards that were once so popular are a little less so today because of the large number of teams and players. Many young children, however, still delight in knowing the names of all the players on their favorite teams and this is a playful use of their rote memory skills.

From the point of view of cognitive growth cycles, the early termination of the cycle for rote memory raises an important question. What becomes of the intrinsic growth forces that motivated its development and what determines its later utilization? If we look at the fate of rote memory, some answers are suggested. In contrast to the preschool child, who spontaneously uses rote memory, the school-age child resists memorization, and educators are up in arms against it. Apparently, therefore, the growth forces that led to the structuralization of rote memory are dissipated once the structures are formed. Thereafter, other extrinsic emotions, needs, and motives apparently come to play the leading role in the activation of rote memory. Digit span, the most commonly used test of rote memory, is particularly susceptible to momentary anxiety and distractibility among adolescents and adults (Rapaport, Sill, & Schafer 1945).

These considerations suggest two corollary hypotheses to that of cognitive growth cycles, namely: (a) the motive forces inherent in formation of cognitive structures are largely dissipated once the cognitive structures are fully formed, and (b) the completed mental structures, which are now bereft of all but structure maintenance forms of intrinsic motivation, require the forces of more abiding psychic energies for their activation and utilization. These corollary hypotheses would seem to be as basic as that of cognitive growth cycles themselves, and we will refer to them again at various points in the discussion.

Perception

In the most general sense, perception can be said to involve the processes by which we read the information which comes to us through our senses. Although perception has to do with all of the senses, I will limit my remarks here to the development of visual perception. In this connection the discussion will lean heavily upon Piaget's (1961) developmental theory and research regarding age changes in this domain.

Perception presents us with an evolution that is much more complex and intricate than the development of rote memory but which nonetheless manifests the characteristics of the cognitive realization cycle described earlier. Unlike rote memory, which does not appear until the emergence of the symbolic function, perceptual processes are already well established at birth or soon after. During the first weeks of life, infants respond selectively to different visual patterns and forms. Moreover, infants appear to prefer more complex forms, as evidenced in their tendency to observe such patterns for longer periods than less complex forms (Fantz, 1965).

These earlier perceptual activities and processes are, however, not truly developmental in the sense that the term is used here because they do not show sequential, age-related changes in performance. They are, in Piaget's terms, "field effects," Gestalt-like organizational structures which are part of the infant's initial equipment. Field effects organize experience according to Gestalt-like principles of good form, closure, and so on, and continue to do so in more or less the same way across the entire life span. Indeed, field effects appear to be basic organizing forms somewhat analogous to those of space, time, and causality that occur in cognition.

In contrast to the appearance of field effects soon after birth, perceptual development proper begins only in the preschool years. Starting at about the age of three, the gradual appearance of what Piaget calls perceptual *regulations* can be seen—perceptual structures which, in their manner of operation, resemble the structures of intelligence. As these structures begin to develop, children start to show the phases of the cognitive realization cycle we have already described with respect to rote memory. That is to say, perception begins to show the stimulus nutriment seeking, the repetition, the gating and storage, and the spontaneous play which are manifested in the realization of other cognitive abilities.

With regard to stimulus-nutriment-seeking activities, we can first refer to anecdotal descriptive data and then to research findings. Elsewhere (Elkind, 1970b) I have suggested that perceptual regulations play an essential role in reading and made the point that printed material can therefore provide the stimulus nutriment for developing perceptual regulations. Montessori (1964) provides the corollary anecdotal evidence and describes in vivid terms children who literally burst into reading and danced about reading everything in sight including signs, labels, and book jackets. During this period children read any and all printed material that was available to them, much as younger children, at the same stage in acquiring rote memory, memorized any material with which they came into contact.

Turning to some research evidence, we found similar phenomena in a study of perceptual exploration (Elkind & Weiss, 1967). One part of the study involved presenting children at different age levels with a card on which 18 pictures of familiar objects were pasted in a triangular array. The child's task was to name every picture on the card. Results showed a striking similarity between kindergarten and third-grade children, all of whom did the same thing, namely, they read the pictures starting at the apex and along the sides of the triangle. This would have been predicted by a Gestalt psychologist since the triangle constitutes a "good form."

What the Gestalt psychologist might have had trouble predicting were the results from the first- and second-grade youngsters. These children surprised us because about half of them read the array from left to right and from top to bottom! That is, they named the picture on one side of the triangle and then its paired opposite on the other side and so on to the bottom of the array. Kugelmass and Lieblich (1970) have recently replicated this finding with Israeli children. The only exception they found was that the Israeli children, schooled in Hebrew, read the pictures on the triangle from *right* to *left* and from top to bottom.

Clearly the tendency to read the figures in this way in the case of first and second graders was in part attributable to the fact that they were learning to read. I have already suggested that reading requires regulations, and these children were also at the age when the development of perceptual regulations is in the ascendance, as we have shown in other investigations (Elkind & Scott, 1962; Elkind, Koegler, & Go, 1962). Learning to read from left to right can thus be interpreted as an exercise for perceptual regulations, and stimuli which permit this activity can be used as stimulus nutriment for the attainment of these abilities. Once the regulations are fully formed, stimulus nutriment seeking disappears and children revert to the path of least effort and Gestalt principles of organization. That is why the third-grade children performed like the kindergarten youngsters. Perceptual regulations have, at that point lost their growth force and hence the readiness to be utilized spontaneously in appropriate situations.

It should be said that these studies also revealed evidence of the final, or play, stage in the cognitive realization cycle. Youngsters who participated in both our study and that of Kugelmass and Lieblich (1970) were also shown a card on which familiar pictures were pasted in a disordered array. First- and second-grade children read the pictures from top to bottom and from left to right, that is, they imposed an organization upon the disordered array. Third-grade children, however, did not limit themselves with respect to top to bottom and right to left. Rather, they explored the array in new and unexpected ways, up, down, and across. It was as if, now being in full command of their perceptual regulations, they could afford to play with different organizations of the stimulus materials.

With regard to stimulus gating and storage we found other results of interest. In an unpublished study we used strips of black tape to unite the pictures on the disordered-array card into distinct rows. The subjects were kindergarten children who were tested on cards with and without lines. On the first testing, the lines had a negative effect and the children made many more errors of commission (naming the same figure twice) and of omission (failing to name the figure at all) on the card with the lines than on the card without the lines. Several weeks later, when the testing was repeated, just the reverse held true. On the second testing the children were effectively able to gate the distracting component of the lines and yet to use them to facilitate their exploration of the array. Performance on the unlined cards improved also, but to a lesser degree. Effective gating, it appears, evolved along with the improvement in perceptual regulations.

As to memory, or storage, of perceptual material, we have recently obtained some interesting data. The studies involved presenting children at different age levels with ordered and disordered arrays of categorizable and noncategorizable figures. Results showed that there was some improvement with age in ability to recall figures. More significantly, however, the data suggest that the ability to recall figures that the child has named, in an ordered or disordered array, varies with his tendency to cluster or group the recalled figures in categories. As studies by Piaget, Inhelder, and Sinclair (1968) have shown with logical materials, our own data suggest that perceptual memory is not a passive but rather an active process. Further, our findings suggest that the tendency to cluster increases with age and, hence, that perceptual memory becomes more active with increasing age and the development of perceptual regulations.

It might be well here to say something about the nature of stimulus nutriment in the growth of perceptual abilities. By and large it appears that children can generally find nourishment for developing perceptual structures in almost any environment. I once tested large numbers of Sioux Indian children on the Pine Ridge reservation in South Dakota. These children had grown up in wickiups in barren fields and valleys with few if any toys, books, or other structured play or educational materials. On the perceptual tests, these youngsters did at least as well as children in the suburbs of cities in the Northeast and Southwest. Indeed, many of the Sioux children were artistically gifted. Even on the borders of the barren badlands they were able to find nourishment for their developing perceptual abilities.

Once perceptual regulations become established, which usually occurs in late childhood, their spontaneous utilization comes to an end. Interestingly, this lack of spontaneous use of perceptual regulations for reorganizing and exploring the visual world appears to diminish at about the same time as the child's spontaneous interest in drawing. The urge to draw, like the urge to perceive creatively, seems to dissipate once the basic abilities (understanding of perspective, etc.) are acquired. Thereafter, other motivations are needed to bring them into operation. This is particularly evident in the Rorschach test, where personal predilections are reflected in reported percepts. In perception, as in rote memory, the control of the attained structures shifts from the growth forces inherent in their formation to extrinsic motivations which then determine the nature and direction of creative perceptual activity.

Language

The past decade has in many ways constituted a new era in the study of language growth and development. Mightily stimulated by the work of Chomsky (1957), investigators have begun to look at the child's acquisition of grammar and his skill in language production. This new trend complements much of the earlier work on language which involved developmental descriptive studies of vocabulary, sentence structure, and parts of speech. Just as earlier works found a sequential development in parts of speech in which nouns appeared earlier than prepositions, there appears to be a comparable sequence in the evolution of children's grammars which suggests that they are also developmental in nature and should, therefore, manifest the same structural growth cycle evident in the formation of other cognitive abilities. Language ability is, however, even more complex than perception and it is not possible to deal with it in any complete or comprehensive way here. Accordingly, I will limit myself to examples from the research which details the growth of "generative grammars" and of semantic structures to illustrate the stages of the structural growth cycle.

In considering the growth of grammar, and of language generally, one point requires special attention, namely, the fact that the child can use his own activity as nutriment to further his own linguistic growth. We will encounter the same phenomenon again when we discuss the development of reasoning. What this means is that evidence for stimulus nutriment seeking in the language sphere generally and in the grammatical sphere in particular can be assessed in terms of the child's increasing tendency to produce language. In this connection Braine (1963) found, for a single child who had just begun to use a two-word open-pivot grammar ("Bobby up," "Bobby go," "Bobby eat," and so on), the following numbers of *new distinct* utterances in successive months: 14, 10, 30, 35, 261, 1,050, and 1,100. This is a dramatic example of stimulus nutriment production, as well as seeking.

Children's learning of grammar also gives many evidences of gating and storage. There is, first of all, the phenomenon of over-regularization, the fact that the child knows the rules but not the exceptions. Children learning English say "feets, comed, broked" because they know the rules and gate out the exceptions. It is really not unlike what children do when they draw, namely, they portray what they know rather than what they perceive. Accordingly, they draw a profile with two eyes because they know a person has two eyes but ignore the fact that from the profile perspective both eyes cannot be seen. In language learning, too, the child may *hear what he knows* rather than what he listens to.

There is considerable evidence that children play with grammatical forms once they are well established. This evidence is particularly prominent in the cultural lore of school children. While the songs and chants of children have many functions, such as providing an introduction to the peer group, they also provide a vehicle for playing with language and expressing mastery of grammatical forms. Here is an example of an old game which has certainly been updated by now.

Three suitors approach a mother and daughter and say, suiting the action to the words,

> Here come three sweeps
> And at your door they bend their knees
> May we have lodgings here, O here
> May we have lodgings here?

The mother replies, "No." The suitors retreat, and then approach again, saying:

> Here come three kings
> And at your door they bend their knees
> May we have lodgings here, O here
> May we have lodgings here?

The mother recants and answers,

> Yes, here is my daughter all safe and sound
> And in her pocket a thousand pound
> And on her finger a guinea-gold ring
> And she's fit to walk with the King.

She hands over her daughter, for whom the suitors pretend to search, then they bring her back to the mother and say,

> Here is your daughter safe and sound
> And in her pocket no thousand pound
> And on her finger no guinea-gold ring
> She's not fit to walk with the King.
>   [Newell, 1963]

This is but one example of the many songs, chants, riddles, and so on that make up the language and lore of childhood (Opie & Opie, 1959). One reason children enjoy these materials so much is, or so it seems to me, the opportunity to play with grammatical structures like that of negation and affirmation in the example. Clearly much of the fun comes from the unexpected negation in the last rhyme. This is really not as farfetched as it seems. Recall the glee of elementary school children when they catch a younger sibling or parent in a grammatical error. To be sure, part of their mirth comes from the feeling of superiority, but what is a feeling of superiority if it is not the feeling of mastery and of the urge to play with what one can now do well?

Similar evidence for cognitive growth cycles can be observed in the semantic aspects of language growth. In the realm of semantics, the repetitious wh- (which, where, why, when) questions of young children are proverbial and reflect the stimulus-nutriment-seeking phase. Here are some examples.

> Do I look like a little baby?
> Can't you get it?
> Can't it be a bigger truck?
> Am I silly?
> Does turtles crawl?
> Did you broke that part?
> Does the kitty stands up?

In talking to a child at this phase, each answer merely elicits another question. It becomes clear then that the adult has become part of a circular reaction in which he provides verbal stimulus nutriment for the child's growing semantic comprehension.

Gating and storage are likewise present at the semantic level. With regard to gating, Piaget (1952) long ago described what he called "parallel play." In such play two children talk *at* rather than *to* one another. One child talks about his new jacket while the other talks about a trip to the store and neither child acknowledges the other's utterance. In such parallel play, the child effectively gates out the semantic input of his companion. It is important to point out that the child could understand the utterances—he certainly does so when he is talking to an adult—but when engaged in play his language accompanies and reinforces his actions; distracting stimuli are effectively gated from consciousness.

Anecdotal examples of semantic storage are easy to come by. Most parents are surprised when a child recalls the name of a person or place he may have seen 6 months or a year ago. We do not expect children to store for such long periods. More experimental evidence comes from the studies of Burtt (1932, 1937), who read his young child passages in Greek, only to find that this facilitated the learning of these passages at a much later point in life. And, more generally, children exposed to a foreign language early in life, even if this experience is not prolonged, seem to learn the language more readily later than young people who have not been so exposed.

Finally, the mastery of elementary semantics involving the distinction between words and things gives rise to a great deal of verbal play. Such play is particularly evident in name calling. Young children are upset when called names by older children because they have trouble distinguishing between the word and the reality. Older children delight in calling others "stupid," "dum dum," "fatso," and so on. While such verbal play has emotional overtones, it also expresses the child's mastery of the distinction between words and reality and the recognition that the two do not always need to coincide.

By and large, the language system, like the perceptual system, seems to be more or less complete structurally by middle childhood. Thereafter, growth in language is a matter of vocabulary growth and increased comprehension associated with the development of reasoning and thought. Again, once the basic structures of language are formed their inherent dynamic seems to be dissipated, and language utilization and efficiency comes under the domination of other forms of motivation. This helps to account for the fact that, while all individuals share the same grammatical structures, there are extraordinary individual differences in volubility and articulateness. These individual differences in linguistic prowess become especially evident in adolescence, when language begins to express the differentiation of individual emotions, motives, and identities characteristic of this period.

Reasoning

As the term is most generally used, reasoning has to do with the processes by which we arrive at knowledge that is implicit in what we already know. In discussing the development of reasoning we will again lean heavily on the work of Jean Piaget. As he has shown (1950), reasoning is the most complex of human mental abilities. With regard to structural growth cycles, for example, we have to allow for a major cycle from birth to the middle of adolescence, the period during which the reasoning structures as a whole attain their final form. In addition there are minor cycles corresponding to Piaget's sensori-motor, preoperational, concrete operational, and formal operational stages. Finally there are subcycles for the attainment of particular concepts such as the conservation of number, of mass and weight, and of volume.

Obviously it is impossible to provide a full discussion of all three levels of structural realization cycles in a presentation such as this one. I do believe, however, that at whatever level we look at the development of reasoning, the behavioral manifestations of active structural realization cycles will be in evidence. To illustrate this assertion, we can look at the attainment of concrete operations in young children. Beginning at about the age of 4 or 5, most children start to develop the mental structures that will make elementary reasoning and mathematical thinking as well as classification and seriation possible (Piaget, 1952a). As these operations come into being we again see evidences of stimulus nutriment seeking, repetition, gating and storage, and eventually play, as the attainment of structures is finalized and consolidated.

Evidence for stimulus nutriment seeking in the attainment of elementary reasoning ability is of both an indirect and a more direct sort. First, with respect to the indirect evidence, children all over the world appear to attain concrete operations at about the same age level (Goodnow, 1969). Indeed, we have more replication studies, and hence more secure data, on Piaget's conservation tasks than on perhaps any other experiment in psychology today. The uniformity of the results across wide variations in cultural background, environmental stimulation, and child-rearing practices suggests that the attainment of operations is not a function of the variations in these general factors. What it does suggest is that children all over the world are able to use whatever stimuli are available to nourish their mental growth.

More direct, if more anecdotal evidence, comes from behavioral observations of children who are moving out of the preoperational stage to the concrete operational stage. Children at this level are inordinately concerned with quantitative gradations, and the preoccupation with "who has more" is very evident. This concern could certainly be interpreted from a psychoanalytic point of view. While such an explanation would probably be justified in part, it does not exclude the stimulus nutriment interpretation. Behavior has multiple determinants, and child behavior directed at obtaining stimulus nutriment could, at the same time, symbolically represent more deep-seated concerns.

Other stimulus-nutriment-seeking behaviors evident during this period are subject to the same dual interpretation. Many preschool children who have learned to count will count over and over again in a manner reminiscent of the circular reactions evident in infancy. The clinician might interpret this behavior as a compulsive action that seeks to undo some feeling of guilt. While this may be true, it is probably again true only in part. The child who counts over and over again is also nourishing his growing quantitative skills. As in the case of language, the child's own activity creates the nourishment for further mental growth.

We see the same duality of interpretation in the case of children's fairy tales. Such tales abound in quantitative terms and gradations. "Goldilocks and the Three Bears" illustrates the point. The three bowls of porridge are of different sizes, the porridge itself is at different temperatures, the beds are of different sizes and degrees of hardness. Again, the elements of the stories could be given a psycho-dynamic interpretation that would make sense. The stimulus nutriment argument also makes sense, however, and children like to hear fairy tales again and again, in part at least because they provide nourishment for the child's growing quantitative abilities.

With regard to stimulus gating and storage, Piaget, Inhelder, and Sinclair's (1968) work on memory is apropos. In one study children aged 3 to 8 were presented with a stepwise arrangement of sticks which were from 9 to 15 cm. in length. The children were instructed to look at the arrangement and told that they were to remember it later. They were allowed to look at the arrangement for as long as they liked. After a week they were asked to recall what they had seen and to demonstrate this with gesture and with a drawing. Six to 8 months later they were again asked to draw from memory the series arrangement which they had not actually seen since the first presentation. After each recall test, the children were given the sticks and asked to make a seriation themselves.

Results of this study were quite remarkable. Initially the stages that Piaget had reported earlier were clearly present in children's drawings and in their constructions. At the first stage (usually 3 to 4 years of age) children drew a number of lines in a row but the lines were roughly equal in length. Then at the next stages (usually 4 to 5 years of age) children either drew the sticks in pairs, one big and one small, or in groups of big and small lines, or in smaller groups of big, little, and middle-sized lines. At the third stage (usually ages 5 and 6) the children drew actual series but with only a few lines in the series. Then, at the fourth stage (usually ages 6 to 7), children were usually able to draw a correct seriation.

After an interval of 6 to 8 months, and without their having been presented with the original seriation again, 90% of the 5- to 8-year-old children had advanced at least one stage in their drawing of the series! One interpretation of this finding is that the memory of the series was not a simple copy of the perceived arrangement but rather a construction resulting from an active assimilation of the stimulus material. In the course of mental development the resulting schemas change as the operations from which they are constructed differentiate and become more hierarchically integrated. These data give evidence that storage during the period of structural growth involves mental activity and reconstruction and is not a passive warehousing of impressions.

With the attainment of concrete operational structures at about the age of 7 and 8, children begin to play with these elementary reasoning structures. The evidence is again anecdotal but familiar. Children of 6 and 7 often tease their younger brothers or sisters by surreptitiously adding liquid to their drinks or by putting the drink to their mouths without drinking so they continue to "have more" even while they are drinking! This behavior implies a sophisticated understanding of continuous quantity and a tendency to play with these ideas. Another trick that older children like to play on younger children is to offer them a dime and a nickel to see which one they will choose. The young child often chooses the nickel, which is larger, and this amuses the older child, who knows the difference between size and amount.

As in the case of interest in fairy tales by younger children, the interest in quantity play and games by older children can be given a dynamic as well as a cognitive interpretation. The enjoyment that 6- and 7-year-old children get out of quantity play of all sorts, including cards and spinner games, is probably determined in multiple ways. It certainly seems, however, that some of the pleasure children take from quantity games arises from the joy of having mastered the abilities required to play them.

It would be possible to give other illustrations of cognitive growth cycles, but the few described above should suffice to describe their major characteristics. While the data for the stages in these cycles—stimulus seeking, repetition, gating, storage, and play—are not as experimental and solid as one would like, the evidence which is available, combined with the anecdotal evidence, is suggestive and seems worthy of more systematic pursuit. Even without additional support, it might still be worthwhile to speculate on the implications of cognitive growth cycles for more general issues of development and for some practical issues of psychology and education. Although the range of such issues is enormous, only three will be dealt with here, namely, the critical-periods question, the question of accelerating mental growth, and the role of intrinsic and extrinsic motivation in learning and performance. Obviously all of these issues are related and their separation is necessary only to simplify exposition.

Issues

Critical Periods

In general, the critical-periods notion within psychology suggests that, at certain points in development, environmental events take on special significance for later growth. Critical periods are rather easy to demonstrate in animals, and the imprinting of chicks during the first 17 days of life is well known. Whatever organism cares for the chick prior to the seventeenth day of life comes to be treated by the chick as if it were its parent. Critical

periods in human development are less easy to identify. There does appear to be a "primary socialization" period during the last trimester of the first year of life wherein the infant attaches itself to a particular person or to several adult figures and shows fear of the rest. Likewise, development theories such as Freud's and Erikson's suggest that environmental events of particular kinds are essential at different points of development.

The conception of cognitive growth cycles is somewhat parallel to the notion of critical periods but emphasizes the importance of internal rather than external direction during the formative period of any particular mental ability. At the same time, however, the notion of cognitive growth cycles also suggests that during the formative period of any mental ability, maximum growth will occur (a) to the extent that the child has a wide variety of materials upon which he can nourish his abilities (i.e., stimulus seeking must be successful), and (b) that he is allowed sufficient time to engage in repetitive practice and play with the materials.

The foregoing statements, however, raise rather difficult questions. First of all, it is important to ask about the content of the stimuli upon which a child nourishes his emerging mental abilities. It has already been suggested that, while children can use a wide range of stimulus materials as nutriments, the kind of stimuli they actually use may have lasting effects. Language is the best example of this proposition. At birth, an infant is capable of learning any language in the world, but as he is exposed to and acquires a particular language, he establishes lifelong preferences and linguistic habits.

Although we have no evidence of this kind of effect in other cognitive domains, it is at least possible that something similar could happen to the perceptual and rational abilities, albeit in a more complex and subtle way. Children brought up in a particular kind of visual environment (in the city, on a ranch, etc.) might learn lifelong preferences for certain forms of environment and visual vistas. Obviously these preferences are complicated by all sorts of affective and interpersonal elements, but in part, at least, they could also be attributable to the kinds of visual environments children use to nourish their perceptual abilities.

The same holds true in the cognitive domain. It is at least possible that the kinds of materials upon which children practice their budding mental abilities determine long-range preferences. Children, say, who find most of the nourishment for their quantitative thinking in fairy tales may have different quantitative preferences as adults than children who nourished their quantitative thinking primarily upon physical materials. Likewise, in the perceptual domain, children who develop their perceptual abilities on the pictorial materials provided by books read to them by parents may have more preference for reading than children whose perceptual abilities are nourished on other types of material. Indeed, this is one way of looking at social-class and ethnic-group differences in academic achievement. It is at least possible that some children get "imprinted" on intellectual kinds of nourishment during critical periods of mental growth while others do not and that these differential experiences set up lifelong preferences in these pursuits. It is a hypothesis that seems worthy of exploration in a more systematic way.

Finally, the critical-periods hypothesis also raises the question not only of "what kind" of nourishment but also of "how much." Again, the question is a difficult one to answer in a few words. There is probably a range of stimuli inputs that children can accommodate to and assimilate without too much difficulty. Children can adapt to too little nourishment by a kind of recycling of what they have (dropping a material but picking it up and playing with it again later in a different way). Likewise, gating and storage enable the child to keep out a certain amount of stimuli when the environment is too rich for his needs.

When, however, environmental stimulation becomes so excessive that gating no longer works and the child is overwhelmed, the situation is different. So too is the situation when, for one reason or another, there is really not enough stimulation for the child to adequately nourish his growing mental abilities. Although we do not have too much evidence in these domains, what we do have is less than encouraging.

In some cases, brain-injured children give the impression of young people unable to adequately gate out environmental stimuli. Such children sometimes appear quite distractible and at the mercy of every momentary sight and sound that is above threshold level. It is at least possible that the perceptual deficit of such children is attributable, at least in part, to their failure to adequately nourish their perceptual abilities during the period when these abilities were being formed.

In the case of stimulus nutriment deprivation we have even less evidence. Sensory-deficient children, such as the blind and the deaf, are nonetheless able to compensate through other sensory avenues. Emotionally disturbed and autistic children present special problems of interpretation. Such children may be deprived of stimulus nutriment because so much of their time is spent seeking the affective nutriment they are so badly lacking. A recent study by Strassman (1970) suggests that mental and perceptual retardation are directly related to the degree of emotional disturbance as judged by hospital personnel. It is not really clear, however, whether these are true deficits or whether they reflect deficiencies in performance attributable to the young person's illness.

In summary, cognitive growth cycles can be considered critical periods of a sort. During these cycles the child needs stimuli to nourish his growing mental abilities. What kind of stimuli he receives during this period, as well as how much, can possibly have lasting effects both in terms of adult preferences for stimulation and in terms of the adequate development of the mental abilities in question.

Accelerating Mental Growth

Throughout this paper, I have tried to show that there is both qualitative and quantitative evidence for proposing that various mental abilities have cycles of growth that are related to age. The demonstration of age-related processes, however, always raises the question of the fixity of the relation and whether or not the relation can be altered by training or by environmental manipulations. The answer to the question will of necessity have to be the old standby, namely, *it depends*. The possibility of accelerating the cognitive growth cycles will depend upon (a) the particular mental ability in question, (b) the particular children whose mental abilities are to be accelerated, and (c) the aims of acceleration. Let us look at each of these factors in a little more detail.

The mental ability. As a general rule it might be said that the earlier a mental ability appears and the shorter its growth cycle, the less susceptible it will be to environmental manipulation. Rote memory ability, for example, appears early and seems to have a relatively short growth cycle. Accordingly, one would expect it to be relatively impervious to special training aimed at maximizing this ability earlier than it would appear without such training. It seems that rote memory remains limited to the retention of about seven bits of information throughout life (Miller, 1956). Only the use of special memory aids and much motivation help to improve "memory."

If we look at perception, however, a somewhat different picture emerges. Some data suggest that children may not spontaneously maximize their perceptual growth as rapidly as they might. In several training studies (Elkind, Koegler, & Go, 1962; Elkind, Larson, & Van Doorninck, 1965) we were able to improve children's age-related level of perceptual performance. At the same time, however, we also found that the extent of change was related to age, that older children benefited more than younger children from training, and that the age differences between the groups were not affected by the improvements made at successive age levels.

It looks, therefore, as if perceptual structures do not realize themselves as rapidly or as fully as they might and that their growth cycles can be speeded up or maximized with special training. This may be particularly true for abilities such as part-whole perception which appear to require fairly specific stimuli (namely, pictures) for their full realization. We have found that black inner-city children do more poorly on part-whole integration than upon figure ground organization and reorganization. It seems likely that figure ground stimulation is probably more universal than are pictures. One would expect that in cases such as part-whole integration, where abilities have not been maximized due to absence of appropriate stimulus nourishment, training will be most effective.

The foregoing discussion raises the question as to whether there is an optimal rate of growth for any particular mental ability. Certainly the many and varied attempts to train children on Piaget's conservation tasks (cf. the review by Brainerd & Allen, 1971) indicate that it is very difficult to accelerate the development of concrete operations in a general way over and above improving performance on skills related to the training tasks. These data, together with our data from the perceptual training studies, suggest that there may be optimal rates of development for particular cognitive abilities but that these rates may not always be maximal and that training can, in such cases, accelerate the growth process. We need to turn now to the consideration of subject factors in acceleration of mental ability.

The children. It is perhaps unnecessary to say that the age relation of particular cognitive growth cycles will vary with individual differences in overall ability. The gifted child will, for example, often pass through the cognitive growth cycles much more rapidly than children of more average ability. On the other hand, retarded children may never manifest some cognitive growth cycles at all. The growth cycle of formal operational, hypothetico-deductive thinking may never appear in the development of the child with limited intellectual endowment.

In this connection it might be well to remark on some apparently paradoxical data on these individual and group differences in rate of mental development. It is generally true that brighter children seem to attain or maximize their mental structures earlier than children who are less endowed. It is also true that less rapid development of abilities is often related to ultimately higher levels of ability. The human infant takes much longer to develop many skills than the chimpanzee but he eventually catches up and goes farther. Likewise there is some evidence (Schaefer & Bayley, 1965) that heavy, rather lethargic babies are eventually brighter than very active, nervous babies. Hence the paradox: Among individuals within the same species, rapid attainment of intellectual abilities is correlated with better than average ability at maturity. As between species, however, just the reverse appears to hold true, and the slower the rate of development for the species, the higher the ultimate level of ability attained. Accordingly, while the long period of human infancy can be used to explain man's superiority over animals, prolonged infancy cannot explain individual differences in intellectual ability among men alone. Indeed, within the human species, children with the shortest infancy (i.e., who walk, talk, etc., earliest) are likely to be the biggest, brightest, and healthiest (Terman, 1925) of the species.

With respect to the acceleration issue, the effects of individual differences are quite predictable. Very simply put, it is easier to accelerate a bright child than it is a dull one. In general the bright child has a much more voracious appetite for stimuli than the slower child and can assimilate it more rapidly. Training aimed at accelerating the cognitive growth of bright children is thus much more likely to succeed than such training aimed at children of average ability. A case in point is the work of Moore (1965), who taught gifted children to read with the "talking typewriter." But this device has been much less successful when used with ghetto children who lack the preparation and ability of Moore's original group.

In this connection, a word or two is in order about ethics and values. It is clear that we can do many things in the way of accelerating cognitive growth in children, particularly in domains where children have not spontaneously maximized their abilities. Yet there are dangers in such attempts because we always pay a price for what we do. We must always ask the ends to which we wish to accelerate, whether the acceleration is worth the cost to the child in what he will miss for what he will gain and for ourselves in terms of the time and effort we must expend. Just because we can do something does not mean that we should therefore go ahead and do it, and this is particularly true when we are concerned with the mental growth of children, which brings us to the issue of the aims of acceleration.

Aims of acceleration. Perhaps it is the American pioneering spirit that makes American psychologists, as soon as they hear of stages, begin thinking of ways to bypass and overcome them. In some cases, as Wohlwill (1970) has recently suggested, the aim seems to be more to demonstrate what a certain methodology can do than it is to achieve some particular educational goal. But many investigators are concerned with accelerating mental growth to achieve educational ends. These ends differ depending upon whether the children are advantaged or disadvantaged. Without arguing the legitimacy of these aims, their developmental justification needs to be discussed.

In the case of advantaged children there is a great deal of social pressure to formalize education at the preschool level in an effort to maximize growth during this "critical period" for learning. I have discussed this issue in detail elsewhere (Elkind, 1969, 1970a) and want to deal with it here only in the context of cognitive growth cycles. From the point of view of cognitive growth cycles, the learning ability most prominent during this period is rote memory (and it is generally agreed that mediational processes do not appear until about age 5 or 6), which is the least susceptible to environmental influence. While it is true that children can do impressive things with this ability, it hardly seems to be the ability upon which one would want to build academic skills. Greater attention to the kind of learning preschool children are most proficient in might dampen the ardor of those who wish to begin academic training early.

With respect to disadvantaged children, the picture is somewhat different. It is generally agreed that the greatest handicap of these youngsters lies in the domain of language, not because they lack language but because they speak a different dialect, quite an elaborate one, from that of middle-class youngsters. Because the language growth cycle is active during the preschool period, this is the time to help these children acquire the dialect that they will need in school. Preschool programs with a heavy language emphasis could then be beneficial in preparing ghetto school children for later academic work.

In short, if acceleration or maximization of intellectual ability seems to be a meaningful goal, then it should be undertaken with some attempt to assess the developmental status of the child in terms of the cognitive abilities in ascendance at that stage in his life. Educational programs appropriate to those abilities would seem the most likely to maximize mental growth and provide the best preparation for future growth.

Intrinsic and Extrinsic Motivation in Learning and Performance

A basic tenet of the cognitive growth cycles posited in this paper is that they are motivated by intrinsic growth forces which are largely dissipated once the structures in question are fully formed. While a certain degree of stimulus nutriment is probably required to maintain these structures in functioning order, the major impetus for their utilization, once the growth cycle is at end, must come from more abiding emotions, needs, and motives. This switch-over of cognitive mechanisms from intrinsic to extrinsic motive forces raises many different kinds of issues, not all of which can be dealt with here. Among the most important of these issues, however, is the role of intrinsically and extrinsically motivated structures in learning and development. It is to this issue that the present section is primarily addressed.

Since Kant's revolutionary compromise between nativism and empiricism, it has been usual to distinguish between the form and the content of thought. Form is that which the individual brings to experience whereas content is what the individual takes from it. For Kant, however, and for the Gestalt psychologists as well, the forms or categories of thought were regarded as innate and more or less fixed at birth. Among Piaget's greatest contributions was his discovery and elucidation of the fact that the forms of thought do themselves evolve with age. As a consequence of Piaget's work we today regard *both* the form and the content of thought as undergoing an evolution in the course of individual development.

While both the form and content of thought change with age, the mechanisms of this transformation are different for the two forms of mental evolution. By and large, the forms of thought involve structural changes and hence presuppose the cognitive growth cycles that have been described in this paper. The content of thought, on the other hand, is acquired by the application of fully formed structures, under the guidance of extrinsic motives, to particular environmental events. So, while both the form and the content of thought evolve from an interaction between the subject and the world, in the case of form the interaction is intrinsically motivated, whereas in the case of content the motivation is extrinsic.

This delineation of the relation between the form and content of thought might be extended to the processes of development and of learning. Both development and learning (in both the classical and operant senses) involve the subject in interaction with the environment. Development, however, is primarily concerned with cognitive growth cycles, intrinsic motivation, and the formation of mental structures. Learning, in contrast, is concerned primarily with associative processes, with extrinsic motivation, and with the acquisition of mental contents.

This analysis suggests why it can be said that development determines learning. Development gives rise to the structures that are utilized in learning (White, 1965). Put somewhat differently, learning is always limited by the cognitive structures available to the individual at any given point in his development. Since the various mental abilities develop at different rates, their effective utilization will of necessity be dependent upon their structural completion. Possession of mental structures does not, however, guarantee their utilization, which now depends upon extrinsic motivation. It is because mental structures derive from intrinsic motivation but become subject to extrinsic motivation that we have the well-known distinction between *competence* and *performance* (Flavell & Wohlwill, 1969).

This distinction, it should be emphasized, becomes prominent only *after* structures are fully formed. During the cognitive growth cycle of particular mental abilities, the child almost always performs to the full extent of his competence. But once the structures are formed and their utilization comes under the control of other motivations, performance becomes a much less reliable index of underlying competence. If, however, we have prior evidence of the cognitive growth cycle with respect to particular abilities, we can determine when poor performance is merely a matter of appropriate motivation or of deficient cognitive structures. Attention to evidence regarding cognitive growth cycles might thus have practical value in determining whether or not deficient performance reflects deficient competence.

One other point needs to be made with respect to cognitive growth cycles and learning in relation to education. A great ideal has been made, of late, of the importance of intrinsic motivation in school learning. It often sounds as if children want to learn all of the time and that it is only poor schools and poor teachers that block or hinder this spontaneous love of learning. The conception of cognitive growth cycles, however, makes it clear that such a view of learning is rather an overgeneralization and quite extreme. It could do actual harm if, as has already happened in some schools and among some children, the belief is inculcated that all learning must be fun and that anything that is uninteresting is, for that reason, not worthwhile.

The conception of cognitive growth cycles suggests a more modest stance. It makes clear that there are many times that a child is intrinsically motivated in a particular subject area. During that period it suffices to provide him an adequate diet of materials to nourish his interest. But it would be a mistake to count on that intrinsic motivation too long, or to blame school or teachers for its dissipation. The child who is constantly involved in numbers during the emergence of quantitative thinking will lose that intrinsic motivation regardless of what the school or teacher does. At that point other extrinsic motivations, whether these be grades, social rewards, or something else, have to be employed.

In short, cognitive growth cycles suggest that learning will not always be "fun" and that what is "fun" at one point in development will not be "fun" at another point. Education, like life itself, must of necessity be a combination of things we want to do and enjoy doing with other things that we have to do because they need to be done. Certainly we should try to make education interesting to young people, but we must at the same time help them to distinguish it from entertainment and to recognize that learning to do what we don't want to do, but what needs to be done, can be one of the most beneficial effects of any educational system.

Conclusion

The present paper has argued that mental abilities develop at different rates and times and that each shows, in the process of reaching maturity, a cognitive growth cycle. This cycle involves, at the outset, stimulus nutriment seeking and repetitious behavior and, at the termination, play as an expression of mastery. Such cognitive growth cycles were said to be motivated by intrinsic growth forces which are largely dissipated once structure formation is completed. Thereafter, more abiding emotions, needs, and motivations take over the activation of the mental abilities in question. These cognitive growth cycles were then illustrated with respect to rote memory, perception, language, and concrete operations. Implications of cognitive growth cycles for critical periods, for the acceleration of mental growth, and for intrinsic and extrinsic motivation in learning and performance were then discussed.

The hypothesis of cognitive growth cycles expresses my own particular standpoint with respect to psychological science, which might as well be made explicit. First, I believe that psychology has tried to bypass the natural history phase of inquiry, the phase of description, classification, and labeling, without much success. There is still a tremendous job of classifying human behavior to be done. To become a truly experimental science we need a much more solid empirical base than we have now. I thus make no apology for the anecdotal nature of some of my observations. We need first to look carefully at all behavior before we can really hope to influence and explain it.

A second conviction is that we still have no single theory that will encompass all of human behavior. Consequently, it seems to me rather fruitless and unproductive to contrast theories which are more likely to be complementary than contradictory. Whether we are talking about Skinner and Piaget or Freud, Adler, and Jung, it is likely that each theory carries a certain measure of truth. Rather than adhere dogmatically to any single theory, a loose adherence to all viable theories would broaden our chances of understanding behavior and of arriving at a truly comprehensive theory of human intelligence and personality.

Finally, and closely related to the last point, is the belief that no piece of behavior is the exclusive province of any theory and discipline. The psychoanalyst cannot say that dreams are his province only and should not be examined from any other vantage point. Likewise, the learning theorist cannot say that, for example, discrimination learning is his province only and shall not be looked at linguistically or cognitively. It is likely that most behavior can be observed simultaneously from many points of view and that these viewpoints could complement rather than contradict one another. For now and for a considerable time in the future we will have to live with multiple complementary models for the same behavior.

In closing this discussion of cognitive growth cycles, I should say something of its origin. The idea is in many ways an expression of the values expressed above. In a very real sense it is an amalgam of ideas from a lot of different writers of varied theoretical persuasions.

All that I have tried to do is to bring these ideas together in an integrated and systematic way. While I cannot credit all those whose ideas are represented here, I would be remiss if I did not indicate that much of what I have said about cognitive growth cycles is either implicit or explicit in the seminal writings of Jean Piaget.

REFERENCES

Bloom, B. S. *Stability and change in human characteristics.* New York: John Wiley, 1964.

Braine, M. D. S. The ontogeny of English phrase structure: The first phase. *Language,* 1963, **39**, 1–13.

Brainerd, C. J., & Allen, W. T. Experimental inductions of the conservation of "first-order" quantitative invariants. *Psychological Bulletin,* 1971, **75**, 128–144.

Burtt, H. E. An experimental study of early childhood memory. *Journal of Genetic Psychology,* 1932, **40**, 287–295.

Burtt, H. E. A further study of early childhood memory. *Journal of Genetic Psychology,* 1937, **50**, 187–192.

Chomsky, N. A. *Syntactic structures.* The Hague: Mouton, 1957.

Elkind, D. Preschool education: Instruction or enrichment. *Childhood Education,* February, 1969, 321–328.

Elkind, D. The case for the academic preschool: Fact or fiction. *Young Children,* January, 1970, 132–140. (a)

Elkind, D. *Children and adolescents.* New York: Oxford University Press, 1970. (b)

Elkind, D., Koegler, R. R., & Go, E. Effects of perceptual training at three age levels. *Science,* 1962, **137**, 3532.

Elkind, D., Larson, M. E., & Van Doorninck, W. Perceptual learning and performance in slow and average readers. *Journal of Educational Psychology,* 1965, **56**(1), 50–56.

Elkind, D., & Scott, L. Studies in perceptual development. I: The decentering of perception. *Child Development,* 1962, **33**, 619–630.

Elkind, D., & Weiss, J. Studies in perceptual development. III: Perceptual exploration. *Child Development,* 1967, **38**, 553–561.

Erikson, E. *Childhood and society.* New York: Norton, 1950.

Fantz, R. L. Visual perception from birth as shown by pattern selectivity. *Annals New York Academy of Science,* 1965, **118**, 793–814.

Flavell, J. H., & Wohlwill, J. F. Formal and functional aspects of cognitive development. In D. Elkind & J. H. Flavell (Eds.), *Studies in cognitive development: Essays in honor of Jean Piaget.* New York: Oxford University Press, 1969.

Goodnow, J. Problems in research on culture and thought. In D. Elkind & J. H. Flavell (Eds.), *Studies in cognitive development: Essays in honor of Jean Piaget.* New York: Oxford University Press, 1969. Pp. 439–464.

Groos, K. *The play of man.* New York: Appleton, 1914.

Kugelmass, S., & Lieblich, A. Perceptual exploration in Israeli children. *Child Development*, 1970, **41**, 1125–1132.

Miller, G. A. The magical number seven, plus or minus two: Some limits on our capacity for processing information. *Psychological Review*, 1956, **63**, 81–97.

Montessori, M. *Spontaneous activity in education*. Cambridge, Mass.: Robert Bentley, 1964.

Moore, O. K. From tools to interactional machines. In *New approaches to individualizing instruction*. Princeton: Educational Testing Service, 1965.

Newell, W. W. *Games and songs of American children*. New York: Dover, 1963 (First published 1883).

Opie, I., and Opie, P. *The lore and language of school children*. London: Oxford University Press, 1960.

Piaget, J. *The psychology of intelligence*. London: Routledge & Kegan Paul, 1950.

Piaget, J. *Play, dreams, and imitation in childhood*. New York: W. W. Norton, 1951.

Piaget, J. *The child's conception of number*. London: Routledge & Kegan Paul, 1952. (a)

Piaget, J. *The language and thought of the child*. London: Routledge & Kegan Paul, 1952. (b)

Piaget, J. *Les mécanismes perceptifs*. Paris: Presses Universitaires de France, 1961.

Piaget, J., Inhelder, B., & Sinclair, H. *Memoire et intelligence*. Paris: Presses Universitaires de France, 1968.

Rapaport, D., Gill, M., & Schafer, R. *Diagnostic psychological testing*. Vol. 1. Chicago: Yearbook Publishers, 1945.

Schaefer, E. S., & Bayley, N. Maternal behavior, child behavior, and their intercorrelations from infancy through adolescence. *Monographs of the Society for Research in Child Development*, 1965, **28**, 3.

Spencer, H. *The principles of psychology*. Vol. 2. New York: Appleton, 1896.

Strassman, L. Perception and the effects of perceptual training on severely emotionally disturbed children. Unpublished doctoral dissertation, University of Rochester, 1970.

Terman, L. M. *Genetic studies of genius*. Vol. 1. *The mental and physical traits of a thousand gifted children*. Stanford, Calif.: Stanford University Press, 1925.

Trembly, D. Age-curve differences between natural and acquired intellectual characteristics. *American Psychologist*, 1964, **19**, 546. (Abstract) Paper delivered to the APA's 72d Annual Convention, September 4–9, 1964, Los Angeles.

Wälder, Robert. The psychoanalytic theory of play. *Psychoanalytic Quarterly*, 1933, **2**, 208–224.

White, S. H. The hierarchical arrangement of learning processes. In L. P. Lipsitt & C. C. Spiker (Eds.), *Advances in child development and behavior*. Vol. 2. New York: Academic Press, 1965. Pp. 187–220.

Wohlwill, J. F. The age variable in psychological research. *Psychological Review*, 1970, **77**, 49–64.

A Cognitive Interpretation of Secondary Reinforcement

LANGDON E. LONGSTRETH[1]

University of Southern California

INTRODUCTION

In one form or another, learning theorists often appeal to the concept of secondary reinforcement (S^r) to account for various patterns of animal and human behavior that appear intractable to simpler analyses. Usually sharing a common S-R frame of reference, but nevertheless differing on many other points (e.g., Hull vs. Skinner), these theorists use the S^r concept to account for apparent instances of learning and response maintenance in the absence of so-called primary reinforcement. That such instances actually occur is seldom questioned. Indeed, the problem was evident to both Hull and Skinner, both of whom made a liberal use of S^r when the occasion seemed to demand it (Skinner, 1938; Hull, 1943).

In truth, there was little evidence for it in those days. It seems to have been invented ad hoc to account for otherwise embarrassing data. Since its introduction, however, a great deal of direct evidence has been adduced. Most textbooks have accepted this evidence as proving the case; they speak as one voice:

"The fact that some forms of reinforcement are secondary or learned, is well established" (Kimble, 1961, p. 167).

"It has received experimental confirmation many times" (Cofer & Appley, 1964, p. 474).

"It is obvious from the studies which have been cited that neutral stimuli may acquire the capacity to serve as a reinforcing stimulus" (Hall, 1966, p. 129).

[1] This paper benefited from critical readings by Donald J. Lewis and Stephen A. Madigan. They are to be blamed for any shortcomings that still exist.

Occasionally, however, doubts have been expressed. Bugelski changed his mind from an earlier positive conclusion based upon the effect of the food magazine solenoid in the Skinner box (Bugelski, 1938) and concluded, "To select out the click and glamorize it into a 'secondary reinforcer' is totally unnecessary, gratuitous, and theoretically harmful" (Bugelski, 1956, p. 271). Myers concluded 2 years later, "The author feels that secondary reinforcement is inadequately defined and inadequately demonstrated" (Myers, 1958, p. 299). A decade later, Bolles expressed a similar opinion: "The attempts to conduct systematic laboratory investigations to disclose how secondary reinforcers are established have often as not failed to obtain any effects at all, much less show how they depend upon experimental parameters" (Bolles, 1967, p. 368). Most recently, the author has joined this critical chorus, concluding, "Not only is the concept of secondary reinforcement often used in a circular way that robs it of scientific meaningfulness, but even more seriously, there is only sketchy evidence supporting the reality of the phenomenon in the first place" (Longstreth, 1970a, p. 317).

So the argument rocks back and forth. The issue is a real one, tied as it is to the systems of Hull and Skinner and their derivatives. Particularly in their extensions to complex forms of human behavior do these theories become crucially dependent upon the S^r concept. Hull wrote, "Most of civilized human learning is apparently effected through secondary reinforcement" (Hull, 1951, p. 28), and Keller and Schoenfeld, speaking for Skinner, referred to it as an "indispensable tool" for the solution of "many vexing and absorbing problems of human action" (Keller & Schoenfeld, 1950, p. 260). Mowrer's 1960 theory, the most recent attempt at a formulation of near universal scope, is completely and inextricably tied to the S^r notion (Mowrer, 1960). According to Mowrer, the reinforcing function of certain stimuli is all that is ever learned, and all behavior is guided by either "hope" or "relief," the two forms in which S^r may occur.

Thus all extant large-scope S-R theories acknowledge their indebtedness to the S^r concept. In the face of occasional attacks from the nonbelievers, moreover, a reaffirmation of the faith seems to appear periodically in the literature. Two of the most recent defenders are Hendry (1969) and Wike (1970). Hendry musters

13 contributors to his book, all of whom conclude they succeeded in isolating S^r effects, and Wike contends that new techniques show the phenomenon to be a real one. It is the purpose of the present paper to carefully examine and evaluate this most recent evidence, and to suggest and defend an alternative point of view. It will be argued that (a) there are still no convincing S^r data; (b) an opposite function, frustration, is the more common result of presenting an S^r without other reinforcers; (c) other data which *seem* to demand an S^r concept are amenable to a cognitive analysis which does not involve S^r; and (d) predictions based on the cognitive formulation support it.

ANIMAL EVIDENCE: A DEMURRER

Wike and Hendry argue that S^r's can be established, but that special techniques are required to show the effect. They agree that the usual learning and extinction measures fare poorly, the latter more so than the former. The new techniques include chain schedules, concurrent chain schedules, second-order schedules, schedules-of-conditioned-reinforcement-with-free-primary-reinforcers, and multiple schedules (Hendry), not to mention token rewards and brief-exteroceptive-stimulus-changes (Wike). Still other methods are described by Kelleher and Gollub (1962) and Kelleher (1966a).

One of the characteristics which may be immediately noted about these procedures, aside from the obvious operant flavor, is their complexity. In chain scheduling, for example, there is no simple one-to-one contingency between a response and a consequence, defining either a learning or an extinction situation. Instead we have the following definition:

> *Chain Schedule or Chained Schedules (CHAIN).* A schedule in which responding during one stimulus is reinforced on a given schedule by the production of a second stimulus, during which responding is reinforced on a given schedule by the production of a third stimulus, and so on, up to final primary reinforcement. A Chain schedule resembles a Multiple schedule except that reinforcement occurs after only the final component, not after each component. A Chain schedule resembles a Tandem schedule except that each component is signaled by a distinctive stimulus. For example, in CHAIN FI 2 FR 5 a response after 2 min in one distinctive stimulus would produce a second distinctive

stimulus, during which the fifth response would produce the reinforcer. [Hendry, 1969, p. 424]

These procedures are quite different from the usual test situations employed to define an "original" or primary reinforcer. The effects of a primary reinforcer are rather easily demonstrated with simple and conventional test situations. These include the procedures necessary to produce (a) learning of a new response and (b) maintenance of a previously learned response, the so-called new learning and extinction tests. In both cases, all that is procedurally required is a simple contingency between the response and the candidate for the title of *reinforcer*. Transsituationality, of course, must also be demonstrated to at least some degree: no one is interested in an event which reinforces just one particular response, or worse yet, just one particular response in one particular species or subspecies.

Accordingly, a candidate for the role of a *secondary reinforcer*, defined as affecting behavior in the same way as a primary reinforcer, should be examined in the same test situations in order to determine the similarity of effects. But when it is, the candidate usually fails the test, as previously noted. What conclusion is therefore generated? *Clearly, if an event or condition fails the tests that by public agreement define a class of phenomena, then that event or condition is not a member of that class.* But Wike, Hendry, and others do not arrive at this conclusion. Instead, *new tests are suggested for secondary reinforcers.* There would then be one set of tests for primary reinforcers and another set of tests for secondary reinforcers. From these different tests one would nevertheless discover a common function for both concepts. Such a position—insisting upon common functions as a result of uncommon tests—seems untenable. But rather than dismissing the whole issue by assigning such questionable reasoning to the S^r proponents, let us instead examine these new test situations and see where they lead us. What data, then, do Wike and Hendry find most convincing in their defense of the concept of secondary reinforcement?

Wike lists several groups of studies. First he acknowledges that the Skinner box, or any other free-responding procedure, for that matter, is a dangerous way to investigate S^r effects due to the confounding of possible elicitation properties—a problem discussed in detail by a number of investigators, including the author (Longstreth, 1966a). Yet, as we shall see, most of the studies cited by Wike employ a free-responding procedure. Exhibit A, for example, is a series of studies by Crowder and colleagues which, according to Wike, "demonstrated that elicitation is inadequate to account for all of the observed S^r effect" (Wike, 1970, p. 58).

Crowder and associates carried out four studies with rats in which yoked controls received the presumed S^r whenever experimental Ss received it for lever pressing (Crowder, Morris, & McDaniel, 1959; Crowder, Gill, Hodge, & Nash, 1959; Crowder, Gay, Bright, & Lee, 1959; Crowder, Gay, Fleming, & Hurst, 1959). It was argued that any eliciting property of the S^r would thus be equated for the two groups, thereby allowing reinforcing effects to appear in isolation. In the first experiment, Ss first received 40 direct food-S^r pairings. Then Ss were confined in a Skinner box until 70 lever presses had occurred, each followed by food and S^r. Then, on the following day, an extinction test session was given. Half the Ss, assigned by either a "haphazard" or "random" method, received the S^r following each lever press. Each experimental S was assigned a yoked control who also received the S^r whenever the experimental S did, but not when the control S pressed the lever. Thus both groups received the same number of S^r's, but a contingency held only for experimental Ss. The results are reported as follows: "During the 50-minute extinction period, the median number of responses in the experimental group was 62; in the control group, 32" (Crowder, Morris, & McDaniel, 1959, p. 301). It is concluded, "Thus, even with facilitation controlled, secondary reinforcement was very much in evidence" (p. 301).

There is no argument with the basic logic of this study, although apparently trivial structural details may be crucial, as we shall soon see. A number of other aspects, though, raise serious qualms. There is the minor fact, for example, that 30 Ss completed the experiment but 42 others were discarded, either for not eating enough or not pressing the lever 70 times in the 50-minute training session. Most rats, then, did not qualify for the test phase. Is anyone really interested in a population of high-eating, fast-lever-pressing, Holtzman albino rats?

The highly condensed presentation of results presents a more serious problem: the previously quoted single sentence is all the *data* we are presented with (excluding the test of significance, $p < .01$), no extinction curves, no latency data, nothing but two medians. Thus there is no way of knowing whether the two groups were equivalent at the beginning of extinction or not, nor is there any way of determining if any extinction occurred in the first place. A proper test of S^r assumes, of course, that the two groups began extinction at the same response rate and that the rate of control Ss then decreased faster than the rate of experimental Ss. A simple report of total medians is not convincing, nor even very relevant. Indeed, the experimental Ss, with more total responses, could nevertheless have extinguished *faster* and even ended with *fewer* responses than control Ss, thus producing the opposite of S^r results. The subsequent studies all suffer from this same problem of inadequate description of the results: in each study the medians are all that is presented.

There are other problems too. As one example, the last study may be compared with the first study. Using the same apparatus and pretraining procedures, Ss first received 100 direct food-S^r pairings. Then they were divided into experimental-control yoked pairs. The members of each pair were placed into separate Skinner boxes until the experimental S had pressed the lever 20 times. Each lever press produced the S^r for both rats. Then all Ss were tested in an identical manner: they were placed into a Skinner box for 50 minutes and the number of responses recorded. Neither food nor S^r was presented. The results were a median score of 98 for experimental Ss and 50 for control Ss. Presumably the 20 response-S^r pairings developed a stronger response in experimental Ss. Now, it will be recalled that in the first study, after 70 *primary* reinforcements, a 50-minute extinction period yielded a median of 62 responses for experimental Ss. In the fourth study, *20* presumed *secondary* reinforcements yielded a median of 98 responses in the same 50-minute extinction period: a 59% increase in number of responses with 71% fewer reinforcements, from primary to secondary at that. With such extreme fluctuations of the dependent variable in directions opposite to what any reinforcement theory would predict, one can understand why nonparametric tests of significance were used. One can perhaps also understand the two following passages from various discussion sections of these reports, the first being the last sentence in the discussion section of the third study: "Our present knowledge, it would seem, does not allow us to predict whether secondary reinforcement will be found in any untried combination of conditions" (Crowder, Gay, Fleming, & Hurst, 1959, p. 309). And after the last study the following passage is found:

> The yoked-box technique can fully control for facilitation only if the above effects are the same for the experimental and the control animals. But most of these effects would seem to depend upon where the animal is and what it is doing when the signal occurs. Thus the signal could waken a control S and/or could move it closer to the bar. The experimental S, however, having just responded, is already awake and next to the bar. In these respects the yoked-box method seems to favor the control S. Should the signal evoke a pawing motion, however, the experimental S clearly would be at an advantage. Which group is favored overall may depend upon the structural details of the particular Skinner box. Hence the yoked-box procedure probably cannot always be relied upon to equalize facilitation in secondary reward experiments. [Crowder, Gay, Fleming, & Hurst, 1959, p. 313]

Thus Crowder and associates end their studies by questioning the relevance of their own findings. Unless there is something in these results that the investigators (and the present author) missed, it is difficult to understand their citation as strong evidence for S^r.

Next, a group of token-reward studies is mentioned as strong evidence for S^r. Included in this group are the early chimpanzee studies of Wolfe (1936) and Cowles (1937), and more recent studies by Kelleher (1957a, 1957b, 1958) and Malagodi (1957a, 1957b, 1957c).

It is popular to refer to the Wolfe and Cowles studies as being among the first to demonstrate the S^r properties of token rewards (e.g., Bolles, 1967). It is doubtful, however, that they should be mentioned outside of a historical context. After pairing white tokens with grapes and brass tokens with absence of food, Wolfe was able to show that responses learned for grapes by his five Ss would sometimes be better maintained by receipt of white tokens than by receipt of brass tokens. This is the extent of the data. The obvious flaws are: (a) in most situations the tokens or grapes were visible *before* the response, thus introducing the elicitation problem; (b) there was no counterbalancing of token appearance (white or brass) with reinforcement treatment (pairing or nonpairing with grapes); (c) when tokens were earned, they were immediately traded for food, and hence the response was followed by delayed primary reward as well as by presumed immediate secondary reward; (d) the order of tests was the same for all five Ss. This last point is as crucial as the others, since the conclusions are based upon response differences from one test situation to another within subjects. The first test situation involved responding for white tokens; the second and third did not, and the fourth did again, but under a slightly different condition. The relevant comparisons are between the first test situation and the others. Order is thus hopelessly confounded with test conditions. That this is not unimportant is indicated by the fact that white tokens in the fourth test session had a very weak effect as compared to their effect in the first session. Wolfe attributed this to the slightly changed conditions rather than to other effects.

Cowles trained two chimpanzees to insert colored discs into a slot machine which delivered a raisin for each disc. A different-colored disc did not produce raisins when inserted. The two chimpanzees developed a decided preference for the food disc as indicated by various choice tests. Then new learning was tested in various tasks wherein one response led to the food disc and another response to the no-food disc or to nothing. Usually the response leading to the food disc was learned at the expense of the other responses. It was therefore concluded that this disc functioned as an S^r.

Criticisms. As in many of the studies to be reviewed here, these Ss were not naive. In fact, both had been used by Wolfe in his investigations of S^r. Additionally, "All had had long experience in various laboratory experiments and were being used by other experimenters contemporaneously with this investigation" (Cowles, 1937, p. 6). Which experiment produced the results? No one can tell. Task confounding was not avoided either. For example, there was no counterbalancing of disc color and pairing or nonpairing with food, nor were there any test comparisons of the food disc with a *neutral* disc that had been paired *neither* with reward nor nonreward. As it is, one doesn't know if the observed effects were due to S^r properties of the food disc or to frustrating properties of the no-food disc.

In short, as clever as they were, one can have a field day with the Wolfe and Cowles studies, pointing out how *not* to conduct an experimental investigation of S^r effects. If this discussion accomplishes nothing else, it is to be hoped that it at least lays to rest the myth that these studies present a convincing case for S^r.

The Malagodi studies led Wike to conclude, "Rats can acquire bar pressing with token rewards of a rubber ball or marble" (Wike, 1970, p. 64). Five rats first learned to pick up a marble and deposit it in a receptacle for food. Then, presumably, they learned to press a lever just for marbles: "The token producing response can be acquired via token reinforcement" (Malagodi, 1967a, p. 1341). *Only it wasn't.* The method section says: "Ss were then shaped to press the lever by the method of successive approximations. When Ss approached the vicinity of the lever, a token was delivered. . . . After depositing the token *and receiving food*, the conditions of production were presented" (p. 1338, italics added). Thus food as well as tokens was used to shape the lever response. How Malagodi and Wike were able to conclude that the lever response was acquired via secondary reinforcement alone completely escapes the present author. But even if food had not been used, the results still would have been inconclusive, since no control group was used: there was no condition where the lever press was followed by *neither* food nor token.

Kelleher presumably maintained lever pressing in two chimpanzees by the presentation of poker chips previously paired with food (Kelleher, 1957a, 1957b, 1958). But that depends upon which study one reads. In the first two experiments, Kelleher himself concluded he had not been able to do so: "This history, however, was not sufficient for establishing a conditioned reinforcer" (Kelleher, 1957a, p. 574). Wike accepted this conclusion only reluctantly, commenting, "This conclusion appears to be a conservative one when we remember that the behavior was maintained for over 200 hours in Experiment II" (Wike, 1970, p. 69).

In a third experiment, with the same two chimpanzees, who now had over 1,000 hours training on poker chips, plus unenumerated hours in undescribed "previous experiments," Kelleher concluded he had finally been successful: the Ss now pressed the key for 60 chips, taking up to 200 minutes, before they could be turned in for food. But there were no control conditions at all. There was no condition, for example, where Ss received a stimulus *not* previously paired with food. Thus, from the point of view of confounding with innumerable experiences in years of previous experiments, from the point of view of self-admitted failure to establish an S^r in most of the studies, and from the point of view of lack of control conditions, one is led to the conclusion that there is no clear evidence here either so far as S^r is concerned. Kelleher himself observed in this last study that the tokens acted as an S^D for responding as well as a (presumed) secondary reinforcer.

Turning from token-reward studies, Wike next asserts that chain schedules have established strong S^r's, and cites two studies by Zimmerman as evidence of "sustained behavior under S^r" (Wike, 1970, p. 71). In the first study (Zimmerman, 1963), an undisclosed number of pigeons was used in a two-key situation, and some of the results from one pigeon are presented. First, a left-key peck produced food plus S^r, and a right-key peck produced only S^r. Under these conditions, the left-key response rate was high and the right-key rate was low, reaching about one-tenth the rate of the former. Yet Zimmerman was able to conclude, "The above results suggest, but do not conclusively demonstrate, that pecking of the right key was maintained by stimuli which were functioning as conditioned reinforcers" (p. 683). They suggest nothing of the sort, it being the case that (a) *some* data from *one* pigeon of an *undisclosed number* are presented, and (b) no control conditions whatsoever are described, such as controls for stimulus generalization, elicitation, etc. But Zimmerman then concludes that S^r effects were convincingly demonstrated by programming various schedules of S^r and asserting that the correlated response rates vary as though S^r were a primary reinforcer. *But these rates are not presented, nor are any tests of goodness of fit described.* Instead, we are simply referred to *Schedules of Reinforcement* (Ferster & Skinner, 1957).

In a second study reported 3 years later, we encounter three pigeons from the previous study plus one new pigeon (Zimmerman & Hanford, 1966). A single key was used, with the S^r presented on an FI schedule of 1 or 3 minutes. Concurrently, food was presented on a VI–3 minute schedule, paired with S^r provided that no key pecking had occurred for 6 seconds—"to eliminate the possibility of accidental unconditioned reinforcement of key pecking" (p. 394). Under these conditions, responding was maintained "indefinitely" (up to 6 months). For control purposes, a neutral stimulus pattern was presented for some 24-minute sessions. Under this condition the response rate was much less than under the presumed S^r condition, leading to the conclusion that S^r effects were demonstrated. There are two reasons for questioning this conclusion: (a) no evidence is presented showing that a temporal interval of 6 seconds between the pecking response and primary reinforcement is sufficient to prevent conditioning, and (b) the S^r stimuli and neutral stimuli were not counterbalanced. This latter point is not insignificant when it is noted that the "neutral" stimulus consisted of a 400-cps tone of undisclosed intensity plus a flashing light of 10 cps. The S^r stimuli, on the other hand, consisted of the click from the food magazine solenoid, absence of blue or yellow key lights, and absence of house lights.

Next, two pigeon studies by Kelleher are cited which demonstrate the effects of "briefly presented exteroceptive stimuli" (Kelleher, 1966a, 1966b). Three pigeons were exposed 111 times to a "second-order schedule" in which one schedule, FI 2, had to be repeated 30 times (FR 30) before reinforcement was forthcoming. A white light was paired with reinforcement, and was also presented for seven-tenths of a second at the end of each FI 2 segment. On test schedules either the light was omitted or a stimulus not paired with reward (darkening of the blue response key) was presented. Examination of the last five sessions showed that (a) response rate increased within FI 2 segments if the end of immediately previous segments had been signaled by the light, and (b) the increase was less or absent if the light signal had not been presented on previous trials, or if key darkening had occurred instead. From this evidence Wike concluded that "profound and highly durable" S^r effects were demonstrated (Wike, 1970, p. 74).

At the risk of appearing redundant, the author must again express his incredulity at this conclusion. All he can discern in this study is temporal conditioning after extended training: when a cue is available to mark the end of each FI 2 segment, S gradually learns to gauge the length of the segment and the usual temporal scallops follow. When the marker is omitted, S has fewer external cues against which to maintain his timing mechanisms, and the temporal scalloping breaks down. There is no need to appeal to S^r to explain such data. The data were inappropriately examined anyway. These studies report response changes *within* FI trials, while the white light was presented *between* FI trials. To demonstrate its S^r property, it would be necessary to show that response rates followed by the white light increased more *from FI segment to FI segment* than response rates followed by a neutral stimulus. The S^r stimulus and the neutral stimulus, of course, would need to be counterbalanced in order to rule out intrinsic stimulus differences. This type of segment-to-segment analysis was not reported, nor were the appropriate counterbalancing controls employed.

Finally, we come to the last major study cited as indicating strong S^r effects, the Saltzman study (Saltzman, 1949). As the author has pointed out elsewhere, the Saltzman study is probably cited more frequently than any other single study as demonstrating clear S^r effects (Longstreth, 1970). What did he do and what did he find?

Rats were fed in a distinctive goal box, black or white, at the end of a straight runway, and subsequently the power of the goal-box color to reinforce the acquisition of a simple position habit in a U-maze was tested. Four groups of rats received the following treatment in the straight runway: Group 1, the consecutive rein-forcement group, received 25 rewarded trials in the same goal box (e.g., black); Group 2, the intermittent reinforcement group, received 25 rewarded trials and 14 nonrewarded trials, all in the same goal box; Group 3, the differential reinforcement group, received 25 rewarded trials in one goal box (e.g., black) and 14 nonrewarded trials in another goal box (e.g., white); Group C, the primary reinforcement group, received the same treatment as Group 1. Position-preference tests were conducted on the last day of training. Counterbalancing procedures controlled for color preference.

Following training, all groups received 15 trials in the U-maze. A choice to the nonpreferred side was called a correct response.

For experimental groups a correct response terminated in the previously reinforced goal box, while an incorrect response led to a different goal box. For Groups 1 and 2 the latter box was one which these animals had not previously encountered; for Group 3 it was the box encountered on nonrewarded training trials. Experimental *S*s received no food in the maze. Group C ran to boxes which were identical, but different from those experienced during training. The box on the nonpreferred side was baited with food for this primary reinforcement group.

The mean number of correct responses for Groups 1, 2, 3, and C were 8.3, 9.0, 10.7, and 10.0, respectively. With theoretical chance performance set at 7.5, all these scores were reported as significant ($p < .05$). It was noted that the superior performance of Group 3 would suggest that S^r established by the differential method is at least as effective as primary reinforcement.

Because of the frequent citation of this study, Lieberman performed an as yet unpublished pseudoreplication in 1967 (Lieberman, 1967). She noted room for two specific improvements in the experimental design. (a) The omission of a nonrewarded control group leaves open the possibility that apparent S^r effects were confounded with unknown variables which affected *all* groups. That is, there was no empirical demonstration that chance performance was, in fact, 7.5 choices in either direction. Lieberman included such a control group; this group encountered a goal box previously paired with food on both sides of the U-maze. (b) The strongest demonstration of S^r effects in the Saltzman study was the performance of Group 3, which encountered a previously nonrewarded goal box on the incorrect side of the U-maze. As Lieberman and others have noted (e.g., Bolles, 1967), this goal box may have been frustrating, and the performance of this group may have reflected aversive properties of frustration rather than S^r properties of the goal-box color previously paired with food. To investigate this possibility, Lieberman had two experimental groups similar to Saltzman's groups: Group E-1 encountered the previously negative goal box on the incorrect side of the U-maze, as did Saltzman's Group 3, and Group E-2 encountered a color which had been paired neither with reward nor nonreward, similar to Saltzman's Groups 1 and 2.

The results of the Saltzman and Lieberman studies are presented together in Figure 1 to facilitate comparison. The main finding is obvious enough: whereas three out of four of Saltzman's groups show evidence of learning (Group 2 shows no evidence of learning), *none* of Lieberman's groups do. Not only is there no evidence of learning over the 15 test trials, but the total number of correct responses between the three groups did not differ significantly either. Lieberman concluded, "Thus the data fail to support Saltzman's conclusion that rats can learn a simple position habit in a maze on the basis of secondary reinforcement" (Lieberman, 1967, p. 30).

Null results, of course, carry a burden positive results do not carry: to be significant, evidence must be presented showing that the null results should *not* have occurred according to the theory under evaluation. Lieberman was aware of this responsibility in advance and took pains to meet it. Thus the original training involved pairings of larger amounts of food with goal-box color than Saltzman used, to circumvent the possibility that simply not enough primary reinforcement was used. Then there is the possibility that, because of unknown and unavoidable differences in lighting conditions of the two laboratories, perhaps the goal-box colors were not discriminable in the Lieberman apparatus, thus precluding demonstration of S^r. To measure this possibility, the last five alley training trials were conducted with the goal-box colors reproduced in the start box, and running speeds were determined. It was found that experimental Ss (Groups E-1 and E-2) ran significantly faster when presented with the color previously paired with food than with the color previously not associated with food. Thus one cannot dismiss these results by suggesting that Ss could not discriminate between the various colors of the goal boxes; they could and did discriminate.

A similar study, using the same apparatus, was conducted as a class project in the spring semester of 1969. The author had spent some weeks developing the notion of secondary reinforcement, and the students had been assigned "Secondary Reinforcement," Chapter 7 of Hull's *Principles of Behavior* (Hull, 1943). No mention had been made of the author's doubts concerning the S^r concept; instead, he defended it enthusiastically. The study was suggested in the context of a simple "demonstration" that would clearly

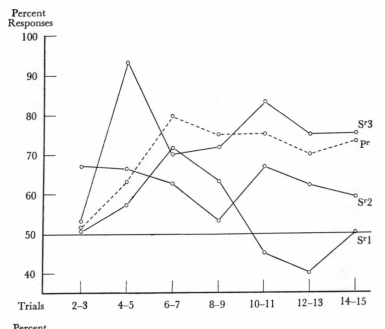

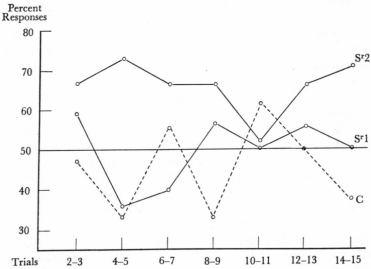

FIG. 1. Saltzman (top) and Lieberman (bottom) data on primary (Pr) and secondary (Sr) reinforcement.

illustrate the concept in action. So far as could be determined by student comments, the eight students fully expected the study to "come out." Incidentally, Lieberman too expected to replicate the Saltzman results; she still owes the author a coke because she didn't.

Ten rats were divided into five pairs. Experimental Ss were placed and fed 40 times in a goal box illuminated through the floor, while control Ss were confined an equal length of time, with the same illumination, in an empty goal box. Then each rat was administered 25 test trials in the U-maze. For each pair of rats, a coin was tossed to determine if S^r would occur on the right or left side. For three pairs it occurred on the right side and for two pairs on the left side. For experimental (S^r) rats, every turn to the S^r side resulted in exposure to the illuminated goal box for 10 seconds, while a turn in the other direction resulted in exposure to an unilluminated goal box. For control rats, test conditions were identical except that food was presented along with illumination on the one side. The comparison, then, similar to Saltzman's, is between an S^r group and a primary reinforcement group.

The results are presented in Figure 2. They show that the primary reinforcement group attained 91% correct responses by the end of test trials, while the S^r group stayed very close to chance. Statistical analyses showed the total number of correct responses between the two groups to be significantly different ($p < .01$). As in Lieberman's study, then, there is no evidence for an S^r effect, in spite of E bias to the contrary.

We have now concluded a review of the studies cited by Wike as demanding a secondary reinforcement explanation. They have been found wanting in every case, in terms of poor or nonexistent control conditions, inadequate reporting of data, small numbers of subjects (approaching the theoretical limit of one in some cases), long and unspecified experimental histories, lack of replicability of results, or various combinations of these features. We have no alternative but to disagree heartily with Wike's argument that the S^r concept is supported by a bed of solid facts. If these facts exist, we have not found them.

There remains Hendry's recent book, *Conditioned Reinforcement* (Hendry, 1969). The edited volume consists of 13 animal research reports, all leading their authors to conclude that S^r was clearly

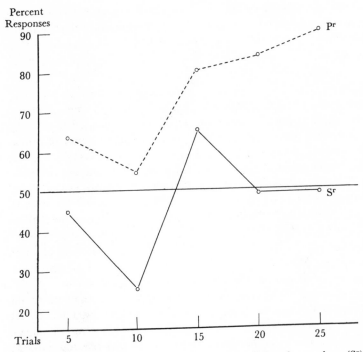

FIG. 2. Longstreth class project data on primary (Pr) and secondary (Sr) reinforcement.

demonstrated. The data and arguments are too copious to review in this chapter, but two observations will reveal the author's overall evaluation. First, the studies are replete with one- to three-pigeon groups, many used in undescribed previous studies, and all used in free-operant tests of S^r effects. The previous review of similar studies reported by Wike is indicative of the amount of historical and procedural confounding one will find in this kind of study. Second, after all is said and done, the editor finds himself forced to disagree with his own contributors. Hendry suggests that what his contributors have been calling an S^r should be relabeled a maintaining stimulus. The next to the last paragraph in the book is worth repeating in full:

> The need to distinguish a maintaining from a reinforcing function comes partly from the fact that a response-produced stimulus that

maintains one operant may not maintain a similar, but different operant. A primary reinforcer is said to be "trans-situational," effective in maintaining an arbitrary operant. Since the effectiveness of a conditioned reinforcer is notoriously difficult to demonstrate in a different environment from the one in which it was established, it seems more prudent and objective to avoid the connotations of the word "reinforcer" by a liberal use of the term "maintaining stimulus" in place of "conditioned reinforcer." Another particular result which argues against calling a maintaining stimulus a reinforcer is Schuster's demonstration that a schedule of maintaining stimuli with a schedule of primary reinforcement is not preferred to the schedule of primary reinforcement alone. Clearly, the maintaining stimulus did not add any incentive value to the option in which it figured even when it was associated with the primary reinforcer. On the other hand, both Marr and De Lorge comment on a case in which a stimulus *not* associated with the primary reinforcer was nevertheless quite an effective maintaining stimulus in a second-order schedule. [Hendry, 1969, pp. 401–402]

In other words, Hendry's conclusion is similar to that of the present author: at best, these studies illustrate an *associative* function of certain stimuli after certain operations. This is part and parcel of the *elicitation problem* so characteristic of operant studies, and as this problem has been discussed a number of times previously, there is no need to dwell upon it here.

HUMAN EVIDENCE: ANOTHER DEMURRER

There are not such enthusiastic supporters of the S^r concept at the human level as there are at the animal level; one does not find books and chapters written in behalf of the existence of the phenomenon in humans. Not that the concept is not accepted; far from it. When it is mentioned, though, it is with the calm assurance that the research phase is over, and one can now apply the concept in the explanation and control of human behavior. As an example of the former, we may present the following passage from a prominent child development textbook:

Many needs are said to come into existence in this way: through persistent conjunction with objects that reduce primary needs (primary reinforcers). Thus, previously neutral objects or events themselves take on reinforcing properties. In many instances the child begins to strive for these secondary reinforcers for their own sake and, hence, is said to have learned a need for them. [Watson, 1965, p. 104]

As an example of the application of the S^r concept to control human behavior, we may note the following typical passage, which describes techniques for the control of autistic children:

The sound of the candy dispenser preceding the delivery of candy served as a conditioned reinforcer. . . . With further training, the delivery of a coin (conditioned reinforcer) sustained the child's performance. . . . Still later, coins sustained the child's performance even though they had to be held for a period of time before they could be cashed in. . . . Even longer delays of reinforcement were arranged by sustaining behavior in the experimental room with a conditioned reinforcer as, for example, a towel or a life jacket which could be used later in the swimming pool." [Ferster, 1961, p. 441]

The thesis of the present author is that the S^r concept has not been established at the human level any better than it has been at the animal level. As he has defended this thesis on two other occasions, it can be disposed of briefly here (Longstreth, 1966, 1970a). The basic points are as follows: (a) A number of studies with human *S*s attempting to establish an S^r function has failed to do so (e.g., Mitrano, 1939; Estes, 1960; Longstreth, 1960, 1966a, 1966b; Donaldson, 1961; Fort, 1961; Myers, Craig, & Myers, 1961; Hall, 1964; Kass, Wilson, & Sidowski, 1964; Loeb, 1964; Kass & Wilson, 1966). (b) Of those reporting positive results, the elicitation problem almost invariably raises its ugly head (e.g., Fort, 1965; Myers, 1960). (c) There is a large number of studies with children showing that a stimulus paired with reward and then presented alone has a function *opposite* to that assigned to S^r, that is, a *frustrating* function (see Longstreth, 1966, 1970a, and Ryan & Watson, 1968, for reviews of these studies). A few comments will be made about this last point insofar as Wike challenged it in the 1969 *Nebraska Symposium on Motivation* (Wike, 1970).

In reviewing the first in a series of studies on S^r and frustration by Longstreth, Wike contended that (a) the conditions may not have been favorable for the development of S^r; (b) with one possible exception, the tests of S^r were not conventional; and (c) frustration theory was not strongly supported anyway. We shall reply to these charges within the context of the same study (Long-streth, 1966, Experiment 1).

In this study, 66 children learned to turn off one light illumination by turning a joystick in one direction (e.g., right) and to turn off a different illumination by turning the joystick in the opposite direction. Marbles were systematically paired with the termination of one illumination but not with the other. When the positive illumination (S+) was presented, a correct response resulted in the immediate termination of S+ and ejection of a marble into a clear plastic tube 2 seconds later. The ejection was accompanied by the noise of the marble ejection solenoid. Two seconds later the next stimulus was presented, either S+ or S−. When the negative stimulus (S−) was presented, a correct response terminated it immediately and the next illumination was presented 4 seconds later. The children were told that when the marbles reached a marker on the clear plastic tube, they could be exchanged for a "prize." Thirty-six training trials were given, 18 S+ and 18 S−. Then extinction began, unannounced, with S needing two more marbles to reach the marker.

There were three extinction groups. In the S + n group, S+ was the only illumination encountered. Two seconds after a correct response, the noise of the marble solenoid was heard as usual, but no marble was delivered. Two seconds later S+ was presented again. In the S+ group, conditions were exactly the same except that the marble solenoid was not activated. In the S− group, the negative illumination was the only illumination encountered. Response measures were amplitude, latency (converted to speed by the use of reciprocals), and number of responses to extinction.

The main extinction results were as follows: (a) Group S + n extinguished first, Group S+ second, and Group S− last ($p <$ .005). (b) Response latency increased most for Group S + n and least for Group S − (the decrements for Groups S + n and S+ were significant, the decrement for Group S − was not). (c) Variability in latency was significantly different for the three groups, being greatest for Group S + n and least for Group S−.

It was argued that these results were the opposite of what one would expect from an S^r point of view. That is, both the termination

of S+ and the noise of the marble solenoid (n) had been systematically paired with the subgoal rewards, marbles, and therefore
should have acquired S^r properties. But the results indicated that
responses followed by both of these stimuli (S + n) extinguished
faster than responses followed by just one of them (S+) or by
neither (S−). Amsel's frustration theory, it was argued, did a much
better job of predicting these results (Amsel, 1958). His theory
assumes that cues previously paired with reward and then presented
alone are aversive, eliciting an unconditioned emotional response.
The emotional response increases drive level, which may activate
avoidance responses. When avoidance occurs, the termination of
emotionality reinforces the previous response, and hence, the
avoidance response is strengthened. With enough extinction trials,
the avoidance response begins to conflict with and finally to dominate the previously rewarded instrumental response, and then
extinction occurs. Frustration, therefore, should have been greatest
for Group S + n and least for Group S−. Hence, the former
group should have extinguished first, and should have shown the
most signs of conflict, as well as of increased drive. This group did,
of course, extinguish first. The latency data support the conflict
prediction. That is, response blockage (e.g., increased latency) is
often assumed to be a sign of conflict, and so is increased variability
in latency. Group S + n showed the greatest increase in latency as
well as the greatest variability, and Group S− showed the smallest
changes in both indexes. The amplitude data, however, did not
support the increased-drive prediction. According to this prediction,
response amplitude on early extinction trials should have first
increased, most for Group S + n and least for Group S−. But no
significant differences were found. In Experiments 2 and 3, however, these changes were observed.

Wike's first criticism, that training conditions might not have
been favorable for the development of S^r, is based upon the argument that the reward, marbles, may not, in fact, have been reinforcing, and that a 2-second delay between S+ and receipt of a
marble may have been too long a delay to impart S^r properties to
S+ anyway. In response, it may first be pointed out that the marbles
were reinforcing; response strength to S+ increased over training
trials significantly more than response strength to S−, as indicated

both by amplitude data (see Figure 1, p. 5, of Longstreth, 1966) and by latency data (see Figure 2, p. 6). Regarding the 2-second delay between offset of S+ and receipt of a marble, in Experiment 2 this interval was changed to 1 second with no change in results. Furthermore, the solenoid noise occurred simultaneously with marble ejection, and yet Group S + n extinguished faster than Group S+. If Wike's reasoning were correct, the opposite should have been found.

Wike's second point, that with one exception unconventional tests of S^r were employed, comes as something of a surprise after the list of new procedures espoused by him. His argument is that one of the S^r components, S+, was presented *before* the response, not after. How can S^r reinforce a response it precedes? There are two answers to this question. (a) S+ was terminated *after* the response, and it was the termination of S+ which was followed 2 seconds later by a marble, not the onset of S+. Thus, according to the S^r assumption, the termination of S+ should have maintained the preceding response in extinction. But it did not. (b) The solenoid noise clearly followed the preceding joystick response, but yet did not function as a S^r; extinction was fastest under condition S + n. Wike acknowledged this fact and agreed that the results support frustration theory. But then he asked, "If Longstreth believes that S^r test conditions are optimal for the production of frustration and frustration produces faster extinction, then how can he account for the results of the many previous S^r studies, using extinction or new learning tests, in which extinction was slower and new learning was better with S^r?" (Wike, 1970, p. 62). The answer by now should be obvious: *What* studies? Indeed, it is perplexing to the author how Wike can ask the question at all, since a few pages later he denies his own answer: "Despite the innumerable investigations of S^r using extinction and new learning tests and involving many variables, convincing demonstrations of S^r have not been evident" (Wike, 1970, p. 75).

Wike's third criticism, that the study did not strongly support frustration theory either, displays a serious misunderstanding of Amsel's theory. According to Wike, resistance to extinction, amplitude, and latency should all follow parallel courses during extinction in order to support frustration theory. Thus he comments, "The failure of S+ and S + n to extinguish faster than S −, when extinction was indexed by amplitude and speed measures, would not appear to be in accord with frustration theory" (p. 60), and, "Two of these predictions, a and c, seem to be contradictory. Why should frustration produce an early decrease in speed but an increase in amplitude?" (p. 61).

The answer, very briefly, is that frustration produces conflict and increased drive. Conflict is indicated by slower speeds (increased latency) and increased drive by greater strength of the response when it does occur (e.g., increased amplitude). It is just this ability of the theory to predict different patterns of development for different indexes of responding that makes it such a convincing formulation.

Our position with regard to human studies of S^r, therefore, is similar to our evaluation of the animal studies: the case has not been proven. In addition, we would insist that a frustration effect rather than an S^r effect seems to be the more reliable consequent of pairing a stimulus with reward and then presenting it alone.

THE DILEMMA

Having argued that S^r effects have not been experimentally demonstrated at either the animal or human level, we now find ourselves in something of a bind. Wike states it succinctly: "At the same time, it is obvious in everyday life that secondary reinforcers, like grades, money and the like, appear to have long-term and powerful effects upon behavior. How can we reconcile the unimpressive results of S^r experiments, employing extinction and new learning paradigms, with these everyday observations?" (Wike, 1970, p. 75).

Wike's solution to the puzzle is to accept these everyday observations as convincing evidence of the power of S^r, and to suggest new tests in order to show its effects in the laboratory. Our solution is different. We reject the everyday observations as having anything to do with S^r. We reject the new laboratory tests of S^r as irrelevant and inconclusive. We argue that the everyday effects can be explained in terms of a cognitive interpretation and that this interpretation can be experimentally investigated in the laboratory. In the following section we develop and defend this point of view.

The Solution: A Cognitive Interpretation

Here is an example of how we would apply a cognitive interpretation to everyday observations of presumed S^r effects. Johnny comes in promptly from play when called by his mother, washes his hands, sits down quietly at the dinner table, and exhibits good manners and proper etiquette throughout the meal. Occasionally his mother or father indicates approval with a smile, a verbalization such as "good," and otherwise exhibits signs of social approval. Suppose a psychologist has been invited to dinner. The question occurs to him, why is this child so well-behaved? If he is of the S^r persuasion, he would probably reason that social approval, having been paired with established reinforcers many times in the child's past, and now presented systematically after episodes of good behavior, secondarily reinforces such behavior and maintains it at a high level of frequency.

We say no. The reason Johnny behaved so well was because he had a plan. The plan was that he intended to ask his parents if he could stay up late and watch a special program on TV. His strategy was that, if his parents were in a "good mood" after dinner, they would be much more likely to grant his request. He therefore behaved in a way calculated to instill the good mood. Social approval from his parents was merely an index of mood state; the greater the frequency of social approval, the better their mood. Thus he behaved in such a way as to maximize the frequency of social approval from his parents. Tomorrow would be another day, and there perhaps would be no special plans for the evening. Johnny perhaps would not come in so promptly for dinner either.

If we may now abstract the description a little, we are saying that human Ss use social approval as information about the likely behavior of its source. If the source's behavior is judged to be important to S, then he will pay attention to it. If, on the other hand, he does not 'see any way in which the source's behavior will affect him, then he is likely to ignore the evaluations. Suppose, for example, that Johnny knew his parents were going out for the evening, and that the baby-sitter would make the decision about how late he could stay up. His good behavior might then have occurred in her presence rather than in his parents' presence. Not that he would ignore his parents' evaluations completely—after all, they would come home sometime, and perhaps would even change their plans if his behavior got too far out of line.

The *power* of the source of social evaluations thus becomes a crucial variable. Power is defined in terms of the probability and quality of the source's future interactions with S in a given situation. We see a *weak power* source as one who may emit all kinds of social approval (and disapproval), but who is judged to have little control over S's behavior or its outcomes in a given future situation. A *strong power* source, on the other hand, is one who is judged to have considerable control over what S can do and what his behavioral outcomes will be in a given future situation. If S wishes to engage in a particular kind of behavior in that situation, and/or if he desires a particular outcome, *and if he can reason*, then he will attempt to manipulate the strong power source in a way calculated to gain his ends; e.g., he will try to predispose the source to act in his behalf when the crucial moment arrives.

The last point, that S must be able to reason, is of some importance. In the simplest case, S must be able to deduce that if his present behavior affects the source's present behavior, and if the source's present behavior is predictive of S's future outcome in situation X, then, if he desires a particular outcome in that situation, he had better pay attention to and manipulate the source's present behavior. If he cannot make the logical jump from the present to the future, then it seems unlikely that he will pay much attention to the source's present evaluations.

We would therefore suspect that our formulation would apply most directly to children beyond the age of four or five. We pick this age because numerous studies suggest that reasoning at younger ages is either very primitive or nonexistent (e.g., White, 1965). Some interesting predictions follow from this notion, the most obvious being that so-called S^r effects should not be much in evidence at younger ages. Of course, one could entertain the idea of two kinds of secondary reinforcement, one kind based upon cognitive mechanisms and the other based upon associative mechanisms (e.g., the Hull-Skinner type of S^r). Perhaps very young children are affected only by the associative type and older children only by the cognitive type, or perhaps older children are affected by both types. However, since we can find no evidence for an associative type of S^r, we would be forced to predict that very young children do not exhibit S^r effects at all, and older children exhibit them in accordance with our admittedly vague cognitive formulation.

EVIDENCE FOR A COGNITIVE INTERPRETATION OF SECONDARY REINFORCEMENT

Background Evidence

There is a good deal of evidence in the psychological literature consistent with our cognitive position. One long line of evidence supports our contention that social approval does not automatically strengthen preceding responses. There is a group of verbal operant conditioning studies which consistently show that verbal response tendencies are not changed by such feedback as "Good" or "Mm-hmmm" or the like unless S is aware of which responses are being reinforced and which are not. (See Dulany, 1962; Spielberger, 1962; and Spielberger & DeNike, 1966, for reviews of these experiments.) Dulany argued that S-R behavior theory is incapable of handling this fact, and described an elaborate cognitive ("propositional") theory to fill the void (Dulany, 1968).

There are studies by Thorndike himself, the originator of the law of effect, suggesting that the "effect" does not always occur. Thorndike discovered that if, during the learning of a task, S was suddenly given a monetary reward for some reason not logically connected to his preceding response—showing up for the experiment, for example—the "reward" had little or no effect upon the probability that the preceding response would be repeated upon presentation of the eliciting stimulus (Thorndike, 1931, 1935). To account for this anomalous result and at the same time retain the law of effect, Thorndike invented the principle of "belongingness": that a reward would have greater response-strengthening effects if the stimulus, response, and reward were related to each other in some meaningful way. As Estes has commented, "His principle seems most foreign in spirit to a theory which depends heavily for its support upon the contention that rewards exert their effects automatically upon preceding stimulus-response associations independently of the learner's awareness of the contingencies involved" (Estes, 1969, p. 84).

Delay-of-reward studies also question the automaticity of reward effects. Contrary to the law of effect, which is defined in terms of the proximity of responses and rewards, these studies show that the crucial variable is *what S does* during the delay (e.g., Saltzman, 1951; Mechanic, 1964; Postman, 1964). Indeed, Buchwald was able to show *better* learning under a delay condition than under a no-delay condition, a finding which shows the extremes to which one might go in disproving the law of effect (Buchwald, 1969). He also presented what might be called a mathematical model of a cognitive theory to account for these results.

Estes has made a distinction between the *informative* and *reinforcing* functions of stimuli, and reports experiments which show that when these two functions are isolated, the reinforcing function of verbal feedback disappears (Estes, 1969). He then proceeds to outline a pure contiguity theory of learning in which rewards play no role in learning at all, but serve instead as incentives, motivating *S* to utilize what has already been learned. Such a position is not unlike the present one, which assumes that S^r's do not affect learning either, but are utilized by *S* for the attainment of incentives which may be quite uncorrelated with the S^r's.

The author has recently carried out a series of experiments which is also relevant here. As only the first of these has been published as yet (Longstreth, 1970b), they will be described in some detail. The studies were designed as a follow-up to a controversy between Greenwald and Postman concerning the automaticity of the law of effect (Greenwald, 1966; Postman, 1966; Nuttin & Greenwald, 1968). According to Greenwald, some neglected work by the Belgian psychologist Joseph Nuttin "strikes at the heart" of the law of effect. What Nuttin presumably demonstrated was that, if some verbal responses are called "right" and others "wrong," retesting resulted in support of the law of effect only if *S* had been led to believe that he would be tested. If he had been led to believe that he would not be tested, that is, that he would not face the learning task again, then the law of effect did not apply; responses followed by "right" were not repeated any more frequently than responses followed by "wrong." If we assume that "right" is an

S^r, then we can immediately see how these results contradict the notion of automatic S^r effects. Postman pointed out a series of methodological flaws in the Nuttin studies, however, which led him to conclude, "It would be difficult to move further outside the boundary conditions of the law of effect" (Postman, 1966, p. 385). He therefore concluded the law had not been tested, and that it was, in his opinion, still a viable law.

The author attempted to throw some light on the controversy by taking heed of Postman's criticisms and repeating the experiments. College students were presented with lists of 10 cards upon each of which was printed an English stimulus word and two German response alternatives (Ss who had studied German were excluded). The S was to pick the German word which was "more similar semantically" to the English word. The purpose given for the study was that E wanted to determine if the "correct" word was recognizable by a naive person. The E then said, "Since I know which word is correct, I'll tell you each time just so you have some idea of how you are doing." For 5 of the 10 cards in each list, E said "right" regardless of what response S made, and on the other half he said "wrong." Crucial lists were presented a second time, without feedback, to measure retention. The key independent variable was that half the Ss had been led to believe that there would be no second test; they were told that each list would be presented just once, and buffer lists were presented once each to confirm this information. The remaining Ss were told that they would be tested, that a specified list would be presented a second time. All Ss were told to "get as many right as you can" when the test list was presented.

This procedure, with minor variations, was followed in five separate experiments. The results are summarized in Table 1, in terms of percent repeated responses under each of the two learning conditions. The results are the same in all five studies. When Ss were told there would be a test, they repeated more "right" responses than would be expected by chance (50%) and fewer wrong responses than would be expected by chance (50%); when they were told there would be no test, these differences were attenuated to nonsignificance in all five studies. The main conclusion is obvious: "right" does not exert automatic S^r effects. Rather, if S is led to

TABLE 1

Summary of Feedback Effects under Test $(+T)$ and No-test $(-T)$ Learning Conditions: Percent Responses Repeated

	Exp. 1 $-T$ $+T$	Exp. 2 $-T$ $+T$	Exp. 3 $-T$ $+T$	Exp. 4 $-T$ $+T$	Exp. 5[a] $-T$ $+T$	Total[b] $-T$ $+T$
"right"	72 90	68 82	62 80	67 74	60 60	65 78
"wrong"	46 22	58 22	52 34	48 30	48 38	51 30
N	10 10	15 15	31 31	18 18	10 10	84 84
Sig.	ns s	sn s	ns s	ns s	ns ns	

[a] In this experiment, an attempt was made to prevent S from encoding relevant information from *either* the test $(+T)$ or no-test $(-T)$ conditions by reducing the intertrial interval. This presumed prevention of rehearsal was successful in reducing performance to nonsignificance under both conditions.

[b] Weighted by sample size.

believe that his performance in a future situation will depend upon repetition of "right" responses and avoidance of "wrong" responses, then he will attempt to encode the relevant information. If he is led to believe that his future performance will not depend upon such responses, then he does not try to encode the relevant information. His future performance, of course, is dependent upon what he has encoded from the learning trial. The effects of "right" and "wrong" thus depend upon his plans.[2]

Dawson (1970) and Dawson and Grings (1968) have recently reported studies of classical conditioning of the GSR which are of interest in the present context. They note that classical conditioning usually results in two kinds of learning: the usual classically conditioned response in which the UCR becomes hooked to the CS, and S's ability to verbalize or otherwise indicate his awareness of the CS-UCS contingency. The former is called classical conditioning and the latter contingency learning. Dawson and Grings began by

2. The fact that percent repetition of "right" responses consistently exceeded the theoretical chance level of 50% in the no-test conditions is not contradictory to this conclusion. (This difference, although not significant in any of the five studies, is significant for the combined results.) Although Thorndike concluded from similar data that rewards have automatic weakening effects (note the close correspondence between fact and theoretical chance for percent "wrong" repetitions in the no-test condition: 51% vs. 50%), other interpretations are possible. A frequency-contiguity theory by Ekstrand, Wallace, and Underwood (1966) accounts for it very nicely, for example, and the author has yet another explanation under development.

accepting the dominant assumption that both kinds of learning occur in the usual paradigm for classical conditioning, and that it should be possible to isolate them. Thus "pure classical conditioning" was attempted in one group and "pure contingency learning" in another group. In the former condition, *S*s were presented with CS-UCS pairings, but contingency learning was minimized by imbedding the pairings in a masking task (paper and pencil tests). The contingency learning group was presented with instructions about the CS-UCS pairings, but no such pairings actually occurred. It was found that only the latter group gave evidence of "conditioned" GSRs, thus suggesting that contingency learning may be essential in the establishment of human GSR classical conditioning.

There were, however, methodological problems which left the data open for other interpretations. Dawson therefore carried out a series of further studies in which these possibilities were investigated. In none of them was he able to show classical conditioning as a result of CS-UCS pairings if contingency learning had been prevented. In all of them he was able to show "conditioning" as a result of contingency learning alone. The conclusion is clear: the "reinforcement" provided by the UCS (electric shock in this case) does not occur unless *S* is aware of its relationship to the CS. Much of what has passed for classical conditioning of the GSR is nothing of the sort, but rather the direct result of contingency learning. Like "right" and "wrong," the reinforcing effects of shock are not automatic, but depend upon the cognitions of *S*.

It may be the case, then, that secondary reinforcers are not the only stimuli which depend upon *S*'s cognitions for a reinforcing effect, but also some, or all, primary reinforcers. A good deal of further research is required before this possibility becomes more than a mere conjecture. That such effects are not limited to shock, however, is already apparent (e.g., Ericksen, 1962; Paul, Ericksen, & Humphreys, 1962). If such a picture does emerge, a very interesting theoretical question is forced: How is animal learning to be accounted for—were Pavlov's dogs "aware" of the CS-UCS contingency? An interesting methodological problem also arises: If contingency learning is possible in animals, how is it to be measured? Nonverbal indexes will have to be developed. Perhaps a dog that looks in the direction of the food source when the metronome sounds has learned the contingency, while a dumb brute that stares straight ahead has not learned it. Some fascinating studies come to mind.

Another line of studies, too long to be summarized in detail, shows that human problem solving often consists of more than a simple strengthening of rewarded responses and weakening of nonrewarded responses; "hypotheses" are elicited which cannot be accounted for by a simple consideration of reinforcement history. Furthermore, these hypotheses, or plans, change systematically as a function of age. After experimenting with subjects of ages 3, 5, 7, 9, 13, and 18, Weir was thus able to conclude:

> Older subjects, particularly adults, enter this task with a strong expectancy that there is a solution which will yield 100 percent reinforcement, or at least 100 percent predictability of when a reinforcement will be delivered and when it will not, and employ complex strategies based on complex hypotheses concerning the nature of the task and the reinforcement schedule. Younger children, on the other hand, are not concerned with, or more likely not capable of, such complex mediating mechanisms, and do not respond on this basis. [Weir, 1968, p. 262]

White reviewed a large number of studies which suggested to him that children below the age of four or five solve problems in a qualitatively different manner than older children or adults (White, 1965). He classified the differences into four groups:

1. The older child uses language symbols as "pure stimulus acts," as cues eliciting responses that the physical referents would not call forth.
2. The older child is able to direct and maintain his attention toward "invariant dimensions of stimuli in a surround of variance."
3. The older child is able to plan about the future and to make inferences about the past.
4. The older child is more reliant on distance receptors and less reliant on the near receptors such as touch, pain, etc.

White concluded that the mental processes characteristic of the older child are incompatible with those of the younger child:

> Let us put the idea more directly and in terms of learning. Suppose the child, before the transition, solves problems according to a set of

processes which we generally describe as "associative".... The changes in the child's behavior from 5 to 7, unlike many other age changes, may not take place by enrichment, elaboration, smoothing, or by any process which transforms and irrevocably alters the original product. Perhaps, instead, a new level of function comes in having the four properties described in Section IV, A [see preceding paragraphs]. We might generally characterize the higher level of function as "cognitive." It needs more detailed description. For the moment, we would like to argue only that the cognitive level of operation depends critically upon the inhibition of associative function or, at least, of the response which associative function is capable of determining. [White, 1965, p. 213]

Specific Evidence

In the first study (Longstreth & Hertel, 1970) we attempted to set up conditions by which we could produce either apparent S^r effects or the opposite (i.e., frustration effects) depending upon the information made available to S's cognitive machinery. We began by asking, Why do human beings work for subgoals such as money? We hypothesized that it is because of the *plans* they have for subgoals: they intend to trade them for other goals. If the information is presented that such trading is impossible, then cognitive mechanisms will bring S to the conclusion that he should cease working for them. If this information is withheld, on the other hand, S will continue working for them even though they are no longer traded for other goals.

The experiment consisted of two phases, training and testing. In training, all Ss (45 children from grades four and five) learned to turn a joystick in one direction to turn off a bright light and in the opposite direction to turn off a dim light. Whenever the bright light was turned off, a marble was automatically ejected 2 seconds later. The S was instructed to insert the marble into a hole in the top of a toy cash register and then push one of the keys. When a key was pushed, a bell rang and the drawer slid out, containing a penny. S was told he could keep the penny, and that he could now turn off another light. While S was attending to the stimulus-response unit, E quietly slipped another penny into the cotton-lined drawer and closed it, preparing the register for the next trial. Thus, for all Ss, turning off the bright light regularly preceded marbles, and marbles regularly preceded pennies.

After seven pennies had been earned, Ss were randomly assigned to three test groups of 15 Ss each. Two experimental groups continued to earn marbles while a control group did not. One of the experimental groups saw that there were no more pennies; when the marble was inserted into the cash register and the drawer opened, the penny was absent. The other experimental group did not receive this information; this group was not allowed to discover that the cash register was empty. This was accomplished by suggesting to them, "Why don't you save your marbles and put them in the cash register at the end of the game?" A cardboard box was then put beside the register and Ss were asked to put their marbles into the box. The control group received no marbles; when they turned off the bright light, it was simply reactivated 5 seconds later.

The dependent variable was the number of times S turned off the bright light. All Ss were allowed to continue responding until they either stopped, expressed a wish to stop, or responded 150 times. The Ss who saw there were *no pennies* responded a median of 10 times; those who were instructed to *save* responded a median of 92 times; and those who received no more marbles (*control*) responded a median of 26 times. These differences were significant when evaluated by Chi Square, $\chi^2(2) = 6.56$, $p < .05$. Mann-Whitney tests indicated that all two-group comparisons were significant ($p < .05$).[3]

These results are not easily accounted for from an S^r point of view. The two experimental groups both received the presumed S^r (marbles) in the test situation. Yet one group showed much less perseverance than a group which did not receive pennies *or* marbles (control), and the other group showed much greater perseverance. From an S^r point of view, both groups should have been more resistant to extinction than the control group. Further, the differences between the two experimental groups should have been in the opposite direction, since the no-pennies group received more of the stimuli previously paired with pennies than the save group. That is, the former group inserted the marbles into the cash register, pushed

3. Means were not analyzed because some Ss were stopped at 150 responses.

the key, heard the bell, and saw the drawer open. All these stimuli, internal as well as external, had previously been paired with marbles and therefore should have functioned as S^r's. Yet this group extinguished much faster than the save group.

From a cognitive point of view, these results are easily explained. While the no-pennies group received more stimuli previously paired with pennies, it also saw that the pennies were absent. A simple application of logical reasoning—work only for pennies; marbles do not produce pennies—leads to the conclusion to stop responding for marbles. The save group, not informed that marbles no longer produce pennies, would not have this logical step to the same conclusion.

The behavior of the control group is less easily explained. If these Ss assumed that marbles were necessary for pennies and that one should work only for pennies, then the absence of marbles should have led to the same rapid extinction that was observed in the no-pennies group. But control Ss were more perseverant than no-pennies Ss. There are two ad hoc explanations that seem reasonable. From a cognitive point of view, the conclusion not to respond may have required more steps of reasoning than was the case for the no-pennies group. That is, the two premises, (a) work only for pennies and (b) there are no more marbles, do not lead to the conclusion to stop working. One must make an additional assumption that marbles are the only way to obtain pennies. With more complicated reasoning required, it would be expected that fewer Ss would arrive at the logical conclusion, and hence the greater perseverance of the control group over the no-pennies group is explained.

A second explanation is frustration. According to Amsel's theory, frustration is maximum when all the stimuli previously paired with reward are presented alone. This was obviously the case for the no-pennies group. Thus it should have experienced more frustration, and hence should have extinguished faster.

There is, of course, no incompatibility between frustration theory and our cognitive formulation: the ability to reason does not immunize one from frustration. It may well be that both processes combined to produce the results of this experiment.

In a dissertation by Jill Lundgren, a different technique was used to examine the relationship between S^r effects and information concerning future rewards (Lundgren, 1970). Under one condition 7-year-old Ss were told that responses leading to the S^r would eventually earn a prize, while in another condition it was made clear that no more prizes could be earned, since E was "out of them." Learning of a new response followed by S^r was then measured in both groups.

The experiment consisted of two phases, a training phase in which a neutral cue was repeatedly paired with social and tangible rewards, and a testing phase in which its S^r properties were measured. In the training phase, experimental Ss were instructed to pull a lever when they heard a buzzer. Pulling the lever resulted in termination of the buzzer and onset of one of two different colored lights (green or yellow). Thirty-two trials were given, with each color appearing 16 times in a random order. Whenever the non-preferred color (determined verbally) appeared, E entered the game room and said, "Good. The green (yellow) light went on. I like that light to come on. That's fine," etc. Further, on every third presentation of that color, S was allowed to choose a prize from a table displaying assorted toys and candies. A control group was treated the same except that no rewards, social or tangible, were presented. When the lever was pulled, a light was activated for 5 seconds and then terminated, with no interactions with E and no toys presented.

In the test phase, a different response was used. Two response buttons were present, with a light source mounted above each. Depression of one button activated the green light and depression of the other button activated the yellow light. S was told to press a button whenever the buzzer came on, and that his responses determined which light was activated.

Half the experimental Ss were told that if they made their winning light (i.e., the one which earned them rewards in the first game) come on often enough, they could earn more prizes. A table of prizes was in the room. This condition is called the Future Reward condition. Remaining experimental Ss were told that there were no more prizes, and the table was empty. This condition is called the No Future Reward condition. Control Ss, who had not received any rewards in the first phase, were rewarded with social and tangible rewards whenever the nonpreferred light color was activated, as experimental Ss had been rewarded in the first phase. The purpose of the control group was thus to determine if those rewards were, in fact, reinforcing in the test situation, a control which is missing from most S^r studies.

A total of 16 test trials was given. The results are presented in Figure 3 in terms of percent choice of the button followed by the S^r color (experimental Ss) or by social-tangible rewards (control Ss). It may be noted, first, that the social-tangible rewards were indeed reinforcing for the button-pushing response: the control group shows a typical learning curve, starting near chance and increasing to about 90% correct responses. Second, the experimental group which was led to believe that activation of the S^r color might result in future rewards (FR) developed a similar preference, which is evident on the first block of trials. (It was possible to exhibit a preference on the first block of trials by observing if the S^r-colored light bulb was mounted to the left or the right, and pushing the response button directly underneath. Control Ss did not yet know which light, if any, would be reinforced and thus were not able to show a preference at the outset.) Third, the experimental group which was led to believe that activation of the S^r color would not result in future rewards did not begin with a response preference nor was one developed; performance began a little above chance and actually receded to almost a perfect chance level (two responses out of four). Statistical analyses confirm these trends: the Control and Future Reward means do not differ from each other, and both are significantly different from means of the No Future Reward condition.

It is clear from this experiment, as from the previous one, that pairing a neutral stimulus with an established reinforcer is not a sufficient condition for the development of an S^r. The S^r effect totally disappeared when S was led to believe that it had no bearing on his future treatment. Moreover, when the opposite belief was engendered, the so-called S^r effect was as strong as the "primary" reinforcement effect, another result which is inimical to S^r theory, since it is hardly assumed that "secondary" effects should be as powerful as "primary" effects.

Turning to the cognitive position, the explanation would proceed from the basic assumption that, to the extent the subject

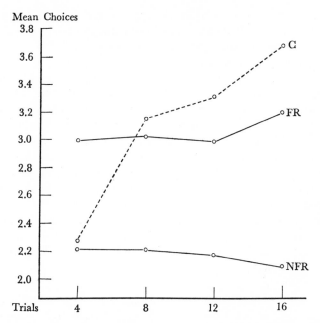

Fig. 3. Lundgren data for two secondary reinforcement conditions (FR and NFR) and a control (C) condition.

reasons about the contingencies between present behavior and future rewards, to that extent will his behavior be guided by the implications of his reasoning. Future Reward Ss were presented with information which allowed them to conclude that pushing the button activating the S^r-colored light would result in future rewards, and their behavior was consistent with this reasoning. The No Future Reward Ss were not presented with such information, and their behavior did not reflect it.

A Prediction

Theories are supposed to generate testable predictions if they are scientifically meaningful. We shall end this discussion of evidence with a prediction and a description of how we intend to test it. Perhaps the data will be in before this paper goes to press.

Suppose S inserts a poker chip in a slot and gets a marble. He then drops the marble in a hole and gets a nickel and a button, both of which he gets to keep. These sequences are repeated over and over. Then a new task is introduced: if S pulls a lever on the left he gets a poker chip; if he pulls a lever on the right he gets a button. He can go back and work at the previous tasks in 10 minutes; until then he must pull a lever (either lever) whenever a buzzer sounds. Which lever will he learn to pull? S^r theory predicts the lever on the right, since buttons were temporally and spatially more contiguous with nickels than were poker chips. The cognitive formulation predicts the lever on the left, because S will realize (deduce) that poker chips are more likely to earn future rewards than buttons.

Of course, there are presuppositions to be demonstrated (e.g., that nickels are in fact reinforcing for lever pulling in this situation) and control procedures to be instituted (e.g., counterbalancing of buttons and poker chips against nickels and marbles; showing that the button is as much a discriminative stimulus as is the poker chip; etc.), but space does not permit a complete description of such details. Assume that whatever control procedures are needed to rule out alternative interpretations are built into the design. Ignoring these qualifications, the formal aspects of the experiment can be schematicized as in Figure 4. We predict that, in any such experiment, R_1 will be learned at the expense of R_2 *to the extent S can reason.* If S cannot reason (e.g., if S is an animal, or a human less

Phase I (training)

$$Sa \longrightarrow Ra \longrightarrow Sb$$
$$Sb \longrightarrow Rb \longrightarrow Sn, S^+$$

Phase II (test)

$$S_1 \longrightarrow R_1 \longrightarrow Sa$$
$$S_2 \longrightarrow R_2 \longrightarrow Sn$$

FIG. 4. Schematic diagram of proposed experiment to separate reinforcing and cognitive effects of supposed S^r's. Sa, Sb, S_1, and S_2 are arbitrary stimuli; Ra, Rb, R_1, and R_2 are arbitrary responses; Sn is an arbitrary neutral stimulus; S+ is an established reinforcer for R_1 and R_2.

than 3 or 4 years of age), then either no preference will develop or, if there is such a thing as an associative S^r effect, a preference for R_2 may develop. We think the latter possibility is remote, simply because we cannot find evidence of an associative S^r effect, Wike, Hendry, and others nonwithstanding.

Some interesting developmental studies within a learning-theory vs. cognitive context are thereby suggested. We hope we will soon be able to carry some of them out.

ADDENDUM

Since the time this paper was presented, the proposed experiment has been carried out. Phase I (training) went as follows: *S* took a paper clip (Sa) from a container and inserted it into a hole; pushed a button which, in conjunction with the paperclip insertion, turned on a light; and turned off the light by pushing a joystick to the left. This sequence of responses following Sa is labeled Ra. Occasionally the joystick response was followed 2 seconds later by automatic ejection of a marble (Sb) into a container resting at the end of a rubber hose. The marble was taken to a counter ("store") and placed in a basket (Rb). A "storekeeper" took the basket and soon returned it with a penny or a nickel (S+) and a piece of wood (Sn) inside. *S* was told he could keep whatever was in the basket, and that he could play the game again by starting at the beginning of the sequence. The sequence of events was thus as described under Phase I of Figure 4: Sa → Ra → Sb → Rb → Sn, S+.

Now for some details. (a) Sb was not presented on every trial in order to heighten interest in the game. When it was not presented, *S* took another Sa and inserted it into the hole. Six marbles were eventually earned, in the order ----M-MM--MM-M. (b) Pennies and nickels alternated irregularly as S+, again to heighten interest. Three of each were earned, for a total of 18 cents. (c) Paper clips and pieces of wood were counterbalanced with respect to Sa and Sn: for half the *S*s paper clips served as Sa and wood as Sn, and the reverse was the case for remaining *S*s.

At the end of Phase I, *E* made Comment A to half the *S*s and Comment B to the remaining *S*s. These comments were followed by a common set of instructions for Phase II (test).

Comment A. "Are you out of paper clips [wood]? Then we can't play this game anymore. If you had gotten enough money, you could have bought one of these prizes here [displaying three Christmas packages]. But you don't have enough money.

"Now let's play another game. If you play it right, you'll be able to play this game again."

Comment B. "Are you out of paper clips [wood]? Then we can't play this game anymore. That's all for this game; we aren't going to play it anymore. I'll turn off the switch here that controls the marble machine [*E* flips a switch that is followed by cessation of a hum emanating from the marble machine].

"Now let's play another game. If you play it right, you can win one of these prizes [displaying three Christmas packages]."

Common instructions. "See these three cups [blue, green, and yellow]? Well, I'm going to put a paper clip in one of them [displaying paper clip and dropping it into one of the cups out of *S*'s line of vision], a piece of wood in another [displaying wood and doing so, again out of *S*'s line of vision], and nothing in one of them. But you won't be able to see me, because I'm going to do it over here where you can't see. Now you pick one of the cups by telling me what color you want. I'll give you the cup you name and you get to keep whatever is in it. You take out whatever is in it and then give me the cup back. I'll always put the things in the same color cups. I won't switch them around. OK, pick a cup now.

[After ten trials] "Which do you want, the paper clip or the wood? Why? [Answers were recorded as near verbatim as possible.] Remember, I always put things in the same cup. If you play the game right, you can [to Comment A *S*s] play the first game again, [to Comment B *S*s] win one of the prizes."

Phase II was continued until the cup containing Sa or Sn was chosen five times in a row, or until 20 trials had ensued. Counterbalancing of cup color and contents was carried out haphazardly (preliminary data and subsequent analyses of these data showed no color preferences in this situation).

In terms of Phase II (test) terminology, Figure 4, the two cups containing paper clip and wood are labeled S_1 and S_2. Choice of either cup is labeled R_1 and R_2, and the contents are labeled Sa and Sn. The third, empty cup is in addition to this outline, and may be represented as $S_3 \rightarrow R_3 \rightarrow$ So, where So indicates that nothing is in the cup.

Two classrooms from the same school provided the Ss for this experiment: first graders and a mixture of fourth and fifth graders. The approximate mean ages of the two classrooms were thus 6 and $9\frac{1}{2}$ years.[4] Age level was orthogonal to instructions (Comments A and B), yielding a 2×2 factorial design with 12 Ss in each cell.

Predictions. The S^r prediction, of course, is that Ss in all conditions will learn to choose the cup containing Sn, since it is the stimulus that has been paired most closely with $S+$. The cognitive prediction is that some Ss will learn to choose the cup containing Sa: those Ss presented with information allowing them to deduce the connection between Sa and a prize, and those able to make the deduction. These Ss are those presented with Comment A who were $9\frac{1}{2}$ years old. This prediction is made as follows:

Comment A Ss were presented with the following information:

1. More money is required to win a prize.
2. Playing the Phase I game is required to obtain money.
3. Sa is required to play the Phase I game.

Presumably, the $9\frac{1}{2}$-year-olds would be more likely to deduce the conclusion, Sa is required to win a prize, than the 6-year-olds.

A second prediction is that, when asked *why* Sa is preferred, $9\frac{1}{2}$-year-old Comment A Ss will be more likely to state the above conclusion: that Sa is needed to play the Phase I game again.

Results. The distribution of Ss who did and did not reach a criterion of five consecutive choices of the cup containing Sa is presented in Table 2. It is clear that in only one condition was there a definite preference for Sa: in the $9\frac{1}{2}$-year-old Comment A condition, where 75% of the Ss reached criterion. Chi Square for the 6-year-old contingency table is not significant, while for the $9\frac{1}{2}$-year-old table, corrected $\chi^2(1) = 4.17$, $p < .05$. The main prediction is thus clearly supported.

4. This study was conducted at Cowan Avenue School, Los Angeles, California. The author is indebted to Donald L. Taylor, principal, and Mrs. Violet Olenhouse and Mrs. Loretta Royce, teachers, whose cooperation and patience made this study possible. William Miller, graduate student, ran some of the subjects; others were run by the author.

TABLE 2

NUMBER OF Ss REACHING CRITERION OF FIVE
CONSECUTIVE CHOICES OF CUP CONTAINING Sa

	6-year-olds		9½-year-olds	
	Comment		Comment	
Criterion	A	B	A	B
Yes	2	1	9	3
No	10	11	3	9
	χ^2(ns)		$\chi^2 = 4.17, p < .05$	

Concerning the S^r prediction, only one S (of 48) chose Sn five times in a row. Clearly, then, Sn did not function as a strong reinforcer in any condition.

The second prediction is that 9½-year-old Comment A Ss would be most likely to respond with the name of the object signified by Sa when asked, "Which do you want, [Sa] or [Sn]?" and with "To play the first game again" or the equivalent when asked "Why?" The number of Ss in each condition responding with this logical reason are presented in Table 3. The prediction is clearly confirmed: Comments A and B had no differential effects on the 6-year-olds, but pronounced effects on the 9½-year-olds. Of the Comment A 9½-year-olds, 83% said something to the effect that they wanted Sa to play the first game again. The most frequent actual response was "To play *that* game again."

TABLE 3

NUMBER OF Ss RESPONDING WITH SA AND A
LOGICAL REASON WHEN ASKED ABOUT
PREFERENCE

	6-year-olds		9½-year-olds	
	Comment		Comment	
Sa, Reason	A	B	A	B
Yes	4	1	10	2
No	8	11	2	10
	χ^2(ns)		$\chi^2 = 8.17, p < .005$	

There is yet another, more demanding, test of the cognitive formulation. Granted that $9\frac{1}{2}$-year-old Comment A Ss were most likely to develop a preference for Cup Sa, and to state that Sa was desired in order to play the first game again, a further prediction is that these two response measures should be related to each other: Ss who learn to choose Cup Sa should do so *because* they wish to play the first game again. The same Ss, in other words, should meet both the performance and the verbal criteria.

Table 4 provides the relevant data. It can be seen that the prediction is supported: 80% of the Ss reaching the performance criterion gave the expected reason when asked why, while only 15% of those not reaching criterion did so. The resulting Phi Coefficient of .63 indicates a sizeable correlation between the two responses.

TABLE 4

NUMBER OF Ss REACHING CHOICE
CRITERION AND GIVING EXPECTED
LOGICAL REASON

Reason	Choice Criterion	
	Yes	No
Yes	12	5
No	3	28
	$\chi^2 = 16.23, p < .001$	

The question of the chicken or the egg can also be asked: Which came first, the reason or the choice? Cognitive theory, of course, predicts that the reason came first and, along with other factors, caused S to develop a choice preference for Cup Sa. Although the present data are not decisive on this matter, it may be noted that of the 12 Ss who met both performance and verbal criteria, 8 gave the correct verbal reason *before* completing the five performance criterion trials. There is nothing here to indicate that performance preceded the logical reason; if anything, the opposite is suggested.

Conclusion. In every way, the results support the cognitive predictions. At the same time the S^r prediction is not supported: a preference for Sn over Sa did not develop in any condition, not even those not producing a preference for Sa. When the learning curves over the 20 performance trials are examined, there is no evidence in any condition of even a positive slope for the Sn choice curves. We are thus led to a rejection of S^r theory at the same time the cognitive position is strongly supported.

It would seem we therefore have a reasonable solution to the dilemma posed earlier—the contrast between laboratory failures to demonstrate S^r effects and strong apparent S^r effects in everyday life (e.g., grades, money, etc.). We would argue that people do not work for money because it has been paired with rewards in the past. They work for it only if they believe it will bring rewards in the future. Since the past usually extends into the future, there is an inevitable correlation between past pairings with reward and beliefs about future usefulness. But there are exceptional circumstances which reveal this correlation to be just that, and not a cause-effect relationship. It is possible, in other words, to separate past pairings with reward from implications about the future. When this is done, as in the present experiment, the S^r-predicted behavior disappears. We may thus conclude that if money were suddenly made worthless, most people would immediately stop working for it, regardless of the number of past pairings between it and other rewards.

Nature, of course, seldom provides opportunities to put hypotheses of this sort to the test—hence the importance of an analytical experimental approach. But it may be noted in passing that a move to a country with different currency is often followed by an immediate abandonment of the "old" currency in favor of the "new" currency; that school children without college plans do not behave as though high grades are particularly reinforcing; that although trading stamps are collected and paired with all kinds of rewards, as soon as the local newspaper announces that "blue-chip stamps will no longer be redeemed in this area," women by the hundreds immediately stop collecting them; that although food has been paired with paper napkins thousands of times in millions of homes, no one collects paper napkins; and that in spite of the fact that my wife has eaten food from pottery dishes for years, she does not collect them, and the dishes she does collect she has never eaten from. Perhaps there is more to be extracted from simple observation than we experimentalists like to think. I don't really think so, though—cases of special pleading have never been convincing to me.[5]

5. I thank Donald D. Jensen of the University of Nebraska for introducing me to the term *special pleading*.

REFERENCES

Amsel, A. The role of frustrative nonreward in noncontinuous reward situations. *Psychological Bulletin*, 1958, **55**, 102–119.

Bolles, R. C. *Theory of motivation*. New York: Harper & Row, 1967.

Buchwald, A. M. Effects of "right" and "wrong" on subsequent behavior: a new interpretation. *Psychological Review*, 1969, **76**, 132–143.

Bugelski, B. R. Extinction with and without sub-goal reinforcement. *Journal of Comparative Psychology*, 1938, **26**, 121–134.

Bugelski, B. R. *The psychology of learning*. New York: Holt, 1956.

Cofer, C. N., & Appley, M. H. *Motivation: Theory and research*. New York: Wiley & Sons, 1964.

Cowles, J. T. Food-tokens as incentives for learning by chimpanzees. *Comparative Psychology Monographs*, 1937, **14**(5).

Crowder, W. F., Gay, B. R., Bright, M. G., & Lee, M. F. Secondary reinforcement or response facilitation? III. Reconditioning. *Journal of Psychology*, 1959, **48**, 307–310.

Crowder, W. F., Gay, B. R., Fleming, W. C., & Hurst, R. W. Secondary reinforcement or response facilitation? IV. The retention method. *Journal of Psychology*, 1959, **48**, 311–314.

Crowder, W. F., Gill, K., Hodge, C. C., & Nash, F. A. Secondary reinforcement or response facilitation? II. Response acquisition. *Journal of Psychology*, 1959, **48**, 303–306.

Crowder, W. F., Morris, J. B., & McDaniel, M. H. Secondary reinforcement or response facilitation? I. Resistance to extinction. *Journal of Psychology*, 1959, **48**, 299–302.

Dawson, M. E. Cognition and conditioning: Effects of masking the CS-UCS contingency on human GSR classical conditioning. *Journal of Experimental Psychology*, 1970, **85**, 389–396.

Dawson, M. E., & Grings, W. W. Comparison of classical conditioning and relational learning. *Journal of Experimental Psychology*, 1968, **76**, 227–231.

Donaldson, T. E. Secondary reinforcement vs. other stimulus effects in extinction and learning of a new response. Unpublished doctoral dissertation, Purdue University, 1961.

Dulany, D. E. The place of hypotheses and intentions: An analysis of verbal control in verbal conditioning. In C. W. Erickson (Ed.), *Behavior and awareness*. Durham; N.C.: Duke University Press, 1962. Pp. 102–129.

Dulany, D. E. Awareness, rules, and propositional control: A confrontation with S-R behavior theory. In T. R. Dixon & D. L. Horton (Eds.), *Verbal behavior and general behavior theory*. New Jersey: Prentice-Hall, 1968. Pp. 340–387.

Ekstrand, B. R., Wallace, W. P., & Underwood, B. J. A frequency theory of verbal-discrimination learning. *Psychological Review*, 1966, **73**, 566–578.

Erickson, C. W. (Ed.) *Behavior and awareness.* Durham, N.C.: Duke University Press, 1962.

Estes, R. K. Number of training trials and variations in stimulus cues as factors effecting extinction in children. Unpublished master's thesis, University of Southern California, 1960.

Estes, W. K. Reinforcement in human learning. In J. T. Tapp (Ed.), *Reinforcement and behavior.* New York: Academic Press, 1969.

Ferster, C. B. Positive reinforcement and behavioral deficits of autistic children. *Child Development*, 1961, **32**, 437–456.

Ferster, C. B., & Skinner, B. F. *Schedules of reinforcement.* New York: Appleton, 1957.

Fort, J. G. Secondary reinforcement with preschool children. *Child Development*, 1961, **32**, 755–764.

Fort, J. G. Discrimination based on secondary reinforcement. *Child Development*, 1965, **36**, 481–490.

Greenwald, A. G. Nuttin's neglected critique of the law of effect. *Psychological Bulletin*, 1966, **65**, 199–205.

Hall, J. Secondary reinforcement or frustration? Unpublished doctoral dissertation, University of Southern California, 1964.

Hall, J. R. *The psychology of learning.* Philadelphia: Lippincott, 1966.

Hendry, D. P. (Ed.) *Conditioned reinforcement.* Homewood, Ill.: Dorsey Press, 1969.

Hull, C. L. *Principles of behavior.* New York: Appleton-Century-Crofts, 1943.

Hull, C. L. *A behavior system.* New Haven: Yale University Press, 1952.

Kass, N., & Wilson, H. Resistance to extinction as a function of percentage of reinforcement, number of training trials, and conditioned reinforcement. *Journal of Experimental Psychology*, 1966, **71**, 355–357.

Kass, N., Wilson, H., & Sidowski, J. B. Effects of number of training trials upon the development of a secondary reinforcer with children. *American Psychologist*, 1964, **19**, 451. (Abstract)

Kelleher, R. T. Conditioned reinforcement in chimpanzees. *Journal of Comparative and Physiological Psychology*, 1957, **50**, 571–575. (a)

Kelleher, R. T. A multiple schedule of conditioned reinforcement with chimpanzees *Psychological Reports*, 1957, **3**, 485–491. (b)

Kelleher, R. T. Fixed ratio schedules of conditioned reinforcement with chimpanzees. *Journal of Experimental Analysis of Behavior*, 1958, **1**, 281–289.

Kelleher, R. T. Chaining and conditioned reinforcement. In W. K. Honig (Ed.), *Operant behavior: Areas of research and application.* New York: Appleton-Century-Crofts, 1966. (a)

Kelleher, R. T. Conditioned reinforcement in second-order schedules. *Journal of Experimental Analysis of Behavior*, 1966, **9**, 475–485. (b)

Kelleher, R. T., & Gollub, L. R. A review of positive conditioned reinforcement. *Journal of Experimental Analysis of Behavior*, 1962, **5**, 543–597.

Keller, F. S., & Schoenfeld, W. N. *Principles of psychology.* New York: Appleton-Century-Crofts, 1950.

Kimble, G. A. *Hilgard and Marquis' conditioning and learning.* (2d ed.) New York: Appleton-Century-Crofts, 1961.

Lieberman, S. M. A study of secondary reinforcement. Unpublished master's thesis, University of Southern California, 1967.

Loeb, J. The incentive value of cartoon faces to children. *Journal of Experimental Child Psychology,* 1964, **1,** 99–107.

Longstreth, L. E. The relationship between expectations and frustration in children. *Child Development,* 1960, **31,** 667–671.

Longstreth, L. E. Frustration and secondary reinforcement concepts as applied to human instrumental conditioning and extinction. *Psychological Monographs,* 1966, **80,** (11, Whole No. 619). (a)

Longstreth, L. E. Frustration rather than S^r effects in children. *Psychonomic Science,* 1966, **4,** 425–426. (b)

Longstreth, L. E. Motivation. In H. W. Reese & L. P. Lipsitt (Eds.), *Experimental child psychology.* New York: Academic Press, 1970. Pp. 311–362. (a)

Longstreth, L. E. Tests of the law of effect using open and closed tasks. *Journal of Experimental Psychology,* 1970, **84,** 53–57. (b)

Longstreth, L. E., & Hertel, R. A test of a cognitive interpretation of S^r effects. Unpublished manuscript, 1970.

Lundgren, J. B. Secondary reinforcement: A cognitive interpretation. Unpublished doctoral dissertation, University of Southern California, 1970.

Malagodi, E. F. Acquisition of the token-reward habit in the rat. *Psychological Reports,* 1967, **20,** 1335–1342. (a)

Malagodi, E. F. Fixed-ratio schedules of token reinforcement. *Psychonomic Science,* 1967, **8,** 469–470. (b)

Malagodi, E. F. Variable-interval schedules of token reinforcement. *Psychonomic Science,* 1967, **8,** 471–472. (c)

Mechanic, A. The responses involved in the rote learning of verbal materials. *Journal of Verbal Learning and Verbal Behavior,* 1964, **3,** 30–36.

Mitrano, A. J. Principles of conditioning in human goal behavior. *Psychological Monographs,* 1939, **51,** (14, Whole No. 230).

Mowrer, O. H. *Learning theory and behavior.* New York: Wiley & Sons, 1960.

Myers, J. L. Secondary reinforcement: A review of recent experimentation. *Psychological Bulletin,* 1958, **55,** 284–301.

Myers, N. A. Extinction following partial and continuous primary and secondary reinforcement. *Journal of Experimental Psychology,* 1960, **60,** 172–179.

Myers, N. A., Craig, G. J., & Myers, J. L. Secondary reinforcement as a function of the number of reinforced trials. *Child Development,* 1961, **32,** 765–772.

Nuttin, J., & Greenwald, A. G. *Reward and punishment in human learning.* New York: Academic Press, 1968.

Paul, G. L., Eriksen, C. W., & Humphreys, L. G. Use of temperature stress with cool air reinforcement for human operant conditioning. *Journal of Experimental Psychology,* 1962, **64,** 329–335.

Postman, L. Short-term memory and incidental learning. In A. W. Melton (Ed.), *Categories of human learning.* New York: Academic Press, 1964. Pp. 145–201.

Postman, L. Reply to Greenwald. *Psychological Bulletin,* 1966, **65,** 383–388.

Ryan, T. J., & Watson, P. Frustrative nonreward theory applied to children's behavior. *Psychological Bulletin*, 1968, **69**, 111–125.

Saltzman, I. J. Maze learning in the absence of primary reinforcement: A study of secondary reinforcement. *Journal of Comparative and Physiological Psychology*, 1949, **42**, 161–173.

Saltzman, I. J. Delay of reward and human verbal learning. *Journal of Experimental Psychology*, 1951, **41**, 437–439.

Skinner, B. F. *The behavior of organisms.* New York: Appleton, 1938.

Spielberger, C. D. The role of awareness in verbal conditioning. In C. W. Eriksen (Ed.), *Behavior and awareness.* Durham, N.C.: Duke University Press, 1962. Pp. 73–101.

Spielberger, C. D., & DeNike, L. D. Descriptive behaviorism versus cognitive theory in verbal operant conditioning. *Psychological Review*, 1966, **73**, 306–327.

Thorndike, E. L. *Human learning.* New York: Century, 1931.

Thorndike, E. L. *The psychology of wants, interests, and attitudes.* New York: Appleton, 1935.

Watson, R. I. *Psychology of the child.* New York: Wiley & Sons, 1965.

Weir, M. W. Developmental changes in problem-solving strategies. In N. S. Endler, L. R. Boulter, & H. Osser (Eds.), *Contemporary issues in developmental psychology.* New York: Holt, Rinehart, & Winston, 1968. Pp. 258–272.

White, S. H. Evidence for a hierarchical arrangement of learning processes. In L. P. Lipsitt & C. C. Spiker (Eds.), *Advances in child development and behavior.* New York: Academic Press, 1965. Pp. 187–220.

Wike, E. L. Secondary reinforcement: Some research and theoretical issues. In W. J. Arnold & D. Levine (Eds.), *Nebraska symposium on motivation.* Lincoln: University of Nebraska Press, 1970. Pp. 39–84.

Wolfe, J. B. Effectiveness of token rewards for chimpanzees. *Comparative Psychology Monographs*, 1936, **12**(60).

Zimmerman, J. Technique for sustaining behavior with conditioned reinforcement. *Science*, 1963, **142**, 682–684.

Zimmerman, J., & Hanford, P. V. Sustaining behavior with conditioned reinforcement as the only response-produced consequence. *Psychological Reports*, 1966, **19**, 391–401.

Preconditions of Inference[1]

MARGARET DONALDSON

University of Edinburgh

The theme of this paper is the nature of the cognitive capacities that lie at the origins of inferential thinking. A fundamental requirement for any system that is capable of inferential activity is that it should be able to operate in terms of relationships of compatibility and incompatibility. That is, it has to be capable of making decisions about whether the cooccurrence of given states of affairs is possible.

A system that can handle relationships of compatibility and incompatibility can, given information about situation X (or X and Y, etc.), survey a further situation Z about which relevant direct information is not available and can classify values of attributes of Z as compatible or incompatible with known values for X and Y. In such a case it may be that the classification of these possible values yields the outcome that all but one are incompatible. Clearly the remaining one is then not only compatible but also necessarily implied.

By way of example, consider the comparatively simple case where we are dealing with the numerical relationships that obtain among three sets of objects, a, b, and c. Suppose that situation X is the relationship between a and b, and situation Y the relationship between b and c. Situation Z, about which direct knowledge is not available, is the relationship between a and c.

Now the kinds of relationship that may obtain can be reduced to three: greater than, equal to, and less than. (This is obviously a reduction by classification of an infinite set of quantified relation-

1. I am grateful to J. Reid and R. Wales for discussions during the preparation of this paper, also to R. Campbell, P. Lloyd, and B. Rowland for reading and commenting on the manuscript. The work was supported in part by a grant from the British Social Science Research Council.

ships—but let us suppose that we are interested in no greater specificity than these three relationships yield.)

The inferential task is to determine, for each of the three possible relationships between a and c, whether it is compatible or incompatible with the combined information that is available concerning X and Y. If we consider all nine possible combinations of values for X and Y (a > b, b > c; a = b, b = c; etc.) we find that seven of these admit of deductive certainty for Z (the way a and c are related to one another), while two (a > b, b < c and a < b, b > c) admit of more than one outcome as regards situation Z. Any system which could fully handle the compatibility-incompatibility relationship would have to come up with the conclusion that, in these two cases, it did not know enough to be sure.

When one starts to consider the capacity for handling compatibility relationships, it is, I think, a useful first step to distinguish the following questions:

1. Is the system one that can make the compatible-incompatible distinction at all?
2. Can it make a particular sort of compatibility judgment—that is, can it make the judgment in regard to a specific set of relations such as, for instance, "more than," "less than," and "equal to"?
3. If it can make this kind of judgment, can it do so exhaustively for a given finite set of possible values?
4. If it can make this kind of judgment, can it do so dependably and "to order"?

We have available to us two main sources of evidence bearing on these questions. On the one hand we can observe how subjects deal with tasks that we have explicitly set them to do; on the other hand we can observe their behavior in situations that are not of our contriving. The evidence from these sources often appears conflicting, but the above four questions may help to suggest how the conflict is to be resolved.

Most attempts to get children to make deductive inferences in specially contrived situations have led to the conclusion that the ability to do this is exceedingly limited or nonexistent until the age of around seven—that is, until the onset of what Piaget calls the period of concrete operational thinking. However, observation of the "spontaneous" behavior of children considerably younger than this can yield instances of what appear to be complicated inferential acts. Where the evidence for this is known to have been carefully recorded it would be obviously foolish to dismiss it as "anecdotal." The following conversation took place between a research worker and a child of just over five, the latter having spontaneously initiated the exchange. The conversation was tape-recorded and is reported verbatim:

S: Is that Mr. Campbell who came here—dead?

E: No. I'm quite sure he isn't dead.

S: Well, there must be two Mr. Campbells then, because Mr. Campbell's dead, under the water.

This occurred four weeks after the news reports of Donald Campbell's fatal accident and three months after a visit to the school by another research worker named Robin Campbell. The child appears to have drawn a valid inference from data derived from two sources remote in time and situation, and her conclusion is stated as something which "must be" so. Her reasoning involves the recognition that the existence of a living person is incompatible with the death of that same person but is, on the other hand, compatible with the death of another person having the same name. (There was, incidentally, no evidence from formal testing of this child to suggest that she was at all advanced; and she came from a home background that was by no means culturally privileged.)

It seems evident that if a child is capable, in any circumstances, of reasoning in this manner, then, at the very least, the answer to the first question with respect to that child is yes; and the answer to the second question is also yes with regard to the particular relations involved in the instance observed. The answer to the third question is not so easily arrived at on the basis of this kind of evidence—and certainly we are not helped at all toward obtaining an answer to question four. Indeed, question four can, in principle, be answered only by asking the child to tackle a number of specific tasks set for him on specific occasions. It seems likely that the discrepant evidence is to be interpreted in terms of this last requirement.

It is not only in young children that the discrepancy can be observed. Older children also often seem to be able to carry out "spontaneously" tasks on which they fail when we sit them down and (however tactfully and skillfully) impose the task upon them. There are a number of possible explanations for this.

The great majority of the tasks we set to children involve at least some verbal component, if only in the shape of some brief verbal instruction. Aside from the issue of language comprehension, there arises the question of the extent to which children at this age are able to regulate their behavior to accord with information verbally communicated to them. Sheldon White (1969) considers an increase in this kind of ability to be one of the main cognitive changes that take place between the ages of five and seven. He points out that while, in free-play situations, children may often engage in one task for long periods of time, the ability to sustain a pattern of behavior in dealing with a task imposed by others is a very different matter. White suggests that there may be a kind of bidirectionality about the difficulty, with inability to sustain a proposition to guide successive behavior segments being accompanied by inability to "integrate successive behavior segments to form a proposition" as shown, for instance, by difficulty in identifying a visual form by haptic exploration. He also discusses the stereotypies, or "motor routines," in young children's behavior and suggests that these may be patterns of response that tend *actively* to intrude and block other behavior. Hence ability to inhibit them may be crucial, and it is possible that growth of motor restraint is a very important factor in the development of ability to accept an imposed task. Finally what White proposes is that the changes he is concerned with may depend on an increased speed of inner reaction which allows a greater number of items of information to enter the child's "span of processing."

White's paper provides a very valuable review of these topics. However there are a number of distinctions which I think may be important and which he does not explicitly draw. At least three separate questions can be formulated:

1. How able is the child in formal test situations to act strictly in accordance with verbal statements if they are of a very simple kind?

2. How able is he to *sustain* (*a*) any kind of behavior, even of the simplest sort, and (*b*) behavior that seems to be guided by a plan or strategy, given in both cases that he has not spontaneously initiated the behavior?
3. How able is he to accept a verbal statement as a basis for reasoning?

The evidence White quotes is mostly relevant to the second question, though his discussion of stereotyped responses bears also on the first. It seems clear that motor routines often do interfere with strict adherence to simple verbal propositions in young subjects, even when there is no call to sustain behavior over appreciable periods. However, in a study by Barbara Rowland and myself (Rowland and Donaldson, unpublished) in which children were given premises in the form "X is in *a*," "X is in *a* or *b*," "X is not in *a*," or "X is not in *a* and not in *b*" to guide their search for a concealed object, there was little indication of interference from stereotyped response patterns although the youngest subject was only three years and one month old. My impression is that much depends on how the constraints imposed by the experimenter's formal task relate to the other constraints which are inherent in the situation. These I have called "circumstantial constraints"[2] since they arise from a kind of force of circumstance which is provided in ordinary life by the entire context of ongoing activity and in test situations by such features as perceptual prominence or some characteristic of spatial arrangement (e.g., spatial proximity to the subject)—and perhaps also by associations with various familiar "real-life" situations. What I am suggesting is that when powerful circumstantial constraints are present and are in conflict with the formal constraints of an imposed task, children find it very difficult to operate strictly in terms of the latter. But it seems that, given an absence of strong contrary circumstantial constraints, children as young as three *are* capable of guiding their behavior to accord with verbally given information. The formal situation is, of course, in such a case effectively quite close to the everyday ones in which they are accustomed to operate.

2. For a more extensive discussion of this topic see Donaldson (1970).

This is very far from being the case when one turns to a consideration of the evidence that bears on the third question. When the child is asked to engage in strict inference from verbal premises presented to him, he is, in certain important respects, in a situation with which he is likely to be quite unfamiliar.

It may be helpful to consider the nature of this unfamiliarity in the light of Von Wright's discussion of modal concepts (Von Wright, 1951). In this essay, Von Wright draws a distinction between alethic concepts and epistemic concepts. Such concepts as *necessary, possible, contingent,* and *impossible* are primarily alethic, that is, concerned with issues of what is, or may be, true. Such concepts as *verified, falsified,* or *undecided* are epistemic, that is, concerned with issues of what is or is not known to be true. (Notice, however, that certain epistemic uses of the alethic terms occur. For instance, the word *possible* is used epistemically, generally as a synonym for *undecided.*)

I have already raised (without so far trying to answer) the question of how soon a child can make the distinction: compatible-incompatible. Such a distinction belongs, of course, in the alethic domain. A correspondingly basic question for the epistemic domain would be: How soon does the child begin to grasp the distinction between what is known and what is not known? Recognition of this distinction will presumably first manifest itself in some sign that the child is aware when there is something that he himself does not know.

For the time being I want merely to leave this further question in the background of the discussion. The point at present is that when a child is asked to engage in a prescribed deductive reasoning task, he must recognize that alethic concepts are now of the first importance. The task requires him to be concerned above all with issues of compatibility, and not to invoke anything which he knows to be true but which is not given in the problem as set to him. Up to the point when he first encounters a situation of this kind, he has been free, in his ordinary dealings with the world, to make use of any knowledge he possesses, no matter how he came by it. Then suddenly he finds himself in a situation were a "correct" response requires that he stop operating in terms of what he already knows to be the case—a situation where certain customary modes of gaining further knowledge (looking to see, asking someone who knows already) are no longer appropriate. He now finds himself presented with a limited amount of information and he is asked to use it to determine whether something or other is or is not so, suspending for the time being whatever else he already knows about the kind of situation that is in question. Further, this may happen to him without any preliminary attempt having been made to explain to him the nature of this new kind of understanding, or the fact that alethic concepts are now of the first importance. In such a situation even a child who is in fact capable of handling alethic concepts (of saying, for instance, "There *must be* two Mr. Campbells") can perhaps not reasonably be expected to manifest this competence, and to exclude rigorously from his thinking any considerations that do not figure in the premises that are given him. In fact, children much older than seven—that is, well beyond the upper limit of the period Sheldon White considers—fail to achieve this kind of exclusion, as I have reported previously (Donaldson, 1963).[3] This earlier study showed that, even in children of 12 to 14, it is still fairly common for a class of errors to occur that have, as their outstanding common feature, a lack of loyalty to what is "given" in the statement of the problem. I called these arbitrary errors since, if the subject is not constrained by the conditions which a problem imposes, he may be held to behave arbitrarily in relation to it. Sometimes the subjects in this study appeared to be constrained, if not by the problem, at least by their prior knowledge of what was "true" in the situations of real life. Sometimes, however, they appeared to make decisions that were unjustified both in the sense that there seemed to be no rational basis for deciding, and that the subject offered no support for his conclusion, simply making up his mind: "It is so."

A recent study by Gilberte le Bonniec (1970) provides many further illustrations of the occurrence of errors of this kind. Le Bonniec is explicitly concerned with the development of modal aspects of reasoning. A task which she uses with preschool children to study the comprehension of conditions which render an act "do-able" involves two dolls, one dressed as a boy, one as a girl. Each doll is provided with a box of plastic pieces which fit together.

3. Even adults do not always manage it. (Cf. Henle, 1962.)

The boy's box contains only straight pieces, the girl's, only round ones. The subject is shown a straight stick and a bracelet both made of the plastic segments, and his task is to infer who made the bracelet, the boy or the girl. The children commonly attribute the bracelet to the girl, which is of course correct; but they tend to do so "because girls like bracelets." On the other hand, one little boy claims that the boy made the bracelet "because Mummies have bracelets," and le Bonniec suggests he had in mind the idea of the bracelet as a present. Another boy will not accept that the girl made the bracelet "because my little sister doesn't know how to do it." These are instances of arbitrary errors that involve appeal to real-life experience. Le Bonniec's work also provides instances of arbitrary and apparently quite unsupported decisions about what is the case—notably about what the color of a hidden object may be. A number of her subjects (in this case aged from five to eight years) simply state what color the hidden object *is*, and show no sign of uncertainty or of any recognition of the possibilities that are open in the situation as it has been presented to them.

That children, in so simple a situation, will decide that they know something which they are very clearly not in a position to know is, on the face of it, a very curious fact. Some of the children are, of course, aware that their decision has the status of a guess— that they are betting on it, so to speak—and they say things which make this clear. Others, however, will say they are sure of the object's color and will appear not to be aware of any other possibility. This kind of finding has been amply confirmed in my own researches; and it might seem to indicate absence of even the most rudimentary grasp of the epistemic notions "known" and "not known."

However, the answer to the question of whether young children have any awareness of this distinction is not so simply given. There is other evidence to indicate that by three years and six months (possibly earlier—that is a cautious estimate) children do not in all circumstances show lack of awareness of this distinction. They appear to understand what it is not to know something and they can be articulate about it. Furthermore they have some under-standing of what it is to be in error. Recently we have been looking at the ability of children between the ages of three and five to judge that a response is right or wrong. It is, of course, notoriously difficult to get children to pass judgment of this kind on anything that is said or done by an adult experimenter. Consequently we have used a talking doll—a toy animal—and have invited the children to "help" him by correcting him when he makes a mistake. It seems clear from our results so far that subjects of three and a half and over are well able to understand what is being asked of them and are able to tell the doll, given of course that they appreciate his error, that he is wrong. (One can easily establish this, in principle, by making the errors very gross at first.) They also respond appropriately when the doll says that he "does not know"—that is, they supply him with information.

I think we can conclude that children of this age do know that it is possible to be in ignorance about whether x or y is the case. This shows also, of course, in their questions. As soon as a child spontaneously asks a question that is truly a request for information, he must be aware, to some extent at least, of a gap in his knowledge and of the existence of a situation in which more than one possibility is open, so far as his information goes. In this connection, however, it is interesting to note that wh-questions and questions to which the appropriate answer is yes or no appear to have a somewhat different status. A paper by Frege (1956) makes some relevant points. In this paper Frege is concerned to distinguish: (1) the apprehension of a thought—or thinking, (2) the recognition of the truth of a thought—or judgment, and (3) the manifestation of the judgment—or assertion.

The first of these occurs, according to Frege, whenever we formulate a "sentence-question," that is, a question which invites a yes or no reply. We then entertain the thought without judgment as to its truth. The form of our language is such that thought without assertion of truth is not too easy to express except in sentences of this kind. The indicative sentence normally has an assertion of truth built into it.

If we want to express a thought without judging it true or false, and without asking a question, we have to use some fairly complicated locution which explicitly expresses possibility or uncertainty: "It might be the case that . . ." or "consider the possibility that . . ." It is interesting to speculate about what might be the effect of having a language where there is some explicit marker to indicate truth or falsehood, the absence of this marker being an indication that no judgment concerning truth is implied. In such a language, *it is blue* would not mean the same as *it is true that it is blue*. Would children learning to speak such a language progress differently in their apprehension of the possible or the merely postulated?

In the absence of information on this point we can at least look at the questions children ask. The relevant issue would seem to be whether, in addition to the wh-questions which are known to be frequent in their speech[4] (and which Frege would call word-questions), they do or do not commonly ask questions of the general form *Is it x?* (i.e., rather than *What is it?*)—for the question *Is it x?* involves the entertaining of two possible outcomes, namely that it is *x* or that it is not *x*. In other words, it does not simply demarcate a region of doubt, it structures or articulates the doubt by means of a hypothesis. Do children ask such questions frequently?

The answer would seem to be that, at a quite early age, they do. Examination of records of spontaneous speech collected during the Edinburgh Cognition Project, (which was run by Roger Wales and myself from 1967 to 1969), shows that such questions are fairly common. Examples from the records are: "Is Neil in the picture?" "Is it flat enough now?" "Are you the biggest?" "Have you got two of them?" These were all recorded when the children were under the age of four.

Therefore it seems that children of this age *can* apprehend—or entertain—a thought without judging it true; they *can*, by the same token, entertain at least a simple pair of alternative possibilities; and they do have awareness of being in a state of ignorance.

Capacities of the kind we have been considering so far are clearly very general in nature. I mean this in the sense that they can, in principle, manifest themselves in the handling of any kind

4. Roger Brown (1968) reports that wh-questions started to appear with some frequency and variety (i.e., not just in a few rigid seemingly unanalyzed forms like "What dat?") from the point which he defines as "Level III" and which occurred, for his three subjects Adam, Eve, and Sarah, between the ages of 21 months and 36 months.

Susan Ervin-Tripp (1970), in a study that concentrates on replies to questions rather than on the production of them, was also concerned primarily with Wh-questions. It is of interest that she found discrimination of questions from other types of utterance to be already well established in her youngest subject at one year and nine months.

of information. That is, it is not knowledge of a particular system (e.g., number) which is at issue—though, of course, there has to be *some* informational context.

The question to which I now want to turn is whether, at the bases of inference, there are capacities of a more specific nature. Is it, for instance, possible that we might be specifically equipped for the apprehension of certain central concepts like space or time or magnitude, and might be predisposed to make compatibility judgments with respect to them at a very early age?

According to Piagetian theory this is not so. However, recently there have been one or two reports which suggest that the kind of reasoning that Piaget describes as characteristic of the concrete operational period may in fact appear considerably before the age of seven. For example, Bryant and Trabasso (personal communication) claim to have evidence that children of four can make deductive inferences concerning transitivity of length, given a situation in which their memory for the critical information is strengthened. And a year or two ago Mehler and Bever (1967) caused something of a sensation by reporting a finding to the effect that children between the ages of two and three can conserve number.

Discussing this in a later work, Bever (1970) claims that at this age children know, without counting, which row in arrays like (1) and (2) has more circles:

(1)
$$0 \quad 0 \quad 0 \quad 0$$
$$0\ 0\ 0\ 0\ 0$$

(2)
$$0 \quad 0 \quad 0 \quad 0$$
$$0 \quad 0 \quad 0 \quad 0 \quad 0 \quad 0$$

Nor are they choosing by density, he says, because in arrays like (3):

(3)
$$0 \quad 0 \quad 0 \quad 0$$
$$0 \quad 0 \quad 0 \quad 0$$

they show no tendency to pick the denser of the two.

To account for these successes, Bever attributes to the children "a primitive capacity to appreciate the relative numerosity of small arrays," a capacity which is later superseded, as a determinant of performance, by perceptual strategies that develop in the age range three to five. The onset of these perceptual strategies is claimed to lead to the typical "nonconserving" errors of the pre-operational child.

So what Mehler and Bever claim to have found is a developmental sequence in which young children achieve a correct response, older ones fall for a time into error, and still older ones overcome the error and achieve success in new ways. In fact it turns out that they are by no means alone in noting sequences of this kind.

A decade ago this would have seemed incredible, for it would have been very difficult to reconcile with current assumptions. No one then doubted that cognitive development proceeds along a straight path marked by a steady increase in the number of correct responses to problems and a corresponding progressive elimination of error. It was widely taken for granted that if children of age *x* failed to produce correct responses in a given situation, then children below age *x* would do so too. This conception of how development progresses was, of course, very much in line with the dominant associationist tradition. In the S-R view of learning, correct responses are progressively strengthened by encounters with the environment while incorrect ones are progressively weakened, the whole movement being essentially "straight forward." Any other view of the matter is indeed very difficult to fit into a behaviorist frame.

It now seems quite clear, however, that another view of the matter is the correct one. In the last seven years or so, evidence has been accumulating of instances in which development is accompanied by a temporary increase in erroneous or inadequate responding. There is now enough of this evidence to make it reasonable to ask whether cognitive growth *characteristically* proceeds in this way. And if this is indeed the case then we must obviously ask what is implied about the nature of the system, and in particular about the possibility of there being primitive capacities which we have failed to detect because their operation is obscured at later ages in some such manner as Mehler and Bever propose.

Without attempting to review the evidence at all exhaustively, I want to quote a number of examples in some detail to illustrate the kind of thing that we now have to take into account. The list is in chronological order.

1. The first instance is in fact not at all recent, but it appears as a quite isolated observation. It is reported by Stern (1924) in discussion of his studies of his own children's responses to line drawings. On this subject he makes the following comment:

> ... for, as a fact, the normal condition in the second year is that pictures only act as rough images calling forth response from the few rough outlines of the child's *schematic concepts*.
>
> This primitive satisfaction with the general impression has the remarkable result that many drawings, recognised at a very early age, later on are not. The child has grown harder to satisfy, more critical; e.g., just because Hilde's idea of a bottle had become more distinct with time, she could not recognise two-and-a-half years later [the drawing] which at (I; 10) she had at once called a bottle.

The drawing in question is like this:

2. The next instance is far removed from Stern's, both with regard to age of subjects and type of activity. In 1963, I reported some findings concerning the responses of children between the ages of 10 and 14 as they tackled verbal problems of a formal deductive kind. I noted that, for these subjects, difficulty in operating with premises containing negatives tended to show an increase from one occasion of testing to the next, the occasions being approximately two years apart. The explanation seemed to be that the more strictly and rigorously the children tried to reason in terms of the premises and the more carefully they tried to check their inferences, the more difficulty the negatives were liable to give them. For instance, Stewart says: "Well, the more I read it, the more it seems to change. . . . Well, at first it seemed no animals

can climb trees,[5] that is to say, they cannot, then I read it over and I thought it meant they can."

Again, Jane says: "I can't get the real meaning of the first sentence. 'No animals . . .' I don't know. 'No animals . . .' If the 'no' wasn't there I could understand it." Two years earlier the same subjects, treating the problems less analytically, did not give evidence of comparable kinds of confusion.

3. The next example is very well known. Ervin (1964) reports that the earliest instances of the use of past tenses in children's speech are provided by a small number of common irregular forms like "came" and "did." That is to say, these are at first used in the correct form by her subjects. Later the same children begin to say "comed" and "doed" (though at the same time they may possibly continue to use "came" and "did"). One explanation might be that the unique irregular tense inflections are learned first as separate lexical items, then later the rule for the regular formation of the past tense in English is acquired by the child and is misapplied to the irregular verbs that he has already been using in the correct way.

4. Lunzer (in Vinh-Bang and Lunzer, 1965) gives an account of a study of children's understanding of the transformations over which perimeter and area are, respectively, conserved or not conserved. He looked both at situations where area was conserved while perimeter was varied and at situations where perimeter was conserved while area was varied. Children around the ages of eight to ten could then be observed to be prone to what Lunzer described as "false conservation"—that is, to the conclusion that both area and perimeter were conserved at the same time. Thus they would sometimes maintain, for instance, that a rectangle measuring 5×45 was equal in area to a square measuring 25×25—a situation in which the younger children could easily recognize that this was not so. (This, of course, is not to say that the younger children handled the complete task successfully.) Lunzer believes that his finding is to be explained by the dominance of an expectation that

5. The premise that Stewart was considering was: "No animals that can only move slowly can climb trees." The premises were intended to be obviously false—even absurd—so that it would be easier to recognize genuine deduction when it occurred.

there will be logical consistency between the perimeter and the area—that the fate of the one is somehow tied to the fate of the other.

5. Studies of conservation by Bruner et al. (1966) yield yet another example. In this case the subjects were asked to consider two beakers of the same diameter, the standard (which was half full of colored water) being six inches high and the empty comparison beaker being eight inches high. The task was to say whether, after the water was poured from standard to comparison beaker, the amount would remain the same; and also to predict where the water level would be. Of four-year-olds, 60% predicted the level correctly, but among children of five to seven, only between 20% and 30% were correct. Two kinds of error were made by the older children—and especially by those who were in fact judged to have shown, on pretest, that they could conserve amount. One error was to predict a lower level because the glass was "bigger" or "taller," which appears to be a misapplication of the principle of compensation. The second was to predict a *higher* level because the glass was taller, which appears as a misuse of a notion of proportion, one child saying that the level would be twice as high because the glass was twice as tall.

6. Fischbein et al. (1967) report a study of the understanding of probability by children between the ages of 5 and 14. Their experimental material consisted of small inclined channels along which balls could be rolled. Forks at various positions along the way were used to produce different probabilities that the ball would reach a given point of exit. In the three simplest situations that were studied, all exits were equiprobable, and in each of these cases there was a drop across the entire age range in the percentage of correct responses to the question whether a ball was just as likely to emerge at one place as at another. In the more complex tasks where the probabilities were unequal, correct responses did in general increase with increasing age.

Finally it may be of interest to add to this list a reference to a paper by Seymour Papert (1963). In this paper, Papert, describing an attempt to simulate the genesis of conservation of length, gives an account of systematic errors which arose at the second stage of development and gave the appearance of regression in relation to the first stage. The point that is of interest is that Papert judges these errors "useful if not indispensable" for further progress.

When we come to look at this kind of developmental sequence and think about the implications for cognitive theory, a central question is whether the early successes are, in some sense, spurious, limited, and inadequately based or whether, on the other hand, they indicate the early presence of genuine cognitive skills which are somehow later overlaid or interfered with by other developments. Mehler and Bever are the chief proponents at the moment of the claim that the latter is the correct interpretation. Since what they have to say is of considerable theoretical significance and interest, I want to spend some time discussing it.

Let us look first in a little more detail at the nature of their theoretical position and the evidence they offer in support of it; second, at some other findings relevant to the interpretation of their studies of conservation; and third, at the relevance to the whole question of the instances of "growth error"[6] listed above.

Mehler and Bever's (1968b) theoretical position is that the child of two already has a number of "fundamental cognitive structures" but he cannot make full use of them because of "behavioral limits on such expressive capacities as attention and memory." They argue that as the child grows older he finds ways of circumventing these limitations by developing certain "perceptual strategies." Bever (1970) has since suggested that it is still an open question whether these strategies develop as an outcome of maturation or whether they are inductions from experience since, for instance, most things that look longer have more parts. Either way, the strategies are held to give the child certain worthwhile advantages but to fail in a number of situations where the direct use of the fundamental capacities would have led to success—and notably to fail in the conservation of number.

Actually it is important to note that the task originally used by Mehler and Bever was not, in the strict sense, concerned with *conservation* at all.[7] The crucial question put to their subjects did

---

6. This term is used by Bruner et al. (1966) to describe such errors.
7. In a subsequent paper Mehler and Bever (1968a) allow that this is the case.

not refer to two arrays equal in number but differing in spatial configuration. It referred to two arrays differing in number, but with the numerical difference and the length of the rows conflicting with one another—that is, the longer row having fewer items in it. The evidence on which Mehler and Bever based their initial case was that the youngest subjects tended to choose the shorter row as having more. This is, of course, in principle, a perfectly good *kind* of evidence in support of the claim that these children (who cannot count) have some sort of notion of what Bever calls "numerosity." But it does not show that they will conclude that some property *must* remain invariant across a certain set of transformations, which is what the classic conservation tasks are about. Mehler and Bever give us no reason to suppose that their subjects are convinced that if no elements are taken away and none are added the number *must* remain the same. That is, questions of compatibility simply do not arise.

However, let us consider their evidence in its own right, as bearing on the existence of a primitive apprehension of numerosity even in the face of perceptually confusing factors. If children of two to three respond as Mehler and Bever say they do, then it seems to me we have to accept that some such fundamental capacity has indeed been demonstrated. But attempts to replicate their findings have at this point to be taken into account. One such attempt was made by Rothenberg and Courtney (1968). They claim to have repeated exactly the Mehler and Bever procedure as described in the original paper,[8] and they in fact obtained, with respect to the items using balls of clay (as distinct from items using M & M candies which the children were allowed to eat) a downward trend in percentage of correct responses over their whole age range from two years and eight months to four years and seven months. But they tend to the view that the early successes are spurious. They point out that the row containing more items was always the one which the experimenter had altered and they think this may have drawn the attention of the younger subjects to it. They also suggest that the younger children did not understand the meaning of "more" and

8. Both Hayes (1969) and Rothenberg and Courtney (1968) also used conservation measures of the classical kind and obtained very few successes, but this is not at the moment strictly relevant to the argument.

that the decreasing percentage of correct responses in older subjects occurred because, as they learned to interpret the word, they took it to mean "takes up more space." Finally, Rothenberg and Courtney report that their subjects' choices were powerfully influenced by considerations of proximity. When the row containing more items was closer to the child the task was significantly easier ($p < .001$ for clay, $p < .01$ for M & Ms).[9]

In a further replication by Jean Hayes (1969) there was a similar finding concerning proximity. Over 70% of all choices were choices of the nearer row. However, when the farther row *was* picked, it tended, in the situation used by Mehler and Bever, to be the row that actually did contain the larger number. Hayes therefore concluded that she had some evidence that ability to compare sets differing in number *is* present in children as young as two-and-a-half; but she, too, saw reason to doubt the adequacy of the children's understanding of "more."

Some of our own work in Edinburgh has been relevant to the question of how children interpret "more" (cf. Donaldson and Balfour, 1968; Donaldson and Wales, 1970) though, except in the full conservation situation, we have not looked at perceptually muddling configurations, and we have not worked with children under three. With children of three and a half, however, we obtained results (Donaldson and Wales, 1969) concerning the consistency of the subjects' responses to "same" and "more" which are entirely in agreement with what is reported on this topic by Rothenberg and Courtney and by Hayes. Our subjects, like theirs, were asked two separate questions in each conservation task that they were given: "Does this row have the same number as this row?" and (irrespective of the reply given) "Does one row have more?" The overwhelming tendency among our subjects at age three and a half was to reply yes to both questions. That is, they failed to show any sign that they appreciated the incompatibility of *x has the same number as y* and *x has more than y*. Thus if we had used only the question "same?" we, too, would have obtained apparent conservation from children under four. It seems that the developmental

9. Similar points have been made by Piaget (1968) in a discussion of Mehler and Bever's claim.

sequence of response patterns is represented by the following three levels:

$$
\begin{array}{cccc}
 & \text{I} & \text{II} & \text{III} \\
\text{Same?} & \text{Yes} & \text{No} & \text{Yes} \\
 & \left.\vphantom{\begin{array}{c}a\\b\end{array}}\right\} \rightarrow & \left\{\vphantom{\begin{array}{c}a\\b\end{array}}\right. \left.\vphantom{\begin{array}{c}a\\b\end{array}}\right\} \rightarrow & \left\{\vphantom{\begin{array}{c}a\\b\end{array}}\right. \\
\text{More?} & \text{Yes} & \text{Yes} & \text{No}
\end{array}
$$

Of these, II is, of course, the classical "nonconserving" pattern, while III is the classical "conserving" or "operational" pattern. But at level I the question "same?" is answered "correctly"; and the differences between levels show up clearly only when the answers to both questions are considered together.

This, then, must obviously rank as an instance of quite spurious early success though I am by no means sure that it is to be accounted for, as Rothenberg and Courtney seem to think, merely on the basis of a tendency to answer yes when in doubt.

However that may be, I think it is reasonable to say that, when circumstantial effects such as proximity are allowed for, there is some evidence which suggests that children of two can apprehend numerical magnitude. But this evidence is still far from conclusive,[10] and a good deal of the present uncertainty is linked to our lack of knowledge of how very young children comprehend the crucial words *more, less, same,* and *different*.

It is now time to consider how the other instances of growth error bear on the Mehler and Bever arguments about fundamental capacities and their overlay by perceptual strategies. The first thing to note is that the other instances relate to a considerable range of tasks and to a range of ages running from one year and ten months to adolescence. Thus some explanation that is much more general than Mehler and Bever's is needed to account for them. We are dealing not merely with a characteristic of the preoperational period but with something that looks like a fairly general feature of

10. For instance, Piaget (1968) claims that very young children sometimes use an even more primitive criterion than length, namely that of "crowding" or "heaping," and he argues that, because of this, Mehler and Bever's findings on "numerosity" are not decisive. To this, Mehler and Bever (1968a) reply that they have observed no tendency for children at any age to choose the denser row as having more.

cognitive growth. The obvious first move is to ask what, if anything, the different examples have in common.

The most pervasive feature is that the early successes seem to depend on some restriction on the information which the child even attempts to process. That is, aspects of the situation are virtually left out of account. The errors then arise when attempts begin to be made to integrate these with the other aspects previously handled—that is, they arise in the course of some extension of the information-processing endeavor. This account seems to fit most clearly the Ervin, Lunzer, Bruner, and Fischbein examples; perhaps something further will have to be invoked to account for the instance provided by Stern and for my own finding.

Ervin's subjects make no mistakes so long as they handle a few common verbs as isolated lexical items. Trouble seems to arise when they begin to relate these to the system as a whole.

It is when Lunzer's subjects try to handle area and perimeter as one related system that they judge to be equal areas that are perceptually quite evidently different.

Bruner's subjects can predict water level correctly (in a limited situation) until they begin to try to relate the level to the size of the glass.

Notice that these errors are produced not by the onset of perceptual strategies but more nearly by the abandonment of reliance on them.

Fischbein et al. say in comment on their findings that the intuition of equiprobability among the younger subjects is supported by a reduced capacity for analysis and by a relative indifference with regard to detail. "It comes out through any of them," say the young subjects typically, without bothering to consider the conditions further. Older children, on the other hand, attempt to introduce certain mechanical or geometrical arguments which they claim might favor one channel or another. That is, they try to relate this situation to other kinds of knowledge which they possess, and this leads them to take into account features which are in fact irrelevant.

Of Stern's example, it may perhaps be said that the early success presumably depends on failing initially to attend to imperfections which are later compelling. (Still later the imperfections can be at one and the same time noticed and, for certain purposes, ignored.) So here, too, some increased processing of information is perhaps involved.

However, of all the instances we have reviewed, Stern's seems most suggestive of the existence of a fundamental capacity subsequently, and for a time, overlaid.

Of my own evidence, it may, I think, fairly be said that the difficulty arises because of the onset of increasingly serious attempts to process the negatives in the premises; but in this case we are not dealing with attempts at the integration of information into a wider system so much as with an extension of respect for the deductive requirements—that is, respect for the formal constraints of the task.

I have tried to find some common feature in these errors, but I do not intend to imply that this will be found to be characteristic of all others that may be detected in the future.[11] However that may prove to be, if the phenomenon is pervasive then, whatever the reason, there are a number of implications for the diagnosis of cognitive states and for developmental study in general.

In the first place, it is clearly unsafe to assume that if subject A gives a "correct" answer and subject B gives a "wrong" one, then A is developmentally in advance of B in this area of cognitive operation. What this implies when changes occurring in one group of subjects are compared with those occurring in another group (as in the standard experimental group–control group situation) can easily be shown. Suppose that, among our subjects, three developmental stages are in fact represented. Suppose further that the responses which characterize Stages 1 and 3 are correct (and not readily distinguishable one from another) while responses at Stage 2 are in error; and that the changes in which we are interested involve some movement from Stages 1 to 2, some from 2 to 3, and some from 1 to 3. It is then evident that any estimate of change based on group averages could be grossly misleading. The main safeguard would seem to lie in recognizing that this kind of sequence may occur and consequently in emphasizing the importance of the study of individual longitudinal trends.[12]

11. Roger Wales and I have in fact obtained evidence of a number of others, some of which may call for rather different interpretation.

12. However serious problems remain. For a discussion of this topic see the appendix to Wales and Campbell (1970).

It follows also, as Mehler and Bever (1968b) point out, that if one finds that children of a given age make a particular error, this is no reason for concluding that one has evidence of a basic limitation which makes it unnecessary to give the same kind of test to younger children. It is now clear, as they emphasize, that we must try to study very young children, and we must then tackle the job of mapping the initial state thus discovered on to the "stable state" of the adult. But beyond this point I find myself in fairly fundamental disagreement with them. The disagreement concerns the following feature of their argument.

They begin by claiming that it is important in cognitive psychology to make the distinction between what a person can learn to do and what he is disposed to do naturally within a particular cognitive domain; and to illustrate what they have in mind they make use of a linguistic analogy. A speaker of English *can* utter "Dog is a nice Sam," but he is disposed naturally to utter "Sam is a nice dog," that is, to speak grammatical English. "Dog is a nice Sam" is ungrammatical and so a linguistic theory of English need not take account of it. Having made this unexceptionable point about the study of English grammar, Mehler and Bever then go on to draw the following most curious parallel: "Analogously, we limit the data relevant for other cognitive skills in terms of natural predispositions rather than in terms of ultimate capabilities."

Uttering "Dog is a nice Sam," or some other ungrammatical string, is thus apparently figuring as the counterpart, in this analogy, of ultimate cognitive capabilities. But it would in fact be the counterpart—so far as a counterpart can be found—of some deliberate piece of ineptitude. We *can* be deliberately inept, with respect both to grammar and to inference. We *can* utter "Dog is a nice Sam"; and we *can* maintain that if *x* is bigger than *y*, *y* is bigger than *x*. Neither capability is very interesting.

What *is* of interest is whether it is possible to illustrate effectively by linguistic analogy the distinction between what people are "naturally predisposed" to do and what they are "ultimately capable" of doing. Chomsky (1968), in a discussion that is very much concerned with the question of the extension of linguistic concepts to other cognitive domains, makes the point that in the case of language the grammars that are in fact constructed by different individuals (i.e., the "stable states" attained by adults) vary only slightly, in spite of superficial differences. So here, if he is right, there is a very solidly established norm—a competence that we all hold in common. This seems to me to come close to saying that there is no great gap in this case between what we are naturally predisposed to do and what we are ultimately capable of doing in the sense in which "ultimate capability" refers to some limit upwards from the norm.

One might at this point consider the poets. When Hopkins says that the grandeur of God "will flame out, like shining from shook foil," or asks:

When will you ever, Peace, wild wooddove, shy wings shut
Your round me roaming end, and under be my boughs?

we encounter something that certainly might be taken to demonstrate the existence of such a gap—a gulf, even. But this, of course, need not indicate that Hopkins has constructed a different grammar from the rest of us, only that sometimes—and to great effect—he can choose not to be bound by it. We are dealing with an outstanding instance of the "great differences in ability to use language" which Chomsky refers to as being perfectly compatible with powerful similarities in underlying grammar.

It is possible that, in the case of inferential structures as well as in the case of grammar, there exists a large core of common rules and processes and that, considered in relation to this, the differences which we tend to notice are superficial. At present, however, I am strongly inclined to doubt it and to think that, at least for inferential structures, there probably is a real gap between the norm and some upward limit of capability, a gap not just in ability to put the rules to use but in actual grasp of them.

However, there are actually two issues. In addition to the question of how much we all hold cognitively in common, there is the question of the distinction between what a given individual is disposed to do most of the time and what the same person *can* do on occasion. Mehler and Bever (1968b) quote the familiar example of the different possible interpretations of "if... then" and claim that the use of "if" to mean "only if" is the one to which we are all disposed, hence that the use of "if" in the sense in which nothing is implied concerning "if not" is not a matter of relevance for cognitive theory.

Another instance that they would presumably want to treat in the same way is mentioned by Von Wright (1951). Von Wright points out that the word *possible* can be used epistemically in two ways: (1) in a manner strictly equivalent to its alethic use, meaning "not known to be false," i.e., "either verified or undecided," and (2) meaning the same as "undecided," i.e., "neither known to be true nor known to be false." The second use is, he thinks, the more natural one and probably the more common. He is surely right in this.

The question of the "natural" uses of these terms is clearly of great importance; but this does not imply that the capacity for any "less natural," or immediate, or spontaneous use of them—or of our intellectual powers in general—is something with which cognitive theory has no cause to be concerned. I am sure that it would be unfortunate if, in the present state of our understanding, we were to accept the limitations on the scope of cognitive theorizing that Mehler and Bever propose.

At the same time, these natural uses do seem likely to be of special significance in relation to the question of basic capacities, to which I now want briefly to return.

What I would like to propose is that the natural sense of *possible*, used epistemically, represents a quite fundamental or primitive cognitive intuition, corresponding to the recognition of being in a state of uncertainty—the recognition that there is something which one does not know, yet which is, in principle, knowable. I think this intuition is probably present, at least fleetingly, in very young children, although sometimes, as in Le Bonniec's examples, it seems to fail even the older ones in what look like very simple tasks.

These failures may arise because of some characteristic of the formal task situation (such as confusion about the acceptable basis for reaching decisions, or even a certain feeling of being under pressure to decide something), or else it may be that the intuition remains for some time liable to fluctuation.

It seems at any rate that it must be present in some form at the point of onset of the first attempts to relate what is directly known to what is in doubt by means of relationships of compatibility or incompatibility. It is when this begins that the alethic notion of "possibility" presumably enters in some form or other upon the scene. In the alethic sense, "possible" is in primary opposition, not to "known" or "determined," but to "impossible."

All of this has to rest on some recognition, however dim, that certain states of affairs cannot coexist. It may seem implausible that any such profound apprehension could be present in very young children. Yet some sense of it is arguably implied by the use of any form of language to make descriptive statements. If one such statement is not seen as effectively ruling out a certain number of others, then I doubt whether it can be regarded as meaningful at all.

The point of onset of active attempts to resolve doubt through the use of notions of compatibility and incompatibility is still quite obscure. Even if such a tendency were powerfully native to us, it would not be surprising that its early operations should be difficult to detect.

When a child is willing to say, of two sets of objects, both that x contains the same number as y and that x contains more than y, this may be because he is not concerning himself with issues of compatibility at all; or it may be because he has not mastered a particular relational system; or because he has not mastered the semantics of "same" and of "more" in their reference to that system. These issues are not easy to disentangle. The task of sorting them out is one of the main challenges for cognitive theory at the present time.

REFERENCES

Bever, T. G. The cognitive basis for linguistic structures. In J. R. Hayes (Ed.), *Cognition and the development of language*. New York: Wiley, 1970. Pp. 279–362.

Brown, R. W. The development of Wh questions in child speech. *Journal of Verbal Learning and Verbal Behavior*, 1968, **7**, 279–290.

Bruner, J. S., Olver, R. R., & Greenfield, P. M. *Studies in cognitive growth*. New York: Wiley, 1966.

Chomsky, N. *Language and mind*. New York: Harcourt, 1968.

Donaldson, M. *A study of children's thinking*. London: Tavistock, 1963.

Donaldson, M. Developmental aspects of performance with negatives. In G. B. Flores d'Arcais & W. J. M. Levelt (Eds.), *Advances in psycholinguistics*. Amsterdam: North-Holland, 1970. Pp. 397–412.

Donaldson, M., & Balfour, G. Less is more: A study of language comprehension in children. *British Journal of Psychology*, 1968, **59**, 461–471.

Donaldson, M., & Wales, R. J. Development of basic cognitive skills: Report to Social Science Research Council (United Kingdom), 1969.

Donaldson, M., & Wales, R. J. On the acquisition of some relational terms. In J. R. Hayes (Ed.), *Cognition and the development of language.* New York: Wiley, 1970.

Ervin, S. Imitation and structural change in children's language. In E. H. Lenneberg (Ed.), *New directions in the study of language.* Cambridge, Mass: M.I.T. Press, 1964. Pp. 163–189.

Ervin-Tripp, S. Discourse agreement: How children answer questions. In J. R. Hayes, (Ed.), *Cognition and the development of language.* New York: Wiley, 1970. Pp. 79–107.

Fischbein, E., Pampu I., & Minzat, I. L'intuition probabiliste chez l'enfant. *Enfance,* 1967, **20**, 193–208.

Frege, G. The thought: A logical inquiry. In P. F. Strawson (Ed.), *Philosophical logic.* London: Oxford University Press, 1956. Pp. 17–38.

Hayes, J. The effects of proximity, length and number in two types of conservation experiment. Research Memorandum MIP-R-57. Edinburgh: Department of Machine Intelligence and Perception, 1969.

Henle, M. The relation between logic and thinking. *Psychological Review,* 1962, **69**, 366–378.

Le Bonniec, G. *Etude génétique des aspects modaux du raisonnement.* Paris: Travaux du Centre d'Etude des Processus Cognitifs et du Langage, 1970, 1.

Lunzer, E. Les co-ordinations et les conservations dans le domaine de la géométrie. In Vinh-Bang & E. Lunzer, *Conservations spatiales,* Paris: Presses Universitaires de France, 1965. Pp. 59–148.

Mehler, J., & Bever, T. G. Cognitive capacity of very young children. *Science,* 1967, **158**, 141–142.

Mehler, J., & Bever, T. G. Reply to J. Piaget. *Science,* 1968, **162**, 979–981. (a)

Mehler, J., & Bever, T. G. The study of competence in cognitive psychology. *International Journal of Psychology,* 1968, **3**, 273–280. (b)

Papert, S. Etude comparée de l'intelligence chez l'enfant et chez le robot. In L. Apostel, et al., *La filiation des structures.* Paris: Presses Universitaires de France, 1963. Pp. 131–194.

Piaget, J. Quantification, conservation and nativism. *Science,* 1968, **162**, 976–979.

Rothenberg, B. B., & Courtney, R. G. Conservation of number in very young children: A replication of and comparison with Mehler & Bever's study. *Journal of Psychology,* 1968, **70**, 205–212.

Rowland, B., & Donaldson, M. Comprehension of disjunction and negation in young children. Unpublished manuscript, University of Edinburgh, 1970.

Stern, W. *Psychology of early childhood up to the sixth year of age.* London: Allen & Unwin, 1924.

Von Wright, G. H. *An essay in modal logic.* Amsterdam: North-Holland, 1951.

Wales, R. J., & Campbell, R. On the development of comparison and the comparison of development. In G. B. Flores d'Arcais, & W. J. M. Levelt (Eds.), *Advances in psycholinguistics.* Amsterdam: North-Holland, 1970. Pp. 373–396.

White, S. Some general outlines of the matrix of developmental changes between five and seven years. Paper read at the International Congress of Psychology, London, 1969.

Nonverbal Communication[1]

ALBERT MEHRABIAN

University of California, Los Angeles

A SEMANTIC SPACE FOR NONVERBAL BEHAVIOR [2]

One of the most troublesome aspects of research in any relatively unexplored area of study is the determination of basic categories or dimensions that cut across most of the phenomena of interest. In the study of nonverbal communication, this has been an ever present problem in that numerous categories can be selected from the following realms: communication behaviors such as facial expressions, verbalizations, movements, and postures; referents such as feelings and attitudes; communicator or addressee attributes such as personality, psychological well-being, age, sex, and status; and communication media such as face-to-face, telephone, and video interactions.

For instance, one can ask, what are the important behaviors to explore in studying nonverbal communication? Immediately one faces the problem that although any behavior is in principle communicative, since it is observable and bears some kind of significance, some behaviors are more a part of communication than others (e.g., facial expressions in contrast to foot movements). The selection of nonverbal cues for study has sometimes been based on expressive qualities—that is, pathology-related (e.g., Braatoy, 1954; Deutsch, 1947, 1952; Deutsch & Murphy, 1955; or Reich, 1945); or personality-related (e.g., Allport & Vernon, 1933)

1. This study was supported by National Science Foundation grant GS 2482 and by United States Public Health Service grant MH 13509. I am thankful to the American Psychological Association, Academic Press, Inc., and Duke University Press for their permission to reproduce modified versions of various segments of papers which are specifically noted below.

2. This section and the application section to follow include modified segments of my article "A semantic space for nonverbal behavior," *Journal of Consulting and Clinical Psychology*, 1970, **35**, 248–257. Copyright © 1970 by the American Psychological Association and reproduced by permission.

attributes. For instance, psychoanalysts such as Braatoy and Reich have interpreted postural rigidity to indicate obsessional tendencies and greater resistance to change. Some clinicians have also been interested in the identification of particular moods or feelings from specific behaviors (e.g., Fromm-Reichmann, 1950). Experimental investigations of this problem led to the identification of seven affects which were consensually coded into facial and vocal expressions, but still did not provide a general framework for the classification of nonverbal behavior (e.g., findings reviewed by Davitz, 1964, or Woodworth & Schlosberg, 1954, Ch. 5).

Thus, the need for a reasonably general set of categories to characterize communication is readily demonstrated. Without it, how can one know what behaviors he should select to study as a part of nonverbal communication? And on what would he base his selection? Indeed, one of the problems has been the apparent arbitrariness with which nonverbal behaviors are isolated as being a part of communication.

In the present approach, the basic categories are developed from a detailed consideration of the referents, and not of the communication behaviors or the communicator-addressee attributes. The dimensions that are used to characterize the referents in turn provide a framework for classifying and studying the effects of the latter factors. Referents were chosen as the starting point because the existing nonverbal communication literature provides adequate evidence to characterize them in a quite general way. Considering some of this evidence, the referents of nonverbal behavior are described in terms of a three-dimensional framework: evaluation, potency or status, and responsiveness. Positive evaluation is communicated by facial and vocal cues (which express variations in liking) and also by several postures and positions (e.g., a closer position, more forward lean, more eye contact, and more direct orientation). Postural relaxation conveys potency or status, and increasing nonverbal activity (e.g., facial or vocal activity) expresses responsiveness to another person.

Facial and Vocal Expressions

One of the first attempts for a more general characterization of the referents of nonverbal behavior and, therefore, possibly of the behaviors themselves, was that of Schlosberg (1954). He suggested a three-dimensional framework involving pleasantness-unpleasantness, sleep-tension, and attention-rejection. Any feeling could be assigned a value on each of these three dimensions, and different feelings would correspond to different points in this three-dimensional space. This shift away from the study of isolated feelings and their corresponding nonverbal cues and toward a characterization of the general referents of nonverbal behavior on a limited set of dimensions was seen as beneficial. It was hoped that it could aid in the identification of large classes of interrelated nonverbal behaviors.

Recent factor-analytic work by Williams and Sundene (1965), Osgood (1966), and Mordkoff (1971) provided further impetus for characterizing the referents of nonverbal behavior in terms of a limited set of dimensions. Williams and Sundene (1965) found that facial, vocal, and facial-vocal cues can be categorized primarily in terms of three orthogonal factors: general evaluation, social control, and activity.

For facial expression of emotions, Osgood (1966) suggested the following dimensions as primary referents: pleasantness (e.g., joy and glee versus dread and anxiety), control (e.g., annoyance, disgust, contempt, scorn, and loathing versus dismay, bewilderment, surprise, amazement, and excitement), and activation (e.g., sullen anger, rage, disgust, scorn, and loathing versus despair, pity, dreamy sadness, boredom, quiet pleasure, complacency, and adoration). He further noted:

> One would expect to find a close relation between the dimensions operating here and those repeatedly found with the semantic differential technique . . . applied to linguistic signs. Pleasantness and Activation appear to be semantically identical with Evaluation and Activity, two of the three major factors in the general semantic space; what we have called the Control dimension is similar in semantic tone to the Potency factor—*scorn, sullen anger* and the like seem to imply strength and *bewilderment, surprise* and the like weakness—but the relation is not as compelling. [P. 27]

Hand Gestures

In one of the few studies that are available in this area, Gitin (1970) presented 36 photographs of hand gestures to subjects who rated each of the photographs on 40 semantic differential scales. Her first three factors were characterized by the following sets of scales.

Factor I: active-passive, sharp-dull, interesting-uninteresting, tense-sleepy, exciting-boring, curious-indifferent, meaningful- senseless, and intentional-unintentional.

Factor II: pleasant-unpleasant, friendly-unfriendly, good-bad, and beautiful-ugly.

Factor III: submissive-dominant, weak-strong, unarmed-armed, doubtful-certain, shy-brave, and slow-fast.

Gitin's first factor corresponds to our responsiveness dimension, which is referred to as "activation" or "activity" in other studies. Her second factor is the counterpart of our evaluation dimension, and her third factor relates to the potency or status dimension. The semantic differential scales corresponding to these three factors help to further clarify the referential significance of an important aspect of nonverbal behavior (hand gestures) as well as other nonverbal behavior in general.

Thus, at least for facial, vocal, and manual expression, it is interesting to find that similar dimensions characterize the referents of nonverbal as well as verbal behaviors. Such a correspondence is reassuring in that it confirms the expected similarity for cognitive categories, despite the dissimilarity of communication channels. It further suggests that, as with verbal communications, it should be possible to identify other classes of nonverbal communication which relate primarily to one of the three referential dimensions. This indeed seems to be the case for those aspects of nonverbal interaction involving stationary postures and positions.

Postures and Positions

Scheflen (1964, 1965, 1966) provided detailed observations of an informal quality on the significance of postures and positions in interpersonal situations. Mehrabian (1968d, 1969b) reviewed experimental findings relating to the communication of attitudes (evaluation and liking) and status (potency or social control) via posture and position cues. Physical proximity to an addressee, more eye contact with him, a forward lean toward him rather than a backward lean away, and an orientation of the torso toward rather than away from him have all been found to communicate a more positive attitude toward the addressee. A second set of cues which indicate postural relaxation include asymmetrical placement of the limbs, sideways lean and/or reclining position of a seated communicator, and specific relaxation measures of a communicator's hands or neck. This second set of cues has been found to relate primarily to status differences between a communicator and his addressee: a communicator is more relaxed with an addressee of lower status than himself, and less relaxed with one of higher status. Although the relaxation cues are intercorrelated and have been extracted as factors in some experiments (e.g., Mehrabian & Williams, 1969), the proxemic (Hall, 1963, 1966) or immediacy (Mehrabian, 1967a; Wiener & Mehrabian, 1968) cues are not intercorrelated. However, insofar as the set of immediacy cues (a) do together reflect a more positive attitude toward an addressee, (b) can be conceptually related as increasing the physical proximity between a communicator and his addressee, and (c) increase the mutual sensory stimulation between the communicators, there is some basis for grouping the cues as part of a single nonverbal dimension. Mehrabian (1969c) provided the scoring criteria for relaxation and immediacy and suggested a set of weights for the computation of total immediacy and relaxation from specific posture and position variables.

Reanalysis of the fourth experiment of Mehrabian (1968a) using these measures yielded simple relationships, in contrast to the rather elaborate ones which were reported in that study. Mehrabian's (1968a) factorial design included two levels of liking of the addressee (liked versus disliked), two levels of status relative to the addressee (high versus low), addressee sex, and communicator sex. For the standing communicators of this experiment, analysis of variance of the immediacy measure indicated only one significant effect: communicators were more immediate with liked than disliked addressees. A similar analysis of the relaxation scores yielded two effects: communicators were more relaxed with lower- than with higher-status addressees, and they were also more relaxed with females than with males.

Findings by Mehrabian and Friar (1969) for communicators in a seated position were reanalyzed with a factorial design which included communicator and addressee sex and two levels each of attitude and status. The results of this reanalysis indicated that communicators who were seated assumed a more immediate position to liked than to disliked addressees; female communicators were generally more immediate to their addressees than male communicators; and when the communicator was of lower status than the addressee, there was no significant effect due to addressee sex.

The analysis of the relaxation scores obtained in the Mehrabian and Friar (1969) study indicated that a communicator was more relaxed when he was of higher status than his addressee; furthermore, for male communicators there was greater relaxation with moderately disliked than with moderately liked addressees, there being no corresponding difference for female communicators. Finally, opposite-sexed communicators were more relaxed with each other than same-sexed communicators.

A third study which also provided data that was reanalyzed for immediacy and relaxation involved the communication of five degrees of attitude toward an addressee (Mehrabian, 1968b). The results of that study indicated a direct linear relationship between immediacy and attitude. Also, relaxation was a decreasing linear function of positive attitude toward an addressee. There was one final interaction effect due to Communicator Sex × Addressee Sex × Attitude. The means for this effect indicated that, in all instances, relaxation linearly increased with increasing dislike of the addressee, with the exception that male communicators who addressed an extremely disliked male exhibited their lowest level of relaxation. This was interpreted as being the result of vigilance elicited by a threatening other.

Incidentally, Wiener and Mehrabian (1968) also used the concept of immediacy to elaborate a method for inferring positive-negative communicator attitudes from different classes of verbal behavior. The inference of communicator attitudes on the basis of their method independently supplements any explicit (verbal) information that a communicator provides about his feelings.

Their approach is based on an analysis of the forms of the communicator-object relationship in verbal contents that are ostensibly equivalent with respect to the *explicit* communication of feelings. For example, the two statements "I am looking at X" and "We are looking at X" vary with respect to the form of communicator-object relationship (i.e., the relationship between "I" and "X"), but both statements are neutral with respect to the expressed feeling toward X. Similarly, "I dislike X" and "I dislike X's habits" vary with respect to the form of communicator-object relationship, but both statements are ostensibly equivalent with respect to the speaker's feeling toward X. Such variations have been categorized with respect to the degree of "nonimmediacy" between the communicator "I" and the object "X" in the communication. Communicator-object "nonimmediacy" is a measure of the degree of attenuation of directness and intensity of interaction between the communicator and the object, as inferred from verbal contents. In the above examples, "We are looking at X" is categorized as less immediate than "I am looking at X," since the former involves a dilution of the interaction with X. Again, "I dislike X's habits" is categorized as less immediate than "I dislike X," since the former restricts interaction to some aspect of X.[3]

Encoding studies by Gottlieb, Wiener, and Mehrabian (1967), Mehrabian (1965, 1966a, 1967b), and Mehrabian and Wiener (1966) have consistently shown that communications about liked persons or events contain greater verbal immediacy. Decoding studies by Mehrabian (1966b, 1967c, 1967d, 1968c) have also consistently shown that more immediate communications are judged by untrained subjects as conveying greater liking. Thus, the immediacy phenomena and hypothesis that have been elaborated for postural cues have greater generality and may be applicable across a diversity of communication channels.

In sum, the findings from studies of posture and position and subtle variations in verbal statements show that immediacy cues primarily denote evaluation. Postural relaxation cues denote status or potency in a relationship. It is interesting to note a weaker effect:

3. Acknowledgment is given to Duke University Press for their permission to use a slightly revised version of the preceding two paragraphs which originally appeared in my "Attitudes in relation to the forms of communicator-object relationship in spoken communications," *Journal of Personality*, 1966, **34**, 80–93. Copyright © Duke University Press.

less relaxation of one's posture does also convey a more positive attitude toward another. One way to interpret this overlap in the referential significance of less relaxation and more immediacy in communicating a more positive feeling is in terms of the implied positive connotations of higher status in our culture. A respectful attitude (i.e., when one conveys that the other is of higher status) does indeed have implied positive connotations. Therefore it is not surprising that the communication of respect and the communication of positive attitude exhibit some similarity in the nonverbal cues which they require. However, whereas the communication of liking is more heavily weighted by variations in immediacy, that of respect is weighted more by variations in relaxation.

The studies reviewed above were not designed within the framework presently being proposed; rather, the framework evolved from those studies. The general correspondence of the findings with those of Gitin (1970), Osgood (1966), Osgood, Suci, and Tannenbaum (1957), and Williams and Sundene (1965) suggested further exploration of the approach for other nonverbal cues. Therefore, this framework is used below to discuss various aspects of facial movement, vocal, and verbal communication.

Movements and Implicit Aspects of Verbalizations

There have been several approaches to the study of movements and of the more subtle qualities of verbalizations. One set of studies investigated the interdependence of behaviors in different channels. For instance, a study by Boomer (1963) showed a direct correlation between speech disturbance (particularly the filled pause) and a composite measure of head, hand, and foot movements of one patient. Dittmann and Llewellyn (1969) explored the differential occurrence of movements at various positions of a phonemic clause —"a string of words, averaging five in length, in which there is one and only one primary stress and which is terminated by a juncture" (p. 99). Head and hand movements occurred more frequently with primary-stressed words, but this relationship accounted for only 7% of the variance in body movement. This finding suggested that "if a person wishes to convey the idea that what he is expressing is important or difficult to conceptualize or exciting, he will introduce movements along with his speech to get this extra information across. The timing of these movements will tend to follow the pattern of timing he is familiar with: that is, early in encoding units or following hesitations in speech" (p. 105). One implication of the findings, of course, is that there are other determiners of movement besides the structural qualities of the statements which they accompany.

According to Condon and Ogston (1966) and Kendon (1967b), one such source of movements is the synchronous quality of interpersonal interaction. These investigators have attempted a microanalysis of movement sequences of participants in a conversation. Some of the forms of synchrony are "movement mirroring," "punctuation," as in the Dittmann and Llewellyn study, and "speech analogous" movements.

> There is a small amount of research which suggests that when subjects are exposed to an input that has a rhythmic organization, such as music, they tend to move in time to it . . . and that if they are already performing some activity, such as tapping, or typing, they may bring the rhythm of this activity into relation with the rhythm of the input. . . . We have seen here, both from the data we have reported on, and also very strikingly from the data reported by Condon and Ogston, that the synchrony of the listener's behavior to that of the speaker may be very precise indeed. The precision of the synchrony suggests that the listeners are responding to a rhythm with which they are thoroughly familiar. This rhythm is, of course, largely the rhythm of speech, the rhythmical character of the syllabic pulse, and for those who have a given language in common this rhythm must be familiar. . . . It seems plausible, thus, that the minute synchrony observable between interactants is a product of their attention to an input where rhythmical structuring is highly familiar to them. [Kendon, 1967b, pp. 36–37]

A third approach has attempted to develop typologies for movement. Such attempts are exemplified by the work of Birdwhistell (1952), Efron (1941), and, more recently, Ekman and Friesen (1969b) and Freedman and Hoffmann (1967). Ekman and Friesen (1969b) suggested a quite thorough system for categorizing movements and related it to the systems of the other investigators. More evidence is needed for the referential significance of the proposed categories, and there is a need for the empirical justification of the separate categories proposed by these investigators.

A fourth approach has focused on the emotion- and attitude-communicating significance of nonverbal behavior. Mahl, Danet, and Norton (1959) suggested that movement information complements verbal messages by anticipating, contradicting, or concurring with the referents of the verbal channel. More specific work by Ekman and Friesen (1967) on the referents of movements of various body parts showed that stationary positions communicate gross affects (i.e., attitudes), whereas movements and facial expressions communicate specific emotions. Along similar lines, Kendon (1967a) and Exline and his colleagues have explored the many-faceted significance of eye contact with, or observation of, another (Exline, 1962, 1963; Exline & Eldridge, 1967; Exline, Gray, & Schuette, 1965; Exline & Winters, 1965). Rosenfeld (1966a, 1966b) used a role-playing paradigm in which his subjects were requested to interreact with someone and elicit varying degrees of liking from him. The nonverbal behaviors of the subjects were the dependent measures and indicated that higher speech rates, lengthier communications, frequent verbal reinforcers to the addressee, gesticulation, smiling, positive head nods, and less frequent self-references were associated with the attempt to elicit more liking.

In the two studies described below, it was assumed that in certain interpersonal situations, the nonverbal communication of attitudes is either more appropriate or a necessary concomitant of the communicator's affect. For instance, Zaidel and Mehrabian (1969) found that communicators were able to express variations in negative affect better than variations in positive affect, whether using facial or vocal channels. Perhaps nonverbal expressions of negative attitude are practiced more than positive ones because it is seldom appropriate to express negative feelings openly. Thus, they are delegated to the subtle, nonverbal channels more frequently than are positive feelings, and people become more proficient at expressing their negative feelings nonverbally.

In other situations, such as being under stress, once again nonverbal channels may become salient indicators, particularly when the communicator is unwilling to express his feelings explicitly. Early psychoanalytic interest in nonverbal behavior was primarily motivated by this assumption (e.g., Deutsch & Murphy, 1955), and the recent interest in the detection of deceit from nonverbal behaviors also seems to be related (Ekman & Friesen, 1969a).

The importance of nonverbal behaviors is also highlighted in situations in which unfamiliar persons interact and one seeks to influence the other (as in political speeches or advertising). Verbal expression of feelings toward another is less permissible in these situations than is an argument or information relating to the topic in question. In the experiments summarized below, the interactions involved dyads, mostly between peers. One member of each dyad was a confederate of the experimenter and exhibited a prearranged set of behaviors designed to seem "normal" for that situation. The other member of the dyad, the actual subject, was observed through a one-way mirror and his behaviors were video recorded.

Perceived and Intended Persuasiveness. In the first two experiments reported by Mehrabian and Williams (1969) subjects presented messages to someone else, employing varying degrees of persuasion. Subjects' nonverbal, vocal, and verbal behaviors were recorded and analyzed. The movement cues rated were lateral swivels in a desk chair, rocking, head nodding, gesticulation, self-manipulation such as scratching or tapping one part of a hand with another, and leg and foot movements. Measures relating to the facial expressions included facial pleasantness and activity. Measures relating to verbalizations were length of communication in terms of number of words or duration, speech rate, the unhalting quality of speech, speech error rate (Kasl & Mahl, 1965; Mahl, 1959), volume, and activity (Huttar, 1967; Starkweather, 1964). The criteria for scoring these categories of nonverbal behavior have been summarized by Mehrabian (1969c).

The analyses of these data led to the postulation of an activity dimension for nonverbal behaviors. The variables grouped under this dimension included facial and vocal activity, speech volume, and speech rate. Whereas immediacy and relaxation indicate variations in liking and status, respectively, activity communicates responsiveness (e.g., note Bentler's, 1969, data for adjectives), and is a function of the salience of the addressee.

The findings from the persuasion studies indicated simply that a communicator's activity increases with his intention to persuade, and the perceived persuasiveness of a message is correlated with the level of activity exhibited nonverbally by the communicator. Both studies reported by Mehrabian and Williams (1969) yielded this one major effect relating activity and persuasion. A second, though weaker, relationship occurred between attempted persuasiveness and immediacy: communicators were more immediate to an addressee when they attempted to be more persuasive. Further, in two experiments, more immediate communications were also perceived as more persuasive.

Thus, findings for the nonverbal concomitants of persuasion can be readily summarized: nonverbal positive responsiveness to an addressee enhances the perceived persuasiveness of a message, and when a person attempts to be persuasive, he exhibits more positive responsiveness to the addressee.

Deceit. In three experiments we have explored the nonverbal concomitants of deceitful and of truthful communications (Mehrabian, 1971a). A variety of paradigms were used in which a subject communicated deceitfully or truthfully to someone else. All the behaviors noted in the preceding discussion of persuasion were recorded and scored. Findings from two of the experiments indicated that immediacy toward an addressee is greater when one is truthful than when deceitful.

In the first experiment, the subject was either promised a reward for successful deceit or threatened that he would be shocked if his deceit was detected. Subjects who were promised a reward were more immediate when truthful than when deceitful, but there was no corresponding significant difference when subjects were threatened with shock. The second experiment involved role playing of deceit versus role playing of truth, and subjects were found to be more immediate while they were role playing at being truthful than when role playing at being deceitful.

Relaxation was not a discriminator between deceit and truth in any of the experiments. Subjects in the first experiment who anticipated possible reward were more relaxed than those who anticipated possible shock. In the second experiment, while being deceitful, high-anxious males were more relaxed than low-anxious males. In contrast, while being deceitful, female high-anxious communicators were less relaxed than female low-anxious communicators. There were no corresponding effects in the truthful conditions. The second experiment also indicated that males were generally more relaxed than females. Finally, in the third experiment, extroverts were more relaxed than introverts.

Thus, these deceit studies provided further validity for the relaxation cues, and suggested a relationship between immediacy of postures and deceitful versus truthful communication, while not providing any relationship between activity level and deceit.

The experimental data reviewed thus far provided a preliminary basis for grouping nonverbal and implicit verbal communication cues, and indicated the primary significance of each of three sets of cues in a variety of social situations. These three sets of cues provide a way of objectively characterizing social interaction. To facilitate further exploration of the interrelationships among these cues and their relation to the personality of participants and the social situations in which they interact, the following section touches on the theoretical significance of these groupings.

A Rationale for the Choice of Semantic Dimensions

It is of some interest to speculate briefly about why the three proposed referential dimensions emerged as particularly relevant in nonverbal communication. Our answer is based on the premise that nonverbal behavior is a developmentally earlier and more primitive form of communication which man shares with animals (e.g., Werner, 1957; Werner & Kaplan, 1963). Such a premise implies that nonverbal behavior reflects very basic social orientations which are correlates of major categories in the cognition of social environments (Piaget, 1960). Positive-negative affect and evaluation are basic cognitive distinctions made from early infancy and retained in adult life—they determine approach and avoidance tendencies toward objects or persons. The evaluation of objects and persons is a crucial aspect of intelligent functioning and even of survival. It is therefore not surprising that people possess behavioral correlates for this cognitive distinction—the immediacy cues—which are ever present in social interaction.

The second dimension, status or potency, relates to social control. It is particularly salient in the social life of animals, as observed in the phenomenon of territoriality (e.g., Calhoun, 1962) and is a major determiner of social interaction patterns among humans. This is especially evident in highly stratified, authoritarian cultures but can be seen in even the most democratic societies (e.g., Hall, 1966).

Responsiveness is conceptualized as the nonverbal-social counterpart of the orienting reflex (e.g., Maltzman, 1967). As such it is another elementary and basic aspect of social life. The degree of responsiveness to another indicates his salience for oneself and is elicited by nonneutral events or persons (extreme instances being unusually reinforcing or threatening ones). In cognition (as in responsiveness) unusual events of either positive or negative quality are grouped and reacted to similarly, as exemplified by the concept of mana in many primitive cultures (e.g., Cassirer, 1953–1957). The differential responsiveness of humans or animals to various aspects of their social environment is characteristic of their alive quality and distinguishes them from the inanimate world. Together with the preceding two cognitive distinctions (evaluation and judgment of social power) it is a basic aspect of intelligent (adaptive, *à la* Piaget, 1960) functioning.

Noting the rather general quality of these cognitive and behavioral dimensions for both animal and human social systems provides a plausible basis for using data obtained from the social interaction of animals. Primates, in particular, can provide complementary information about certain aspects of affect and attitude communication in humans. For instance, Sommer (1967) summarized some of the research which related the spatial arrangement of persons in a variety of social situations to their social status. A number of the studies Sommer reviewed were motivated by the more familiar phenomenon of territoriality observed in animals (e.g., Ardrey, 1966; Lorenz, 1967; McBride, 1964). Even informal observation of chimpanzees living together reveals impressive differences in the postures, positions, movements, and facial expressions of dyads differing in status. Since status or potency is readily specified in terms of size or strength in such animal social systems, investigation of the nonverbal correlates of potency is considerably simplified and may yield nonverbal interaction cues that have transcultural relevance. More generally, the observation of animal social interactions can complement the study of individuals of a single culture (e.g., American college students) and provide corroboration for identified dimensions of social interaction.

FACTOR ANALYSES OF IMPLICIT COMMUNICATION CUES[4]

Two recent experiments were designed to explore the relationships among nonverbal and implicit verbal behaviors in a waiting situation with a stranger (Mehrabian, 1971b; Mehrabian & Ksionzky, 1971c). In both of these experiments, one of the pair of strangers who waited together was an experimental confederate, but this was not evident to his partner, the subject in the experiment. Confederates were initially coached in detail regarding where to stand, how to orient, how much eye contact to have with the subjects, the degree of their facial pleasantness and positive vocalization, and the number and length of their verbal utterances. Two different sets of 22 confederates, equally divided as to sex, were trained and participated in each of the two experiments. The training of confederates and the use of a large number of them was designed to minimize the confounding of results by confederate attributes or physical appearance.

In the experimental situations, one subject and a confederate of the same sex were led into a "waiting" room while the experimenter ostensibly went to prepare the materials for the experiment. Actually, this 2-minute waiting period was the experiment proper, and both the subject's and the confederate's behaviors were recorded on video and audio tape. This method was quite effective in eliciting spontaneous and natural social behaviors from subjects.

Experiment I

In the Mehrabian (1971b) study, the waiting room was 9 × 20 feet in size and was empty except for a table placed in one corner.

4. I am indebted to Academic Press, Inc., for their permission to use rewritten segments, including Tables 1 and 2, of my "Verbal and nonverbal interaction of strangers in a waiting situation," *Journal of Experimental Research in Personality*, 1971, **5**, 127–138.

Thus, both the confederate and the subject were standing. A standing rather than a seated arrangement was used to make possible the exploration of distances and orientations in relation to other cues. The confederate's behaviors toward the subject were predetermined to be either slightly positive or negative, as follows.

Confederate slightly negative toward the subject: The confederate, who entered the waiting room ahead of the subject, took a preassigned position near one corner and faced diagonally across to the opposite corner of the room. He stood with his legs in a moderately asymmetrical position and both feet resting flat on the floor. His hands and arms were moderately relaxed—his arms in a slightly asymmetrical position or held behind his back, or one arm hanging loosely with the other holding that forearm. In general, then, the confederate's posture was intended to communicate a moderate level of relaxation that seemed natural in the waiting situation. The confederate had been trained to look toward the subject's head 25% of the time, and to do so especially if the subject addressed him. The confederate's facial expressions, which were also scored, obtained a mean rating of 1.5 on a scale ranging from 0 (no positive expressions) to 4 (extremely positive expression). As the confederate entered the waiting room with the subject, he looked at the subject and smiled once, and did not exhibit any negative facial expressions during the waiting period. He never initiated a conversation, nor did he ask any questions, but he always responded if the subject initiated a topic or made a remark. His responses were brief, averaging 1.5 words.

Confederate slightly positive toward the subject: In this condition the confederate's behaviors were identical to those in the slightly negative condition, with the following exceptions. His facial expressions were more positive, having been rated 2.6 on the same 0-to-4 scale. The confederate initiated conversation once for every three verbal initiations of the subject. In a typical initiation, the subject's question was first answered and then a similar question was asked in return (e.g., "I'm majoring in chemistry; how about you?"). The verbal responses of the confederate were longer than in the preceding condition, averaging 4.5 words.

Each confederate was partner to approximately 12 subjects and served in only one condition, the slightly positive or the slightly negative. All confederates received the same information, regardless of the condition they served in. They were told that the experiment was to study the ways in which strangers interact in a waiting situation, that we were using several confederates to ensure generality of results, that to ensure comparability in the behaviors of various confederates we needed to train them in great detail, and that more natural behaviors would be elicited from subjects if they remained unaware that their partners were experimental confederates. In the final portion of the experiment, the subjects were requested to answer questionnaire measures of affiliative tendency, sensitivity to rejection (Mehrabian, 1970d) and achieving tendency (Mehrabian, 1968e, 1968f, 1969a).

Each subject's behavior during the 2-minute waiting period was observed and recorded through a one-way mirror. Observers scored eye contact and distance, since these are difficult to score from video recordings. The remaining dependent measures and confederate behaviors were scored subsequently from the audio and video recordings. The entire set of dependent measures from the waiting period are included in Table 1. Two observers independently scored the audio recordings first and then scored the video recordings for movements. Reliability estimates for the dependent measures have been provided by Mehrabian (1969c) and justified averaging the pair of scores obtained by the two observers for each dependent measure.

The names of the variables in Table 1 are self-explanatory. Rate measures, unless otherwise specified below, were in terms of number of units (e.g., movements, statements) per minute. Speech rate, speech volume, and vocal activity (i.e., a composite of intensity range and fundamental frequency range) were estimated on scales ranging from 0 to 4. The positive-negative quality of both the vocal component and the verbal contents was scored on scales ranging from -2 to $+2$. A statement was defined as a simple sentence or an independent clause; a subject's statements were also subdivided into "declaratives," "questions," and "answers." Verbal reinforcers (e.g., "yeah," "uh-huh," "really?" and "hm-mm") were scored as a separate category and did not qualify as statements. Speech duration of the subject (or the confederate) was the percentage of the waiting period during which he talked.

Behavioral data from the waiting period were factor analyzed, and varimax rotation of the primary factors yielded the groupings listed in Table 1. Variables are listed in order according to the magnitude of their loadings, and direction of loading for each variable on the corresponding factor is also indicated. Each subject's z scores for the variables of a given factor were summed algebraically to serve as a composite score for that factor. For instance, an "intimate-close position" score was simply a subject's z score for "shoulder orientation" minus his z score for "distance."

TABLE 1

SUMMARY OF THE FACTORS CHARACTERIZING SOCIAL INTERACTION
IN MEHRABIAN's (1971b) STUDY

	Direction of Loading on Factor
Factor I: Affiliative Behavior	
1. Total number of statements per minute	(+)
2. Number of declarative statements per minute	(+)
3. Number of questions per minute	(+)
4. Percent duration of subject's speech	(+)
5. Percent duration of confederate's speech	(+)
6. Percent duration of eye contact with confederate	(+)
7. Head nods per minute	(+)
8. Pleasantness of facial expressions	(+)
9. Number of verbal reinforcers per minute	(+)
10. Positive verbal content	(+)
11. Hand and arm gestures per minute	(+)
12. Pleasantness of vocal expressions	(+)
Factor II: Responsiveness to (or Salience of) Target	
1. Vocal activity	(+)
2. Speech volume	(+)
3. Speech rate	(+)
Factor III: Relaxation	
1. Leg and foot movements per minute	(−)
2. Rocking movements per minute	(−)
3. Body lean	(+)
Factor IV: Intimacy (or Close Position)	
1. Shoulder orientation away from confederate	(+)
2. Distance from confederate	(−)
Factor V: Behavioral Index of Distress	
1. Percent duration of walking	(+)

To compute an affiliative behavior index, however, it was noted that a number of the variables were simply redundant measures of amount of speech. Therefore, the corresponding index included only "statement rate" as the representative measure for the various related cues:

Affiliative behavior =
    total number of statements per minute
    + percent duration of eye contact with the confederate
    + head nods per minute + pleasantness of facial expressions
    + number of verbal reinforcers per minute
    + positive verbal content + hand and arm gestures per minute
    + pleasantness of vocal expressions

Since the cues for affiliative behavior are of primary interest, the intercorrelations among the variables in this first factor are reported in Table 2.

The intercorrelations among the variables subsumed within the first factor and reported in Table 2 show that positive affect cues were significantly correlated with various indexes of amount of conversation. Together, the positive affect cues in verbalization (e.g., verbal reinforcement rate, positive verbal content, positive vocalization), positive affect cues in nonverbal behavior (e.g., eye contact, head nods, pleasant facial expressions, gesticulation), and various indicators of amount of conversation (total number of statements per minute, duration of speech) defined a unitary dimension of social behavior. These intercorrelations provided support for Mehrabian and Ksionzky's (1970) hypothesis that affiliative behavior is not simply the exchange of verbalizations, but rather encompasses a broader realm of social cues which consist of the exchange of positive reinforcers. Their model of affiliative behavior was based on the assumption that affiliation is elicited by positive reinforcement and is discouraged by negative reinforcement. The correlational data of the present experiment support this basic assumption of the interdependence of affiliation and exchange of positive reinforcers.

One result was contrary to expectations: distance and orientation were not found to be part of the primary affiliative behavior factor. Rather, together they defined a separate factor referred to as

TABLE 2

CORRELATIONS AMONG VARIABLES DEFINING THE AFFILIATIVE BEHAVIOR FACTOR[a]

	2	3	4	5	6	7	8	9	10	11	12
1. Total statements per minute	.99	.74	.87	.78	.73	.62	.56	.54	.54	.46	.35
2. Declarative statements per minute		.75	.86	.75	.73	.61	.55	.54	.53	.46	.33
3. Questions per minute			.63	.69	.66	.47	.43	.62	.49	.22	.32
4. Percent speech duration of subject				.79	.67	.52	.52	.45	.47	.51	.32
5. Percent speech duration of confederate					.70	.55	.52	.53	.51	.36	.32
6. Percent duration eye contact with confederate						.52	.59	.44	.41	.41	.33
7. Head nods per minute							.41	.37	.40	.22	.30
8. Pleasantness of facial expressions								.32	.38	.30	.33
9. Verbal reinforcers per minute									.39	.20	.29
10. Positive verbal content										.16	.44
11. Hand and arm gestures per minute											.19
12. Pleasantness of vocal expressions											

[a] With 254 cases, correlations of .17 are significant at the .01 level.

"intimate–close position." This finding was surprising since smaller distances have consistently been found to be correlates of greater liking. More direct orientation has also been found, though less consistently, to correlate with positive attitudes toward the listener (Mehrabian, 1967a). In the present experiment the absence of a correlation between affiliative behavior and a smaller distance or a more direct orientation may have been due to the averaging of distances and orientations over the total interaction duration. Earlier experiments have usually been based on the initial choice of distance or orientation (e.g., Mehrabian, 1969b). Perhaps the averaging minimized the attitudinal significance of a subject's initial choice of distance from the confederate.

Although the initial distance and orientation may be more indicative of like–dislike of the other, the present close position factor could also be indicative of some other aspects of social interaction considered by Sommer (1967, 1969). In several of his experiments, Sommer found a consistent difference in the pattern of seating depending on the activity of the subjects, such that cooperative situations typically involved a closer position (i.e., smaller distance and less direct orientation) relative to competitive ones. Other studies have also shown an inverse relationship between distance and orientation, and have led some investigators to posit a limited tolerance for intimacy: the increasing intimacy due to a smaller distance is compensated for in terms of less direct orientation (e.g., Argyle & Dean, 1965; Argyle & Kendon, 1967). The results of the present experiment showed only a few effects for this intimacy (or close position) factor, but did serve to identify it as a part of social interaction which is distinct from affiliative behavior. In other studies where there are variations in the prior familiarity of subjects, or experimentally determined variations in their mutual interdependence in a task, the intimacy index may be of greater value.

The results of the factor analysis indicated that the measure of highest loading on affiliative behavior was "total number of statements per minute." Thus statement rate (i.e., total number of simple sentences or independent clauses uttered per minute) is a more satisfactory measure than speech duration, though it is somewhat more cumbersome to score. When audio tape recordings of social interaction are available and a more stable index of affiliative behavior is desired, scores for total statement rate, verbal reinforcer rate, positive verbal content, and positiveness of the vocal component can be standardized and summed. Such an index can serve as a convenient dependent measure for most studies of affiliative behavior. The obtained intercorrelations of these verbal cues with nonverbal communications of positive affect serve as assurance that such a composite measure that is based on the verbal interchange is reasonably representative of general affiliative behavior.

A consideration of the literature in the nonverbal communication area led to the postulation of three orthogonal dimensions for characterizing the nonverbal aspects of social interaction: communications of liking (which include all of the nonverbal cues within the first factor), responsiveness to the target (or, alternatively, the salience of the target for oneself), and potency or status as conveyed by greater relaxation (Mehrabian, 1970a). The present results show that when verbal cues are also considered within the complex of social interaction, the same three factors emerge, and that most of the verbal cues which measure amount of verbal interchange are part of the first factor, liking-affiliation. The second factor, responsiveness, is correlated only slightly with the communication of liking, and reflects the extent to which the subject is reacting to another, whether in a positive or negative way. For instance, in persuasive communication situations in which the nonverbal expression of liking may be construed as manipulative and insincere, it has been found that increased attempts at persuasion are associated with increased responsiveness to the listener, but with only slight increases in actual positiveness toward the listener (Mehrabian & Williams, 1969).

Postural relaxation has been found to be a correlate of higher status of the speaker relative to his listener. The composition of the relaxation index is somewhat different for standing and seated positions. For seated postures, asymmetry in positioning of the limbs and the degree of reclining or sideways lean are the best indicators; for standing positions, sideways lean of the body again serves as a measure of relaxation, but rocking movements and leg and foot movements while in the same place are also important indicators.

In addition to the above factor analytic results for the inter-relationships among the various cues, the experiment yielded a number of relationships between the factors characterizing social behavior, the experimental condition, and the personality of the participants. Highlights of these results are briefly summarized below. Subjects reciprocated the positive (or negative) behaviors of experimental confederates; those with higher scores on a measure of affiliative tendency communicated more positive affect and were more in tune to the degree of positiveness they received from a confederate. Two kinds of significance were attached to bodily tension, depending on the degree of positive attitude communicated simultaneously. Tension in the generally more positive high affiliators conveyed respect, but in the slightly negative subjects who were sensitive to rejection, it conveyed vigilance. There was also more tension during interaction with others of higher status. With same-sexed targets, females affiliated more than males, and were more intimate and submissive. Birth order failed to relate signif-icantly to either affiliative behavior or the questionnaire personality measures of affiliative tendency, sensitivity to rejection, or achieving tendency.

Experiment II

This experiment by Mehrabian and Ksionzky (1971c) explored the contribution of a different set of experimental factors to the social interaction of a subject with an experimental confederate. The dependent measures, however, were essentially the same as those in the preceding experiment and were similarly scored and factor analyzed. The 22 experimental confederates were initially coached to behave in the slightly positive way described under Experiment I. The confederates were unaware of the experimental condition to which a subject was assigned. The audio and video recordings were scored using criteria given by Mehrabian (1969c). Two raters independently scored each category and their scores were averaged. No information about subjects' personality scores was available to the raters, since those questionnaires were scored last.

The measures taken during the waiting period were factor analyzed and a principal component solution was obtained.

Varimax rotation of the primary factors yielded the groupings of these cues given in Table 3. For each factor in Table 3, the variables are listed starting with those having the highest loadings, on down to the variable with the lowest loading on the factor. Table 3 also provides the direction of loading of the variables on their corresponding factors.

TABLE 3

SUMMARY OF FACTORS CHARACTERIZING SOCIAL INTERACTION
IN THE MEHRABIAN AND KSIONZKY (1971c) EXPERIMENT

	Direction of Loading on Factor
Factor I: Affiliative Behavior	
1. Total number of statements per minute	(+)
2. Number of declarative statements per minute	(+)
3. Percent duration of eye contact with confederate	(+)
4. Percent duration of subject's speech	(+)
5. Percent duration of confederate's speech	(+)
6. Positive verbal content	(+)
7. Head nods per minute	(+)
8. Hand and arm gestures per minute	(+)
9. Pleasantness of facial expressions	(+)
Factor II: Responsiveness to (or Salience of) Target	
1. Vocal activity	(+)
2. Speech rate	(+)
3. Speech volume	(+)
Factor III: Relaxation	
1. Rocking movements per minute	(−)
2. Leg and foot movements per minute	(−)
3. Body lean	(+)
Factor IV: Ingratiation	
1. Pleasantness of vocal expressions	(+)
2. Negative verbal content	(−)
3. Verbal reinforcers given per minute	(+)
4. Number of questions per minute	(+)
5. Self-manipulations per minute	(+)
Factor V: Behavioral Index of Distress	
1. Percent duration of walking	(+)
2. Object manipulations per minute	(+)
3. Arm position asymmetry	(+)
Factor VI: Close Position	
1. Shoulder orientation away from confederate	(+)
2. Distance from confederate	(−)
3. Head turns per minute (looking around)	(+)

The results in Tables 1 and 3 are in general agreement. The fourth factor of Table 3 was found to be part of the affiliative behavior factor in Table 1. In this study, it emerged as a relatively independent aspect of social behavior and connoted greater dependency and subservience to another. Other data from this experiment showed that such a distinction between affiliative and ingratiating behavior is helpful when situational factors (the cooperative condition of this experiment and, more generally, situations in which one person is less confident of his abilities and/or is in a more subservient role relative to another) force mutual dependency between participants.

The contribution of arm position asymmetry to the behavioral index of distress is a by-product of object manipulation, which in the experimental situation involved the use of one hand only (e.g., writing or drawing designs on a blackboard—another evasive maneuver). Thus, the first two variables of this factor are sufficient for characterizing distress.

Additional results which related the dependent measures to the independent effects in the study indicated that the results for affiliative behavior were mostly consistent with a model proposed by Mehrabian (1970b) and Mehrabian and Ksionzky (1970, 1971a, 1971b). The behavioral correlates of the personality variables were more pronounced when the stimulus cues bearing on those behaviors were more ambiguous. For instance, persons who scored high on a measure of affiliative tendency tended to be more affiliative with the confederates who had not been clearly positive or negative in evaluating them prior to the waiting period. Similarly, those who scored high on a measure of sensitivity to rejection tended to be less affiliative with the confederates who had not been clearly positive or negative in evaluating them earlier on.

A second general result was that the frustration of characteristic goals associated with each of two personality attributes was especially distressing to persons possessing those attributes. For instance, positive affiliators showed more distress when anticipating cooperation with others who disliked them. Also, high achievers, who prize success more than low achievers, showed the highest level of distress when they had to depend on the cooperation of someone who disliked them.

Finally, although the effects of birth order were also explored, it was found to be an extremely disappointing predictor of behavioral cues in social interaction.

Experiments Where Affiliative Behavior (Positive Affect) Is Assessed from Audio Recordings [5]

The preceding two experiments presented the results of factor analyses of verbal and nonverbal cues in social situations. Frequently an experimenter cannot afford the extensive effort which is involved in assessing affiliative behavior (or positive affect communication) from nonverbal cues. In such cases, it is possible to readily obtain a subtle measure of affiliative behavior on the basis of implicit verbal cues. This procedure was used by Mehrabian and Diamond (1971a, 1971b) in four experiments which explored the facilitating and inhibiting effects of various furniture arrangements and two types of objects on social interaction.

The dyads in all three experiments of the Mehrabian and Diamond (1971b) study were strangers (neither one of whom was an experimental confederate) and thought they were waiting for the "music listening" experiment to start. Actually, this waiting period was the experiment proper and their informal social interaction was recorded and studied as a function of various furniture arrangements and objects in the waiting room.

The audio recording of each pair's interaction was subsequently scored for the following: (1) total statement rate—the number of simple sentences or independent clauses of each subject per minute; (2) percent speech duration—the percentage of the 5-minute interaction period during which the subject spoke; (3) percent speech duration for the pair; (4) verbal reinforcer rate—the number of "uh-huh," "yes," or other agreements given to the partner; (5) latency of the initial statement—the duration of silence of each subject before his first statement in the interaction; (6) positive verbal content—rated on a 5-point scale; and (7) negative verbal content—also rated on a 5-point scale.

5. This section includes rewritten segments from Mehrabian and Diamond's "The effects of furniture arrangement, props, and personality on social interaction," *Journal of Personality and Social Psychology*, 1971, in press. Copyright © 1971 by the American Psychological Association and reproduced by permission.

TABLE 4

INTERCORRELATIONS AMONG IMPLICIT VERBAL CUES[a]

	2	3	4	5	6	7
1. Total statement rate	.86	.76	.56	.23	−.42	.31
2. Percent speech duration of subject		.82	.45	.27	−.38	.26
3. Percent speech duration of pair			.58	.50	−.46	.20
4. Positive verbal content				.42	−.39	.03
5. Verbal reinforcer rate					−.26	−.01
6. Latency						−.19
7. Negative verbal content						

a With df = 286, correlations in excess of .16 are significant at the .01 level.

Again, data from all three of the present experiments supported the hypothesis of Mehrabian and Ksionzky (1970) that positive communications of attitude and amount of conversation are correlated and define an affiliative behavior factor. These data indicated that negative contents in communication are not part of this factor. The representative intercorrelations for the various affiliative cues and negative content scores of one experiment are given in Table 4.

Total statement rate, speech duration of a subject, singly or with his partner, frequency of verbal reinforcers, and a separate index of positive verbal content are positively intercorrelated and all of these are negatively correlated with latency of a subject's initial statement.

There are three redundant measures of amount of conversation in Table 4: total statement rate, percent speech duration, and percent speech duration of the pair. To avoid disproportionate contribution from this source to a composite index of affiliative behavior, the best single measure of amount of conversation, total statement rate, was used in computing the following index, where all the variables were first normalized.

Affiliative behavior = total statement rate + positive verbal content
+ verbal reinforcer rate − latency

In addition to the correlational data of Table 4, the experiments in this study provided confirmation that the proposed measure of affiliative behavior is indeed a direct correlate of an individual's affiliative tendency (R_1) and an inverse correlate of his sensitivity to rejection (R_2). For instance, the following regression equation indicates the contributions of the various main effects to affiliative behavior in the first experiment of the study. All variables are normalized in this equation and (O) represents the sum of the angles at which both subjects would have to turn in order to assume a face-to-face position.

Affiliative behavior $= .21R_1 - .14R_2 + .21R_1' - .16R_2' - .23(O)$

The primed factors are the partner's scores on the personality measures. These findings indicate that those with higher scores on the affiliative tendency measure (Mehrabian, 1970d) exhibited more affiliative behavior and especially when their partners were also more affiliative. Further, those who had scored high on a sensitivity to rejection measure (Mehrabian, 1970d) exhibited less affiliative behavior and were even less affiliative with partners who were also sensitive to rejection.

Additional findings of incidental interest were as follows. The first two experiments included all possible combinations of four distances and three orientations for the seating of dyads who were left alone to wait in a room. Both experiments showed that the less direct orientations (such as when sitting side by side on a couch) were less conducive to conversation, and particularly inhibiting for the otherwise more sociable pairs—that is, those in which at least one was a more affiliative person. The first experiment also included measures of relaxation, and indicated a general increase in relaxation with increasing distance between the pairs.

The results of this and the Mehrabian and Diamond (1971a) study suggest that just as more immediate positions are assumed to those who are better liked, more immediate positioning of persons in social situations may facilitate the communication of liking.

MULTICHANNEL COMMUNICATION [6]

Now that the significance of individual cues in communication has been reviewed, we will consider more complex communica-

6. This section includes modified segments from Mehrabian and Ferris's "Inference of attitudes from nonverbal communication in two channels," *Journal of Consulting Psychology*, 1967, **31**, 248–252; and Mehrabian and Wiener's "Decoding of inconsistent communications," *Journal of Personality and Social Psychology*, 1967, **6**, 109–114. Copyright © 1967 by the American Psychological Association and reproduced by permission.

tions—those involving the simultaneous use of messages in several channels. The basic issue behind the study of multichannel communications is the meaning or function of inconsistent versus consistent (redundant) messages. The concept of inconsistent communication (e.g., double bind communication, Haley, 1963; Schuham, 1967; Weakland, 1961) has received considerable attention in the past decade, but only recently has it been formulated as a measurable phenomenon.

Implicit in any discussion of inconsistent communication is a referent. In an inconsistent message, various components denote contradictory referents, whereas information provided by various components of a consistent message is redundant. We have seen that the referent of any message can be described in terms of the liking, potency, and responsiveness which it signifies. Thus there can be inconsistency in the denotation of a referent on any one of these three dimensions. In most of the studies to be reviewed, positive-negative feelings (levels of liking) were the referents of communication. However, the methods and questions are also applicable to the study of communications of potency and responsiveness.

There are several interrelated issues in the study of multichannel communications: (a) How does one combine consistent or inconsistent communications of attitude received in several channels to infer the attitude implied in the entire message? (b) Why do people use inconsistent communications at all? If the joint combination of inconsistent verbal and nonverbal cues leads to a certain attitude which could also have been communicated with a consistent message, why is the inconsistent message preferred in some cases? (c) Are inconsistent communications more difficult to decode? Do they involve more inaccuracy or ambiguity? (d) If inconsistent communications *are* more difficult to decode, do they contribute to the development of psychopathology in one who frequently receives them, as double bind theorists have suggested?

Both a communicator's verbalizations and his nonverbal behaviors express his attitudes, and the referents implied by his verbalizations may be either consistent or inconsistent with those implied in his nonverbal behaviors. How, then, is the total attitude inferred from a complex (i.e., multichannel) message a function of the attitude communicated in each channel alone? For instance, if a communicator uses two channels, verbalizations and facial expressions, to indicate his attitude, how is the total expressed attitude a function of the attitudes expressed in the facial and verbal components separately?

Whereas there have been many studies of nonverbal attitude or feeling communication in single channels, investigation of feelings or attitudes transmitted in two or more channels simultaneously is just beginning. Gates (1927) found that children were more accurate in their judgments of facial than of vocal expressions of feeling. Unfortunately, her method allowed only a tentative conclusion that discrimination of feeling is easier on the basis of facial than of vocal cues. But there was some corroboration of Gates's findings in studies by Levitt (1964) and Zaidel and Mehrabian (1969). In the Levitt study communicators were filmed as they attempted to convey six emotions facially and vocally, using neutral verbal materials. The decoding of facial and vocal stimuli in combination was only as accurate as the decoding of facial stimuli alone, and both conditions were more accurate than the decoding of vocal stimuli alone. This finding indicates that in a two-channel facial-vocal communication of emotion, the facial channel contributes more than the vocal channel to the decoding of the total message. The Zaidel and Mehrabian findings more directly indicated that variations in liking are conveyed more readily with facial than with vocal expressions.

Williams and Sundene (1965) also explored the characteristics of two-channel communications of emotion. They used the semantic differential method (Osgood, Suci, & Tannenbaum, 1957) to obtain judgments of the same emotions communicated facially, vocally, and in facial-vocal combinations. All three modes of communication were found to be recognized in terms of three factors: general evaluation, social control, and activity.

It should be noted that none of the foregoing studies investigated two-channel communications in which the emotion communicated in the facial expression was inconsistent with that communicated vocally. While experimental studies of multichannel communications from any particular population (e.g., children or adults) were lacking, theories about the effects of such communications were proposed. Bateson, Jackson, Haley, and Weakland (1956) proposed a "double bind" theory of schizophrenia according to which schizophrenics develop maladaptive responses because they are the frequent recipients of inconsistent attitude communications. A double bind communication is defined as involving two or more inconsistent attitude messages which are assumed to elicit incompatible responses from the addressee. For example, a mother asks her son to come over and kiss her while she nonverbally communicates indifference to what he is requested to do. It is assumed that the child is left with the dilemma of responding to either the verbal or the nonverbal component, knowing that response to either one will elicit a rebuff. The recipients of frequent double bind messages are assumed to learn to respond with their own double bind messages. In the example considered, the child may respond with, "I can't come because my leg hurts," or "I can't come because Trap is holding me," the hurt leg and Trap (a nonexistent companion) being figments of his imagination.

Whereas it is assumed that double bind communications lead to the development of maladaptive patterns of interpersonal functioning, Haley (1963) also conceptualized most psychotherapeutic processes as being interpretable within a beneficial double bind paradigm. His thesis was that applications of the beneficial double bind serve to successfully eliminate the secondary gain which is associated with a symptomatic behavior and therefore eliminate that behavior.

The above assumptions can be partially clarified through investigation of the ways in which multichannel attitude communications are decoded.

A Linear Model for the Inference of Attitudes from Multichannel Communications

Mehrabian and Wiener (1967) and Mehrabian and Ferris (1967) investigated the combined effects of consistent and inconsistent verbal-vocal communications and consistent and inconsistent facial-vocal communications of attitude, respectively. Both studies involved nine sets of communication stimuli.

In the Mehrabian and Wiener (1967) study, verbal-vocal communications were prepared so that three degrees of positive verbal content were associated with each of three degrees of vocally expressed attitude. Having been judged for amount of liking conveyed, the words *honey*, *thanks*, and *dear* were selected as instances of positive contents (the judgments of these words had comparable mean values and standard deviations). Similarly, the words *maybe*, *really*, and *oh* were selected as comparable instances of neutral contents; and the words *don't*, *brute*, and *terrible* were selected as comparable instances of negative contents.

Two female speakers were employed to read each of the nine selected words in positive, neutral, and negative tones. For the positive, neutral, and negative tone conditions, respectively, the speakers spoke the words, regardless of content, to convey liking, high evaluation, or preference; a neutral attitude, that is, neither liking nor disliking; and an attitude of dislike, low evaluation, or lack of preference toward the target person. All possible combinations of two speaker conditions, three vocal conditions, three content conditions, and three instances of each content condition were recorded on tape.

To obtain the independent effects of the vocal and content components of these recordings and to relate them to the effects of the total vocal-content message, Mehrabian and Wiener (1967) had three different groups of subjects listen to the recorded messages. One group was asked to judge the degree of liking conveyed by each message, relying only on the meanings of the words used and not on the intonation. The second group was asked to judge the degree of liking conveyed by each message, relying only on the vocal component and not on the meanings of the words used. Finally, the third group formed their judgments of liking on the basis of all the information combined in each message.

The results showed that the vocal component in the various messages primarily determined subjects' judgments of affect from the total messages (i.e., content and vocal components combined), and that the content component of inconsistent messages had a negligible contribution to the affect inferred from such statements.

In the Mehrabian and Ferris (1967) study, 25 subjects first rated the amount of liking implied by each of 15 written words.

From these judgments, the word *maybe* was selected as an appropriate neutral verbal carrier of vocal communications. Three female speakers were then instructed to vary their tone of voice while saying the word *maybe* so as to communicate like, neutrality, and dislike toward an imagined addressee. Each speaker said the word *maybe* twice in the same way while her statements were being audio recorded.

The facial communications of three degrees of attitude were selected in a similar manner. Photographs of three female models were taken as they used facial expressions to communicate like, neutrality, and dislike toward another person. On the basis of subjects' judgments of the vocal and facial communications, three vocal communications (i.e., positive, neutral, and negative) obtained from each of two speakers and three facial communications obtained from each of two models were selected. The facial attitude communications of a given value (e.g., positive) were selected to match the vocal attitude communications of the same value. Standard deviations of judgments as well as their means were matched. In other words, for the Mehrabian and Ferris (1967) experiment, the independent effects of all vocal communications of like-dislike were comparable to the independent effects of all facial communications of like-dislike within each of the three levels of liking.

Thus, in both experiments, the separate effect of each component was independently assessed. It was therefore possible to express the dependent measure, the degree of attitude inferred from the total message, in terms of the values of the separate components. The results of the Mehrabian and Wiener (1967) study indicated that most of the variability in judgment of total attitude was accounted for by variations contained in the vocal component.

In the Mehrabian and Ferris (1967) study, the combined effect of the facial and vocal components was a weighted sum of their independent effects, since there was no significant interaction between them. The following regression equation summarizes the approximate relative contributions of facial and vocal components to interpretations of combined facial-vocal attitude communications:

$$A_{Total} = .60A_{Facial} + .40A_{Vocal} \tag{1}$$

A_{Total} represents attitude inferred on a scale of -3 to $+3$ from the two-channel communications. A_{Facial} represents attitude communicated in the facial component alone on the same scale. Similarly A_{Vocal} represents attitude communicated in the vocal component alone. The findings given in equation 1, together with those from the Mehrabian and Wiener (1967) study, suggest that the combined effect of simultaneous verbal, vocal, and facial attitude communications is a weighted sum of their independent effects as follows:

$$A_{Total} = .07A_{Verbal} + .38A_{Vocal} + .55A_{Facial} \qquad (2)$$

where all four attitude variables are measured on the same scale (e.g., a scale of liking ranging from -3 to $+3$).

In general, then, it is hypothesized that when there is inconsistency between verbally and nonverbally expressed attitudes, the nonverbal portion will dominate in determining the total message. For instance, when there are inconsistencies between attitudes communicated verbally and posturally, the postural component should dominate in determining the total attitude which is inferred. The results reported earlier for communication of attitude via posture and position cues make it possible to test this hypothesis. Also, in two recent studies, Argyle, Salter, Nicholson, Williams, and Burgess (1970) and Argyle, Alkema, and Gilmour (1971) provided support for the proposed hypothesis. They found that nonverbal cues make a greater contribution than verbal cues to the communication of a more dominant (or potent) or a more positive attitude.

A note of caution is in order regarding the summary of findings given in equation 2. The Bugental, Kaswan, and Love (1970), Mehrabian and Wiener (1967), and Lampel and Anderson (1968) studies indicated that attitudes conveyed in various channels interact to determine the total inferred attitude. Therefore, equation 2 is only a first-order approximation. More detailed study of the main and interactive effects of various channels is needed and might include the preparation of videotaped stimuli involving four channels of communication: verbal, vocal, facial, and immediacy of position cues.

For example, three levels of verbal attitude could be combined with each of three levels of vocal, facial, and position cues. To facilitate analysis of the results, the levels of the three attitudes communicated in each channel would be equated so that, for instance, the positive facial cues were equal in value to the positive vocal, positive verbal, and positive position cues. Thus, 81 types of communication stimuli, with replications over different communicators of both sexes, would yield a large set of stimuli for decoding. Addressees could vary in personality characteristics (e.g., affiliative tendency) or level and kind of psychopathology. The dependent measures could include not only mean judgments for each of the 81 communication types, but also the variability and latency of judgments. By examining the variability of responses to inconsistent communications, one could assess the difficulty in decoding them. Such difficulty could be measured also from the latency of judgments of total attitude and might have some additional implication for double bind theory, which suggests that addressees should take a longer time, or have more disagreement, in judging the total attitude conveyed in inconsistent or ambiguous messages.

Such a study would provide detailed answers to the question of how one combines consistent or inconsistent communications to infer an attitude for the entire message, and whether inconsistent communications involve more inaccuracy or ambiguity, thus making them more difficult to decode. If several replications of the 81 stimuli were used, the analysis of variance of the data obtained from each subject (e.g., as suggested by Anderson, 1962, 1964) would provide a direct check on the linear model proposed in equation 2, since it would indicate the extent to which the inferences of total attitude deviate from linearity. For instance, it is hypothesized that the coefficients in the equations for pathological individuals (weighted sums such as equation 2) are more varied than those of normals. This hypothesis is based on the assumption that more maladjusted individuals tend to be more idiosyncratic or nonconsensual in their weighting of each component in a total message—that is, in the ways they make inferences from complex communications.

When Are Feelings Communicated Inconsistently?[7]

To this point we have considered the ways in which consistent and inconsistent communications are decoded. There still remains the question of why a person selects an inconsistent message when he has the choice of using a consistent message to convey the same attitude. Why does he select sarcasm, for instance, a message in which he uses a negative vocal component with positive content (e.g., "I really like that!"), thereby communicating a negative attitude to the addressee? He might also have communicated negative attitude in both the verbal and vocal channels. The question, then, is the significance of consistency or inconsistency per se. Could it be that redundancy contributes to intensity? One interesting implication of the linear model summarized in equation 2 is that the effect of redundancy (i.e., consistent attitude communication in two or more channels) is to intensify the attitude communicated in any of the component channels. Thus, pushing a child away while turning away from him communicates a more negative feeling toward the child than only pushing him away or only turning away from him. Similarly, holding and kissing a child communicates a more positive attitude toward him than only holding or only kissing him.

The model in equation 2 indicates that inconsistent attitude communications can be readily classified into two categories—one in which the total impact is positive and another in which it is negative. Positive inconsistency is evidenced when someone verbally insults another while smiling (a girl says, "I don't like you much," to her boyfriend with a smile and loving vocalization). Negative inconsistency might involve an irritated facial expression accompanied by positive vocal and/or verbal expressions (someone yells, "Oh, that's beautiful! Just great!" when angry). These two categories can in turn be distinguished from consistent attitude communications in which all the components are judged as either positive or negative in quality.

Given these distinctions, the problem can be restated in two

7. Acknowledgment is given to Academic Press, Inc., for their permission to use, in this section, rewritten segments from my paper "When are feelings communicated inconsistently?" *Journal of Experimental Research in Personality*, 1970, **4**, 198–212.

parts: When are inconsistent negative attitude communications preferred, with preferences for consistent negative attitude communications of the same degree used as a baseline; and when are inconsistent positive communications preferred, using consistent positive attitude communications as the base of comparison? Thus, it is important to experimentally and/or statistically control for the attitudinal level of the messages produced by, or given to, subjects in various situations.

Mehrabian (1970e) used such controls in four experiments briefly described below. For each inconsistent communication used as a stimulus, a consistent control communication was obtained which contained an equal degree of the same overall attitude. Subjects expressed their preferences for each kind of message in a variety of social situations. In one set of analyses of covariance, preferences of inconsistent positive communications were the dependent measure and preferences of consistent positive communications were the covariate. A second set of analyses of covariance involved preferences of inconsistent negative communications as the dependent measure and preferences of consistent negative communications as the covariate.

In all the four experiments, two channels of communication, verbal and vocal, were employed. The inconsistent positive communications involved positive vocal and negative verbal components, and the inconsistent negative communications involved negative vocal and positive verbal components. The control stimuli for these two sets of messages consisted of moderately positive verbal and vocal communications on one hand, and moderately negative verbal and vocal communications on the other. Several instances of each of the four types of communication were recorded on tape. Subjects listened and indicated preferences for these while imagining a variety of social situations.

The study was an exploratory search for relationships. In the absence of any experimental literature bearing directly on the problem, the choice of factors was made on tentative grounds. The factors included negative affect-arousing cues in combination with social situations varying in formality.

The two personality variables explored in the study were communicator social approval-seeking tendency, as measured by the

Crowne and Marlowe (1960) Social Desirability scale, and communicator anxiety as measured by the Mandler and Sarason (1952) Test Anxiety Questionnaire. These two variables were selected because higher social approval-seeking tendency and anxiety were expected to make the overt expression of negative feelings more difficult.

The results of each experiment showed that consistent communications of attitude are preferred over inconsistent ones, and that among inconsistent communications, the positive are less preferred than negative ones. These findings corroborated informal observations made during the preparation of the stimuli, where it was noted that subjects had greater difficulty producing the inconsistent messages, a difficulty which was even more pronounced when the inconsistent messages were positive. The implication is that, because of their less frequent use, inconsistent messages are more difficult to produce, and that less frequent use reflects a lower preference for them. Another observation during preparation of stimuli was that inconsistent communications of attitude frequently rely on facial expressions. For instance, when subjects were instructed to say something negative with a positive vocal component, they actually used a neutral vocal component but assumed a positive facial expression, so that audiotape recordings of their statements did not really reflect the intended inconsistency. It thus seems that any further exploration of preference for inconsistent messages should include facial as well as verbal and vocal expressions.

The second generalization that emerged from Mehrabian's (1970e) data related preference for inconsistent communications to formality of communication situations. The experiments included a series of factors for various aspects of formality. In some conditions, the situation was simply described as formal versus informal; in others formality was implied by indicating that the addressee was of a higher rather than lower status. Still others involved the presence versus absence of bystanders or observers, the assumption being that observers in a situation tend to increase its formality. A fourth manipulation involved an explicit versus implicit insult from the addressee as a cue to which the communicator responded. It was expected that a situation in which the addressee was explicitly insulting would be more informal than one in which an insult was implicit. A final manipulation involved the addressee's tolerance for criticism, based on the assumption that persons who can tolerate criticism tend to elicit more informal interaction than those who cannot.

The results for all these formality factors showed 16 effects in support and 2 opposed to the following generalization: inconsistent communications are preferred more in the more informal communication settings.

Without exception, the remaining results from the four experiments were consistent with the following general conclusions: (1) The verbal component of an inconsistent message conveys evaluation of an addressee's action, and therefore is the basis for selecting a message when the addressee behaves pleasantly versus unpleasantly. (2) The nonverbal component of an inconsistent message conveys evaluation of the addressee's person, and therefore is the basis for selecting a message when the addressee is liked versus disliked.

Also, without exception, the significant effects indicated that the more anxious subjects had more preference for positive inconsistent messages and less preference for negative inconsistent messages. This finding showed that more anxious persons were less willing to convey negative feelings to the person of the addressee, since they preferred messages with positive nonverbal components and avoided those with negative nonverbal components. There were no consistent results for communicator social approval-seeking tendency.

The individual difference measures included in the study were selected to reflect a communicator's unwillingness to express negative feelings to others. A measure of sensitivity to rejection was not available when the study was designed, so measures of communicator anxiety and approval-seeking tendency were used; however, it was felt that a direct measure of sensitivity to rejection (e.g., Mehrabian, 1970d) would be more appropriate since such persons would be more hesitant to openly convey negative feelings to others.

The research summarized in equation 2 showed that different nonverbal cues exhibit similar relationships to verbal cues when they accompany the latter. Thus, one extrapolation of the findings of the Mehrabian (1970e) study is that even when other nonverbal cues are also involved and contribute to inconsistency, the preceding interpretations of the findings still hold: verbal components of inconsistent messages convey evaluative attitudes toward another's actions, whereas the nonverbal (e.g., facial or postural) components convey evaluative attitudes to the person himself. In general, then, positive inconsistent messages should be more frequent with liked than disliked addressees and when the addressee's actions are unpleasant. In contrast, negative inconsistent messages should be more frequent with disliked than liked addressees and when the addressee's actions are pleasant.

Inconsistent Communications and Psychopathology[8]

A more direct test of the double bind hypothesis was made by Beakel and Mehrabian (1969). They explored the frequency of occurrence of consistent and inconsistent attitude communications of parents toward their more or less disturbed adolescent children. According to the double bind hypothesis, it is expected that parents of the more disturbed children communicate inconsistency in attitude more frequently than parents of less disturbed children.

In the experiment, inconsistency of communication was assessed from the attitudes conveyed verbally and posturally. Postural, rather than facial or vocal, cues were selected because of their more subtle quality. We could have relied on facial cues, but in the presence of an "evaluative" therapist it seemed that parents would be less able to censor their communication of attitude via postural cues than to censor or control their facial expressions.

A sample of 21 families who had a disturbed adolescent member were the subjects who provided the communications analyzed in the experiment. Verbalizations and postures were measured from audio and video recordings of adolescents and their parents as they discussed a family problem stemming from the child's disturbance. In no case were the participants aware that their actions were being

8. This section includes rewritten segments from Beakel and Mehrabian's "Inconsistent communications and psychopathology," *Journal of Abnormal Psychology*, 1969, **74**, 126–130. Copyright © 1969 by the American Psychological Association and reproduced by permission.

recorded through a one-way mirror. All family members were seated during the session.

Three clinical psychologists, who were familiar with the problems presented in the entire sample, ranked the 21 adolescents concerned for severity of pathology, without regard to diagnostic classification. The communication data in the experiment were taken from the parents of the five adolescents receiving the lowest severity scores and the parents of the five receiving the highest scores.

The results of the experiment did not support the double bind hypothesis; there was no greater incongruity in the postural-verbal communications of parents of more disturbed adolescents than in the communications of parents of less disturbed adolescents. Two different measures of incongruity were employed. For one incongruity measure (based on separate judgments of the verbalizations and postures of the parents), there was no significant difference in incongruity of communications between parents of the more and of the less disturbed group. For a second incongruity measure (based on anticipated postures in comparison to actual postures for a verbalization), the mothers of the less disturbed group of adolescents were found to show a greater amount of incongruity. Thus, the data generally failed to support the hypothesis and, for one measure, provided contradictory evidence for the communication of mothers. These findings which contradict the double bind hypothesis are consistent with the conclusions which Schuham (1967) drew from his review.

Whereas the findings involving the incongruity measures are difficult to interpret in terms of the double bind idea, those from measures of degree of positive-negative attitude communication can be interpreted. The parents of the more disturbed adolescents showed more negative attitudes toward these adolescents (in their verbalizations, but not in their posture) than parents of the less disturbed adolescents.

The relationship between psychopathology of children and the negative attitude messages of their parents can be due to either or both of the following. The parents may have more negative feelings toward these more disturbed children because the latter create more problems for them than less disturbed children do for their parents. Alternatively, initially negative attitudes of the parents may have contributed to the psychopathology of the children. In either case, negative attitudes of parents at least contribute to the maintenance of the children's maladjustment. In discussing their findings, Mehrabian and Wiener (1967) suggested, "It could be argued that unusually frequent negative attitude communicating messages do contribute to severe psychopathological functioning ... for example, indiscriminate negative reinforcement is not conducive to learning the numerous interpersonal and social skills which are lacking in individuals classed as schizophrenics" (Mehrabian & Wiener, 1967, p. 114). Rogers's (1959) conceptualization of psychopathology also suggests a relationship between negative attitude communications of parents and psychopathology of their children. In his theory, greater psychopathology of a child is associated with greater degrees of "conditional positive regard" of parents toward the child. "Conditional positive regard" refers to the conditional quality of the love or liking of one person toward another.

One way to interpret and measure Rogers's concept of conditional versus unconditional positive regard is simply in terms of the frequency and/or intensity with which one individual expresses negative attitudes toward another. Thus, it is not so much the distinction between attitudes communicated toward a person's actions and attitudes toward that person himself which is the critical variable, as Rogers would suggest. Rather it is a question of the intensity of total negative attitude expressed toward another person.

In sum, the findings of the Beakel and Mehrabian (1969) study show that exploration of the overall quality of positive-negative attitude, rather than inconsistency in attitude communication, is a more useful avenue for investigating the relationship between communication patterns and psychopathology.

Applications

In a variety of contexts, we have seen that nonverbal behaviors are more important or basic (possibly because they are more difficult to censor) than verbal ones: untrained observers assign greater weight to the feelings communicated nonverbally in vocal and facial expressions than to the feelings expressed verbally. Further, some nonverbal channels are more subtle than others. For instance, communications of attitude or status with posture and position cues are more subtle and probably less subject to censorship or deliberate control than are facial or vocal expressions of the same attitudes. Finally, some of the findings show individual differences in channel preference for the expression of unacceptable feelings (e.g., Zaidel & Mehrabian, 1969).

The preceding generalizations can serve as a basis for applying the findings of implicit communication in both everyday and experimental situations. In social psychological experiments, it is sometimes important to obtain valid indexes of a communicator's feelings and attitudes toward a certain group of persons, beliefs, or experiences, but the experimenter may not feel confident about his subject's verbal reports. For example, if the topic of experimentation deals with prejudice, honest and explicit verbal responses may be confounded by a subject's social approval-seeking tendency or by the general social discouragement of openly expressing certain attitudes or feelings (e.g., males being discouraged from admitting they are afraid or feel threatened). Consequently, the researcher must rely on more subtle measures. Some of the nonverbal or implicit verbal cues which have been considered in this study lend themselves readily to the assessment of attitudes in such experimental situations. For instance, suppose an experimenter wishes to explore prejudice toward Negroes, and creates a situation to test the effects of cooperative or competitive interaction on attitude change. Verbal and postural immediacy measures could be obtained both before and after the subject's interaction, and changes in the degree of postural or verbal immediacy would serve as indexes of attitude change and also provide a basis for assessing the generalization of new attitudes toward other Negroes as well.

Nonverbal and implicit verbal cues can also be used in everyday situations, for example to assess candidates' attitudes as expressed in their political speeches. Exploring these findings for persons from different cultures may yield valuable applications in the context of diplomatic negotiations as well. These would provide not only clues to determine which nonverbal behaviors inadvertently communicate misleading attitudes (e.g., Hall, 1959), but also ways to assess the attitudes of various participants in negotiations where the verbal communications are not sufficiently informative. A by-product of the less controlled nature of implicit cues is that they help not only to identify feelings or attitudes that a communicator is hesitant to express because of social pressure or conformity, but also to detect deceit.

The subtle quality of nonverbal cues has been used intuitively in various forms of advertising to induce particular attitudes toward various products. They can be used yet more systematically, since implicit cues lend themselves in a variety of ways toward maximizing the persuasive impact of communications (Mehrabian & Williams, 1969).

The concepts of reinforcement-learning theory are receiving increasing attention and application in behavior modification. When using the principles of instrumental learning to modify interpersonal behaviors, the choice of reinforcers is quite critical. This is especially the case when the person being influenced is not dependent upon the person who reinforces or influences (i.e., he is not a child, a hospital patient, or a prison inmate). When the client and the modifying agent are of equal status, having potentially equal power to materially reinforce each other, social reinforcers can serve as important vehicles for the modification of behavior (Mehrabian, 1970c). Social reinforcers may be viewed as ways of communicating liking or respect and higher status to a person whose behaviors are being shaped. For instance, head nodding is a way of communicating respect to the addressee, as in agreement with him. Thus, it is expected that both cues should function as reinforcers, and the findings show this to be the case (Krasner, 1958; Matarazzo, Wiens, & Saslow, 1965). Communications of agreement and head nodding show respect and positive attitude, but the analyses and groupings of nonverbal cues in terms of liking and status differences (respect) suggest that the cues which primarily express liking are also quite relevant and important in the shaping of interpersonal behavior. The findings we have reported provide a basis for the experimental control of the level and kind of social reinforcers that can be used to explore the function of nonverbal cues in behavior modification. Experimenters could select from a diversity of nonverbal cues those which are best suited to their particular experimental requirements. For instance, they could explore the differential effectiveness of the communication of respect versus the communication of liking in shaping the behaviors of different types of subjects, such as children versus adults.

The use of inconsistent reinforcers in the shaping of behavior may also be of some interest here. What, if any, is the value of using inconsistent messages, such as positive or negative inconsistent messages, in the process of social influence? Haley (1963) suggested that one way to view the typical psychodynamic therapy is in terms of inconsistent messages to the client. For example, the therapist verbally asserts an unwillingness to be directive, because being directive would imply his higher status in the situation and might be resented by the client. But both informal observations and recent experimental findings have shown that even those who completely deny a directive therapeutic role nevertheless use nonverbal cues to shape their clients' behaviors (e.g., Truax, 1966). Since they have denied the use of shaping in their procedures, psychodynamically oriented therapists have not presented a theoretical analysis of the rationale for such a method. The choice of this method is nevertheless significant and requires analysis. Why is it that such inconsistency is used?

Mehrabian (1970c) suggested a possible rationale for the development of this technique among psychoanalytic or Rogerian therapists. This same technique can be experimentally explored with a variety of simple methods by shaping a subject's behaviors through systematic use of inconsistent cues, the experimenter's nonverbal cues being used for shaping while his verbal cues are neutral or even contradictory. The differential effectiveness of such inconsistent messages in shaping the behaviors of different types of subjects should be of considerable interest. It would seem that when the verbal component includes a denial of manipulative intent but the nonverbal cues nevertheless systematically communicate liking or respect, more effective shaping of another person's behavior will result, particularly when that other person is openly resistant to influence or manipulation by a peer.

Some additional applications of findings from studies of implicit communication can occur in the exploration of characteristic attitude communications. Concern for individual differences in nonverbal behavior (expressive qualities) was partially responsible for the study of nonverbal behavior in the first place. Conceptualizing the referents of nonverbal behavior in terms of evaluation, potency, and responsiveness, it is expected that (1) affiliative dispositions correlate with more immediate nonverbal behaviors toward others; (2) dominant personality dispositions correlate with relaxation; (3) anxious or disturbed individuals exhibit less relaxation and, depending on the form of psychopathology, possibly less immediacy, as in the case of withdrawn schizophrenia; and (4) depressive tendencies, which are associated with withdrawal and less responsiveness to people in general, are reflected in low levels of activity.

Individual differences can be explored also by investigating preferences for expressing negative feelings in more or less obvious channels. It is assumed that the various channels of attitude communication, in the order listed, convey increasingly obvious negative feelings: verbal nonimmediacy (Wiener & Mehrabian, 1968), postural nonimmediacy, negative vocal, negative facial, and negative verbal communications. For instance, Zaidel and Mehrabian (1969) found that in the relatively obvious facial and vocal channels, high social approval seekers were less able to communicate variation in negative feelings than low social approval seekers.

In general, then, individual differences in the use of implicit communication cues can be conceptualized in three ways: (1) in terms of the three-dimensional framework (i.e., consistent individual differences in the expression of positive feelings and differences in the expression of dominance and responsiveness); (2) in terms of a person's tendency to use implicit and nonobvious, versus more obvious and explicit, channels to express his feelings; and (3) as one aspect of social skills—the appropriate communication of attitude and status through nonverbal cues. At one extreme, pathology can be detected from grossly inappropriate manifestations of immediacy or tension-relaxation, as when a communicator is too immediate with an unfamiliar addressee or when his tension level communicates fear to an addressee who is not actually threatening. Variations in the effectiveness of more normal individuals in their social dealings may be partially due to the attitude or status which they typically convey. For instance, an individual who indiscriminately assumes a generally high level of postural relaxation with addressees of different status may experience persistent but puzzling problems with high-status others. Finally, individual differences in persuasive ability may be due partially to the ability to communicate appropriate levels of positive attitude and status to different kinds of addressees.

The relation of characteristic attitude communications to level of psychopathology of the communicator can also be explored. Attitudes could be experimentally assessed from both verbal and nonverbal behaviors, thus yielding not only a measure of the inconsistency in the communication of liking, but also the extent of total negative attitude conveyed to addressees. Such measures could be related in turn to the level of psychopathology of children who are frequent recipients of such attitudes; to their personality; or, finally, to the level of psychopathology or the personality of those who frequently use such communications.

The implicit communications of like or dislike or the characteristic implicit communications of a more or less dominant attitude may contribute to inaccuracy in communications (Mehrabian & Reed, 1968). Thus, knowledge of implicit cues can also assist in a variety of settings where inaccuracy detracts from effective communication, such as between supervisors and employees, or teachers and students.

Overview

The rationale for the research we have reviewed and reported here differs from earlier approaches to the study of nonverbal and subtle verbal behaviors. In contrast to those approaches, which sought discrete nonverbal behaviors and explored their specific referents, or, conversely, identified the discrete behaviors associated with certain feelings, the present approach relies on a multidimensional characterization of the referents of implicit communication as variations in liking, potency, and responsiveness. It has thus been possible to identify, in a variety of channels, the behaviors that consistently convey varying degrees of each of these referents.

The advantage of our approach is that encoding paradigms can be used readily to identify large numbers of behaviors associated with each of these referential dimensions. The disadvantage is that the approach does not permit the identification of specific feelings which may convey varying degrees of each of the referential dimensions. Thus, just as the general characterization of the referents of speech in terms of evaluation, potency, and activity accounts for only about 65% of the referential significance of speech (e.g., Osgood, Suci, & Tannenbaum, 1957, p. 61), likewise the use of a multidimensional framework certainly does not exhaust the referents of implicit behavior. Nevertheless, such a description accounts for about half of the variance in the significance of nonverbal and implicit verbal cues.

The reliance on a multidimensional framework does seem desirable at this point because it provides a reasonably simple and general scheme with which to identify and study quite diverse sets of behaviors. As more work relating to each of these referential dimensions becomes available, it will be not only possible, but desirable, to identify the specific behaviors which convey more subtle shades of feeling (e.g., the Mona Lisa smile), and to place them as points in this three-dimensional semantic space.

This being a paper on "communication research," it seems appropriate to close with a note on methodology. There are two complementary avenues for exploring communication phenomena. In the first, *decoding*, subjects are presented with prepared stimuli and instructed to infer feelings and attitudes from those stimuli. Such a method is advantageous since it allows a comparison of the effects of a number of cues, singly or in combination, on inferred attitudes. It also allows the investigation of the relative effects of these cues for various communicator and addressee groups (e.g., different sex or personality). Finally, possible confounding effects of communications in other channels (e.g., facial expressions, verbalizations, or gestures) can be eliminated. A decoding method yields considerable information because it makes possible the systematic control of a large number of variables.

In the second method, *encoding*, subjects are placed in experimental situations which elicit different kinds of attitude-related behavior. Typical encoding methods employ role playing, in which a subject is requested to assume a certain role or attitude toward his addressee (e.g., Rosenfeld, 1966a, 1966b). Occasionally there are studies which take advantage of existing likes and dislikes or status differences among subjects, and other studies which actually induce like or dislike in a subject toward the addressee (e.g., Exline & Winters, 1965).[9]

Thus, an encoding method, unlike a decoding one, cannot include the systematic study of interactions among communication cues. But a decoding study requires factorial designs for the study of the interactions, and thus limits the number of cues which can be investigated, since a design involving more than six or seven factors is unmanageably large. In an encoding method, although it is possible to study the interactive effects of only one cue at a time with communicator and addressee characteristics, there is no limit to the number of communication cues which can be readily included and interpreted in the design. The use of regression or discriminant analyses (e.g., Anderson & Bancroft, 1955) in conjunction with an encoding method can provide the relative strengths of the various communication cues which connote attitudes.

Almost all communication research is based on either the encoding or the decoding method. There would be some value in a third methodology which encompasses the major advantages of both the encoding and decoding methods. In one such method, stimuli are prepared as they would be with a decoding method. They are then presented to subjects, who are asked to indicate their preference for using these stimuli in various social situations. There are several advantages to this method. First, if the experimenter prepares a series of stimuli which are inappropriate for the communication of the particular referents he is studying, subjects will characteristically show very low preference scores for the use of those stimuli. This informs the experimenter just how well suited his stimuli actually are for the communication of the particular referents—an inference which is not possible when the decoding method is used. This third method allows a systematic control of the communication cues which are employed. Factorial designs can be used to assess the independent and interactive effects of various communication cues in determining a referent, an advantage

9. The preceding two paragraphs were adapted from my article "Significance of posture and position in the communication of attitude and status relationships," *Psychological Bulletin*, 1969, **71**, 359–372. Copyright © 1969 by the American Psychological Association and reproduced by permission.

which is not available with encoding methods. Mehrabian's (1970e) study of inconsistent messages illustrates the use of this third encoding-decoding method.

The latter method does not require the experimenter to possess an advanced understanding of the phenomenon he is about to explore. Extensive knowledge is, however, required to prepare an appropriate set of stimuli when one uses a decoding method. Thus, whereas encoding methods are appropriate in the beginning stages of communication research, the proposed encoding-decoding method is appropriate for intermediate stages, and decoding methods are appropriate during the highly developed phases of such research.

REFERENCES

Allport, G., & Vernon, P. *Studies in expressive movement.* New York: Macmillan, 1933.

Anderson, N. H. Application of an additive model to impression formation. *Science,* 1962, **138**, 817–818.

Anderson, N. H. Note on weighted sum and linear operator models. *Psychonomic Science,* 1964, **1**, 189–190.

Anderson, R. L., & Bancroft, T. A. *Statistical theory in research.* New York: McGraw-Hill, 1955.

Ardrey, R. *The territorial imperative.* New York: Atheneum, 1966.

Argyle, M., Alkema, F., & Gilmour, R. The communication of friendly and hostile attitudes by verbal and nonverbal signals. Unpublished manuscript, Institute of Experimental Psychology, Oxford University, 1971.

Argyle, M., & Dean, J. Eye contact, distance, and affiliation. *Sociometry,* 1965, **28**, 289–304.

Argyle, M., & Kendon, A. The experimental analysis of social performance. In L. Berkowitz (Ed.), *Advances in experimental social psychology.* New York: Academic Press, 1967, Pp. 55–98.

Argyle, M., Salter, V., Nicholson, H., Williams, M., & Burgess, P. The communication of inferior and superior attitudes by verbal and nonverbal signals. *British Journal of Social and Clinical Psychology,* 1970, **9**, 222–231.

Bateson, G., Jackson, D. D., Haley, J., & Weakland, J. Toward a theory of schizophrenia. *Behavioral Sciences,* 1956, **1**, 251–264.

Beakel, N. G., & Mehrabian, A. Inconsistent communications and psychopathology. *Journal of Abnormal Psychology,* 1969, **74**, 126–130.

Bentler, P. M. Semantic space is (approximately) bipolar. *Journal of Psychology,* 1969, **71**, 33–40.

Birdwhistell, R. L. *Introduction to kinesics.* Louisville: University of Kentucky Press, 1952.

Boomer, D. S. Speech disturbance and body movement in interviews. *Journal of Nervous and Mental Disease*, 1963, **136**, 263–266.

Braatoy, T. F. *Fundamentals of psychoanalytic technique*. New York: Wiley, 1954.

Bugental, D. E., Kaswan, J. W., & Love, L. R. Perception of contradictory meanings conveyed by verbal and nonverbal channels. *Journal of Personality and Social Psychology*, 1970, **16**, 647–655.

Calhoun, J. B. *The ecology and sociology of the Norway rat*. Bethesda, Maryland: United States Public Health Service, 1962.

Cassirer, E. *The philosophy of symbolic forms*. New Haven: Yale University Press, 1953–1957. 3 vols.

Condon, W. S., & Ogston, W. D. Sound film analysis of normal and pathological behavior patterns. *Journal of Nervous and Mental Disease*, 1966, **143**, 338–347.

Crowne, D. P., & Marlowe, D. A new scale of social desirability independent of psychopathology. *Journal of Consulting Psychology*, 1960, **24**, 349–354.

Davitz, J. R. (Ed.) *The communication of emotional meaning*. New York: McGraw-Hill, 1964.

Deutsch, F. Analysis of postural behavior. *Psychoanalytic Quarterly*, 1947, **16**, 195–213.

Deutsch, F. Analytic posturology. *Psychoanalytic Quarterly*, 1952, **21**, 196–214.

Deutsch, F., & Murphy, W. F. *The clinical interview*. New York: International Universities Press, 1955. 2 vols.

Dittmann, A. T., & Llewellyn, L. G. Body movements and speech rhythm in social conversation. *Journal of Personality and Social Psychology*, 1969, **11**, 98–106.

Efron, D. *Gesture and environment*. New York: King's Crown, 1941.

Ekman, P., & Friesen, W. V. Head and body cues in the judgment of emotion: A reformulation. *Perceptual and Motor Skills*, 1967, **24**, 711–724.

Ekman, P., & Friesen, W. V. Nonverbal leakage and clues to deception. *Psychiatry*, 1969, **32**, 88–106. (a)

Ekman, P., & Friesen, W. V. The repertoire of nonverbal behavior: Categories, origins, usage, and coding. *Semiotica*, 1969, **1**, 49–98. (b)

Exline, R. V. Effects of need for affiliation, sex, and the sight of others upon initial communications in problem-solving groups. *Journal of Personality*, 1962, **30**, 541–556.

Exline, R. V. Explorations in the process of person perception: Visual interaction in relation to competition, sex, and need for affiliation. *Journal of Personality*, 1963, **31**, 1–20.

Exline, R. V., & Eldridge, C. Effects of two patterns of a speaker's visual behavior upon the perception of the authenticity of his verbal message. Paper presented at the meeting of the Eastern Psychological Association, Boston, April, 1967.

Exline, R. V., Gray, D., & Schuette, D. Visual behavior in a dyad as affected by interview content and sex of respondent. *Journal of Personality and Social Psychology*, 1965, **1**, 201–209.

Exline, R. V., & Winters, L. C. Affective relations and mutual glances in dyads. In S. Tomkins & C. Izzard (Eds.), *Affect cognition and personality*. New York: Springer, 1965. Pp. 319–330.

Freedman, N., & Hoffmann, S. P. Kinetic behavior in altered clinical states: Approach to objective analysis of motor behavior during clinical interviews. *Perceptual and Motor Skills*, 1967, **24**, 527–539.

Fromm-Reichmann, F. *Psychoanalysis and psychotherapy*. Chicago: University of Chicago Press, 1950.

Gates, G. S. The role of the auditory element in the interpretation of emotion. *Psychological Bulletin*, 1927, **24**, 175. (Abstract)

Gitin, S. R. A dimensional analysis of manual expression. *Journal of Personality and Social Psychology*, 1970, **15**, 271–277.

Gottlieb, R., Wiener, M., & Mehrabian, A. Immediacy, discomfort-relief quotient, and content in verbalizations about positive and negative experiences. *Journal of Personality and Social Psychology*, 1967, **7**, 266–274.

Haley, J. *Strategies of Psychotherapy*. New York: Grune & Stratton, 1963.

Hall, E. T. *The silent language*. Garden City, N.Y.: Doubleday, 1959.

Hall, E. T. A system for the notation of proxemic behavior. *American Anthropologist*, 1963, **65**, 1003–1026.

Hall, E. T. *The hidden dimension*. Garden City, N.Y.: Doubleday, 1966.

Huttar, G. L. *Some relations between emotions and the prosodic parameters of speech*. Santa Barbara, Calif.: Speech Communications Research Laboratory, 1967.

Kasl, S. V., & Mahl, G. F. The relationship of disturbances and hesitations in spontaneous speech to anxiety. *Journal of Personality and Social Psychology*, 1965, **1**, 425–433.

Kendon, A. Some functions of gaze direction in social interaction. *Acta Psychologica*, 1967, **26**, 22–63. (a)

Kendon, A. Some observations on interactional synchrony. Unpublished manuscript, Western Psychiatric Institute and Clinic, Pittsburgh, 1967. (b)

Krasner, L. Studies of the conditioning of verbal behavior. *Psychological Bulletin*, 1958, **55**, 148–170.

Lampel, A. K., & Anderson, N. H. Combining visual and verbal information in an impression-formation task. *Journal of Personality and Social Psychology*, 1968, **9**, 1–6.

Levitt, E. A. The relationship between abilities to express emotional meanings vocally and facially. In J. R. Davitz (Ed.), *The communication of emotional meaning*. New York: McGraw-Hill, 1964. Pp. 87–100.

Lorenz, K. *On aggression*. Toronto: Bantam, 1967.

Mahl, G. F. Measuring the patient's anxiety during interviews from "expressive" aspects of his speech. *Transactions of the New York Academy of Sciences*, 1959, **21**, 249–257.

Mahl, G. F., Danet, B., & Norton, N. Reflection of major personality characteristics in gestures and body movement. Paper presented at annual meeting of the American Psychological Association, Cincinnati, September, 1959.

Maltzman, I. Individual differences in "attention": The orienting reflex. In R. M. Gagne (Ed.), *Learning and individual differences*. Columbus, Ohio: Merrill, 1967. Pp. 94–112.

Mandler, G., & Sarason, S. B. A study of anxiety and learning. *Journal of Abnormal and Social Psychology*, 1952, **47**, 166–173.

Matarazzo, J. D., Wiens, A. N., & Saslow, G. Studies in interviewer speech behavior. In L. Krasner and U. P. Ullmann (Eds.), *Research in behavior modification.* New York: Holt, Rinehart & Winston, 1965. Pp. 179–210.

McBride, G. *A general theory of social organization and behavior.* St. Lucia: University of Queensland Press, 1964.

Mehrabian, A. Communication length as an index of communicator attitude. *Psychological Reports*, 1965, **17**, 519–522.

Mehrabian, A. Attitudes in relation to the forms of communicator-object relationship in spoken communications. *Journal of Personality*, 1966, **34**, 80–93. (a)

Mehrabian, A. Immediacy: An indicator of attitudes in linguistic communication. *Journal of Personality*, 1966, **34**, 26–34. (b)

Mehrabian, A. Orientation behaviors and nonverbal attitude communication. *Journal of Communication*, 1967, **17**, 324–332. (a)

Mehrabian, A. Attitudes inferred from non-immediacy of verbal communications. *Journal of Verbal Learning and Verbal Behavior*, 1967, **6**, 294–295. (b)

Mehrabian, A. Attitudes inferred from neutral verbal communications. *Journal of Consulting Psychology*, 1967, **31**, 414–417. (c)

Mehrabian, A. Substitute for apology: Manipulation of cognitions to reduce negative attitude toward self. *Psychological Reports*, 1967, **20**, 687–692. (d)

Mehrabian, A. Inference of attitudes from the posture, orientation, and distance of a communicator. *Journal of Consulting and Clinical Psychology*, 1968, **32**, 296–308. (a)

Mehrabian, A. Relationship of attitude to seated posture, orientation, and distance. *Journal of Personality and Social Psychology*, 1968, **10**, 26–30. (b)

Mehrabian, A. The effect of context on judgments of speaker attitude. *Journal of Personality*, 1968, **36**, 21–32. (c)

Mehrabian, A. Communication without words. *Psychology Today*, 1968, **2**, 52–55. (d)

Mehrabian, A. *An analysis of personality theories.* Englewood Cliffs, N.J.: Prentice-Hall, 1968. (e)

Mehrabian, A. Male and female scales of the tendency to achieve. *Educational and Psychological Measurement*, 1968, **28**, 493–502. (f)

Mehrabian, A. Measures of achieving tendency. *Educational and Psychological Measurement*, 1969, **29**, 445–451. (a)

Mehrabian, A. Significance of posture and position in the communication of attitude and status relationships. *Psychological Bulletin*, 1969, **71**, 359–372. (b)

Mehrabian, A. Some referents and measures of nonverbal behavior. *Behavior Research Methods and Instrumentation*, 1969, **1**, 203–207. (c)

Mehrabian, A. A semantic space for nonverbal behavior. *Journal of Consulting and Clinical Psychology*, 1970, **35**, 248–257. (a)

Mehrabian, A. Some determinants of affiliation and conformity. *Psychological Reports*, 1970, **27**, 19–29. (b)

Mehrabian, A. *Tactics of social influence.* Englewood Cliffs, N.J.: Prentice-Hall, 1970. (c)

Mehrabian, A. The development and validation of measures of affiliative tendency and sensitivity to rejection. *Educational and Psychological Measurement*, 1970, **30**, 417–428. (d)

Mehrabian, A. When are feelings communicated inconsistently? *Journal of Experimental Research in Personality*, 1970, **4**, 198–212. (e)

Mehrabian, A. Nonverbal betrayal of feeling. *Journal of Experimental Research in Personality*, 1971, **5**, 64–73. (a)

Mehrabian, A. Verbal and nonverbal interaction of strangers in a waiting situation. *Journal of Experimental Research in Personality*, 1971, **5**, 127–138. (b)

Mehrabian, A., & Diamond, S. G. Seating arrangement and conversation. *Sociometry*, 1971, **34**, 281–289. (a)

Mehrabian, A., & Diamond, S. G. The effects of furniture arrangement, props, and personality on social interaction. *Journal of Personality and Social Psychology*, 1971, in press. (b)

Mehrabian, A., & Ferris, S. R. Inference of attitudes from nonverbal communication in two channels. *Journal of Consulting Psychology*, 1967, **31**, 248–252.

Mehrabian, A., & Friar, J. T. Encoding of attitude by a seated communicator via posture and position cues. *Journal of Consulting and Clinical Psychology*, 1969, **33**, 330–336.

Mehrabian, A., & Ksionzky, S. Models for affiliative and conformity behavior. *Psychological Bulletin*, 1970, **74**, 110–126.

Mehrabian, A., & Ksionzky, S. Anticipated compatibility as a function of attitude or status similarity. *Journal of Personality*, 1971, **39**, 225–241. (a)

Mehrabian, A., & Ksionzky, S. Factors of interpersonal behavior and judgment in social groups. *Psychological Reports*, 1971, **28**, 483–492. (b)

Mehrabian, A., & Ksionzky, S. Categories and some determiners of social behavior. Unpublished manuscript, UCLA, 1971. (c)

Mehrabian, A., & Reed, H. Some determinants of communication accuracy. *Psychological Bulletin*, 1968, **70**, 365–381.

Mehrabian, A., & Wiener, M. Non-immediacy between communicator and object of communication in a verbal message: Application to the inference of attitudes. *Journal of Consulting Psychology*, 1966, **30**, 420–425.

Mehrabian, A., & Wiener, M. Decoding of inconsistent communications. *Journal of Personality and Social Psychology*, 1967, **6**, 109–114.

Mehrabian, A., & Williams, M. Nonverbal concomitants of perceived and intended persuasiveness. *Journal of Personality and Social Psychology*, 1969, **13**, 37–58.

Mordkoff, A. M. The judgment of emotion from facial expression: A replication. *Journal of Experimental Research in Personality*, 1971, **5**, 74–78.

Osgood, C. E. Dimensionality of the semantic space for communication via facial expressions. *Scandinavian Journal of Psychology*, 1966, **7**, 1–30.

Osgood, C. E., Suci, G. J., & Tannenbaum, P. H. *The measurement of meaning*. Urbana: University of Illinois Press, 1957.

Piaget, J. *Psychology of intelligence*. Paterson, N.J.: Littlefield, Adams, 1960.

Reich, W. *Character analysis*. Trans. by T. P. Wolfe. New York: Orgone Institute Press, 1945.

Rogers, C. R. A theory of therapy, personality, and interpersonal relationships, as developed in the client-centered framework. In S. Koch (Ed.), *Psychology: A study of a science*, Vol. 3. New York: McGraw-Hill, 1959. Pp. 184–256.

Rosenfeld, H. M. Approval-seeking and approval-inducing functions of verbal and nonverbal responses in the dyad. *Journal of Personality and Social Psychology*, 1966, **4**, 597–605. (a)

Rosenfeld, H. M. Instrumental affiliative functions of facial and gestural expressions. *Journal of Personality and Social Psychology*, 1966, **4**, 65–72. (b)

Scheflen, A. E. The significance of posture in communication systems. *Psychiatry*, 1964, **27**, 316–331.

Scheflen, A. E. *Stream and structure of communicational behavior: Context analysis of a psychotherapy session*. Behavioral Studies Monograph No. 1. Philadelphia: Eastern Pennsylvania Psychiatric Institute, 1965.

Scheflen, A. E. Systems and psychosomatics. *Psychosomatic Medicine*, 1966, **28**, 297–304.

Schlosberg, H. Three dimensions of emotion. *Psychological Review*, 1954, **61**, 81–88.

Schuham, A. The double-bind hypothesis a decade later. *Psychological Bulletin*, 1967, **68**, 409–416.

Sommer, R. Small group ecology. *Psychological Bulletin*, 1967, **67**, 145–151.

Sommer, R. *Personal space*. Englewood Cliffs, N.J.: Prentice-Hall, 1969.

Starkweather, J. A. Variations in vocal behavior. In D. M. Rioch (Ed.), *Disorders of communication*. Proceedings of ARNMD, Vol. 42. Baltimore: Williams & Wilkins, 1964.

Truax, C. B. Reinforcement and nonreinforcement in Rogerian psychotherapy. *Journal of Abnormal Psychology*, 1966, **71**, 1–9.

Weakland, J. H. The "double bind" hypothesis of schizophrenia and three-party interaction. In D. D. Jackson (Ed.), *The etiology of schizophrenia*. New York: Basic Books, 1961. Pp. 373–388.

Werner, H. *Comparative psychology of mental development*. (Rev. ed.) New York: International Universities Press, 1957.

Werner, H., & Kaplan, B. *Symbol formation*. New York: Wiley, 1963.

Wiener, M., & Mehrabian, A. *Language within language: Immediacy, a channel in verbal communication*. New York: Appleton-Century-Crofts, 1968.

Williams, F., & Sundene, B. Dimensions of recognition: Visual vs. vocal expression of emotion. *Audio Visual Communications Review*, 1965, **13**, 44–52.

Woodworth, R. S., & Schlosberg, H. *Experimental Psychology*. New York: Holt, 1954.

Zaidel, S. F., & Mehrabian, A. The ability to communicate and infer positive and negative attitudes facially and vocally. *Journal of Experimental Research in Personality*, 1969, **3**, 233–241.

Visual Interaction: The Glances of Power and Preference[1]

RALPH V. EXLINE

University of Delaware

INTRODUCTION

I first became interested in the study of interpersonal visual behavior rather by accident. Several years ago I composed a number of unisexual groups of five persons each according to their relative ratio of affiliation to achievement need. The purpose of the study was to investigate some hunches as to why women were more capable than men in the assessment of interpersonal preferences within task-oriented discussion groups. The task given the group was a structured discussion task which required that the group members speak in a prearranged order two times around the group. The floor was then thrown open to all, and the discussion generally became a free-for-all.

A curious regularity caught our attention as we observed the groups at their work. Whenever a member of an affiliative group spoke, whether male or female, the speaker would evenly distribute a considerable amount of visual attention around the group. When making a general statement, he or she would first rest his gaze upon one person, then another, then the third, and fourth, until the whole group had been encompassed in a rather stately progression. Equally striking were the behaviors of the affiliative listeners. They appeared to rivet their visual attention upon the face of the speaker,

1. Studies reported in this paper were supported by funds from Contracts Nonr 2285(02) and Nonr 2285(07), Office of Naval Research.

163

giving the observer the impression that he was the relatively constant focus of four pairs of orbs.

If, in the general discussion, one affiliator spoke to a point made by another, the two would first engage each other in a mutual glance, usually broken by the speaker to look at the others who sat watching him.

On the other hand, the relatively more achievement-oriented groups provided a marked contrast in visual interaction. The achievement-oriented speaker was more prone to give an initial quick sweep of the group, then focus his attention on notes in hand, or on the middle distance. Occasionally he would sweep the group again before returning to his notes or briefly engage one person who may have inadvertently caught his eye. Neither did the achievement-oriented listeners look steadily at the speaker. They too would peruse their notes, look into the distance, or occasionally look at the speaker when his visual attention was elsewhere.

Hastily constructing a crude symbol system to represent one-way glances, mutual glances, encompassing sweeps, and the like, we confirmed that, in the groups needed to complete our original design, affiliative groups were indeed visually more interactive to a statistically significant degree. While we found the phenomenon interesting, we made no mention of it when publishing the results of the study. Our data collection methods were most primitive; a single observer watched five persons and made some hen scratches on a piece of paper. In addition the observer was a research assistant who had participated in our discussions about the phenomena—by no stretch of the imagination could she be said to be blind as to our expectations. Thus we decided to restrain our enthusiasm until more systematic and better controlled studies of the behavior could be accomplished.

Once alerted to the phenomenon, we found references to it cropping up everywhere in nonscientific literature. Poets used it to signify the communication of affective expression: "Lips and eyes, glances and smiles are the major elements in the arsenal of expression," wrote Ogden in 1961. In more florid style, Magnus, in 1885, declared that "though we were as eloquent as Demosthenes or Cicero . . . yet our skills would not equal the bewitching speech of the eyes."

Novelists have made use of visual interaction to portray the feel of a momentary interaction, or to delineate the nature of a more enduring relationship. As an example of the former we have Hermann Broch's description of a nineteenth-century happening:

> So they smiled frankly at each other and their souls nodded to each other through the windows of their eyes, just for an instant, like two neighbors who have never greeted each other and now happen to lean out of their windows at the same moment, pleased and embarrassed by this unforeseen and simultaneous greeting. Convention rescued them out of their embarrassment, and lifting his glass Bertrand said: "Prosit Pasenow." [H. Broch, *The Sleepwalkers: A Trilogy*]

For an example of the latter, i.e., the glance that characterizes a relationship, listen to Nagio Marsh: "From the time that they had confronted each other he had looked fully into her eyes. It was not the half-unseeing attention of ordinary courtesy, but an unanswering, fixed regard. He seemed to blink less than most people"; and almost immediately following: "At the same time it seemed to her that he and she acknowledged each other as enemies" (Nagio Marsh, *Spinsters in Jeopardy*).

Others have pointed to the more fearful properties of the look. Elworthy (1895) has documented the opinion that belief in the evil eye is one of the most ancient superstitions of the human race, being referred to in the literature of ancient Egypt, Babylonia, Greece, and Rome. In more recent times, Tomkins (1963) has called our attention to contemporary news reports to the effect that English country folk attribute the wildness of pigs to the evil eye and that an American businessman hired an expert to keep employees at work by "glaring at them."

I found concern with the phenomenon was by no means restricted to poets and novelists. The mutual glance has its practical applications. For example, in the film *Yesterday, Today, and Tomorrow*, Sophia Loren was required to perform a striptease. In order to help her do it in professional style, the management hired the coach of the girls at Le Crazy Horse night club in Paris to work with her. According to Miss Loren, he gave her one tip which she found "extremely decisive." He said that a girl cannot undress with style and be convincing if she does not look straight into the eyes of a man, one man, casually selected among the audience. Let me put it in her own words:

> I was very uncomfortable and embarrassed during the shooting of the scene. There was one moment when I thought to drop the strip sequence and beg for something else. Now I can be positive of one thing, if I was able to do successfully the scene it was because I picked one person and performed only for him, looking straight into his eyes. My audience in the film is composed of one lonely spectator, Marcello Mastroianni! [*Life*, April 10, 1964]

Throughout the literature two themes recur—the theme of preference and the theme of power. Both the sociologist Simmel (1969) and the philosopher Sartre (1957) have stressed the role of mutual glances in the establishment of significant interpersonal bonds. According to Simmel, it is the mutual as distinct from the one-way glance which signifies union—whether we seek or avoid such visual contact depends upon our desire for union with each other. Sartre, on the other hand, stresses the threat to individual autonomy inherent in the mutual glance: "Either the other looks at me and alienates my liberty, or I assimilate and seize the liberty of the other" (Scheutze, 1948).

Farfetched? Perhaps, but listen to Norman Mailer (1968) describe a visual experience he underwent in the back of a truck while waiting to be arraigned for his part in the antiwar march on the Pentagon in the fall of 1967:

> They were interrupted by the insertion of the next prisoner . . . , a young man with straight blond hair and a Nazi armband on his sleeve. He was installed in the rear . . . but Mailer was not happy, for his eyes and the Nazi's bounced off each other like two heads colliding . . . . Standing in the truck, a few feet apart from each other, all prisoners regarding one another, the Nazi fixed on Mailer. Their eyes looked like magnets coming into line, and for perhaps twenty seconds they stared at each other. Mailer looked into a pair of yellow eyes so compressed with hate that back of his own eyes he could feel the echo of such hatred ringing. . . . Mailer could feel violence behind violence rocking through his head. If the two of them were ever alone in an alley, one of them might kill the other in a fight—it was not unlike holding an electric wire in the hand. . . .

>   After the first five seconds of the shock had passed, he realized he
> might be able to win . . . now he could feel the hint of force ebbing in
> the other's eyes, and could wonder at his own necessity to win . . .
> the thought of losing had been intolerable as if he had been obliged not
> to lose, as if the duty of his life at that particular moment must have
> been to look into that Nazi's eye, and say with his own, ". . . you
> know nothing! My eyes encompass yours. My philosophy contains
> yours. You have met the wrong man." And the Nazi looked away, and
> was hysterical with fury on the instant. "You Jew bastard," he shouted.
> "Dirty Jew with kinky hair." [*Armies of the Night*, pp. 160–163]

Mailer's vignette would seem to be the living embodiment of
Sartre's position. "Either the other looks at me and alienates my
liberty, . . ." wrote Sartre. "My eyes encompass yours. My philosophy contains yours," exulted Mailer as he sensed the Nazi
giving way.

EMPIRICAL STUDIES

A Questionnaire Study of Comfort with Visual Interaction During Speech and Silence

Several times I have asked classes or audiences to pair up and
silently look into each other's eyes for 30 seconds. A few seconds pass
and some begin to fidget, others giggle, or unsuccessfully try to
suppress laughter. Smiles and nervous grimaces can be observed,
and though some pairs sit silently boring deadpan into each other's
eyes throughout, many more break contact before the half minute
is up. Subjective reports of the feelings engendered by the experience
range from a loss of the sense of self to great tension and awareness
of the other. "Spooky" and "weird" are terms often used to
describe the encounter.

Such behavior and sensations are consistent with the results
we obtained when we asked 500 U.S. and British students to
indicate on an 8-point scale how comfortable they would be with
another who, when speaking, listening, or sharing mutual silence,
would look at the respondent 50% of the time, never, or always.
For each respondent the imaginary other was further classified as to
whether he was older, younger, or a peer of the same or opposite

sex as the respondent. Thus any one respondent would provide nine look-speak-listen comfort ratings for only one of six categories of hypothetical other interactants.

The results are comparable for both national samples and clearly show highly significant effects concerned with the amount of the other's looking, whether the other is speaking, listening, or both are silent, and for the interaction between speech and gaze patterns. Figure 1 represents the first two effects and shows that across all speech and silence conditions respondents anticipate the most comfort with the 50% look and least comfort when the other never looks. Similarly, when we ignore the visual conditions, we see that respondents expect to be most comfortable when the other is speaking, and least comfortable when both are silent.

Table 1 represents the interaction of look and speech conditions, and from it we can see that respondents would find the other's visual attention less aversive when someone is speaking than when both are silent, the reverse being the case for the other's visual avoidance. These relationships are more graphically demonstrated

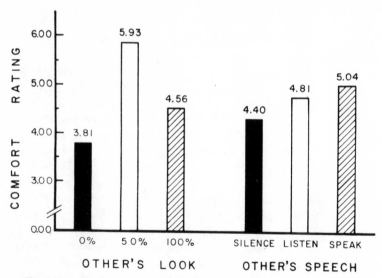

Fig. 1. Mean anticipated comfort ratings made by 360 U.S. students concerning the visual attention or speech behaviors of hypothetical other persons.

TABLE 1

MEAN ANTICIPATED COMFORT RATINGS MADE BY U.S. MEN AND WOMEN OF
THE BEHAVIOR OF HYPOTHETICAL OTHER PERSONS, CATEGORIZED
BY VISUAL ATTENTION AND SPEECH ($N = 360$)

Percent Look Category	Speaking Category							
	Other Speaks		Other Listens		Both Silent		Total Percent Look	
	M	s	M	s	M	s	M	s
0	3.76	1.39	3.28	1.33	4.38	1.70	3.81	1.47
50	6.17	.94	6.01	1.44	5.60	1.53	5.93	1.30
100	5.19	1.85	5.14	1.88	3.34	1.89	4.56	1.87
Means: Look t Speaking	5.04	1.39	4.81	1.55	4.40	1.71		

in Figure 2, where it is clearly seen that one expects to be least
comfortable when another never looks when one is speaking, or
always looks when both are silent. An analysis of written descriptions of the impressions that respondents would form on the basis of
such behaviors of another indicates that the modal impression of the
nonlooking listener is one of rejection or personal disinterest. The
silent starer, on the other hand, is perceived as "queer" or otherwise
deviant.

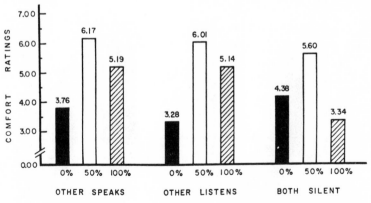

FIG. 2. Mean anticipated comfort ratings made by 360 U.S. students of the
visual attention and speech behaviors of hypothetical other persons.

Figure 3 represents a more detailed breakdown of the comfort ratings elicited by one of the most interesting of our interaction conditions, namely that of the 100% look during complete silence. It is apparent that both men and women are less disconcerted by the silent stares of younger persons than by those of peers or older persons. In addition, while both sexes of respondents would seem to prefer the complete visual attention of a peer of the opposite sex to that of their own, the comfort differential would seem to be much greater for men than for women. Note that men rate their comfort with an attentive male at only 2.70, lowest of all the male comfort ratings. This increases to a rating of 4.27 if the other is a female peer. For women, on the other hand, these same ratings increase from 2.93 to only 3.60. The impact of bedroom eyes would seem to be greater on the male of the species.

The least comfortable lowest mean comfort rating in any of the look-speak-silence conditions for any category of hypothetical other is also to be found in Figure 3. In the American sample this is the

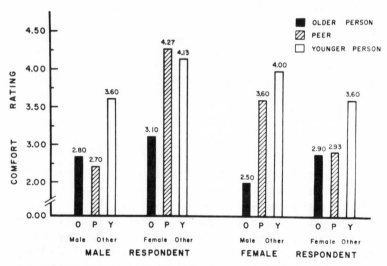

Fig. 3. Mean comfort ratings made by 180 U.S. men and 180 U.S. women of an anticipated 100% look in silence received from hypothetical other persons categorized as to age and sex. ($N = 30$ per mean)

situation in which college-age women are the target, in silence, of the complete visual attention of a male of their fathers' generation (M = 2.50).[2] Though the rho correlation between British and U.S. mean comfort ratings for the 12 age-sex categories in this condition is .87, significant beyond the .01 level, the lowest comfort rating in the British sample is found when women anticipate the complete visual attention of a woman of their mothers' generation. While it is tempting to consider these latter data in terms of homo- and heterosexual concerns, we do not intend to claim that these data represent cross-national differences in the sources of sexual anxieties of British and American women. The differences between means of 2.50 (older men) vs. 2.90 (older women) for Americans, and 1.80 (older men) vs. 1.50 (older women) for British, are not statistically significant. Neither do we know whether the feeling of discomfort is rooted in concern over intimacy, the memory of parental disapproval, or a combination of both factors. Figure 3 does, however, demonstrate a complex interplay of visual attention and speech behavior upon the feelings of comfort which characterize the anticipated interaction of young men and women in like-sex or cross-sex pairs.

It is clear from our questionnaire study that we prefer a moderate amount of visual attention from those with whom we interact in face-to-face situations. The study, however, throws no light upon the reasons for our preferences, nor does it provide us with much direct information about the themes of power and preference to which we earlier referred.

Visual Interaction in Relation to Competition, Sex, and Need for Affiliation

Let us return for a moment to the study first mentioned—the one in which persons with opposite affiliation-to-achievement ratios exhibited such apparently different styles of visual interaction. The study raised questions both methodological and substantive in nature. First, could we record and quantify the phenomena in a way to check upon our impression that the two types of persons showed systematically different visual interaction patterns? Second,

2. Contrast this to the mean rating of 6.73 recorded by women who anticipate listening to a male peer who looks 50% of the time.

assuming that the first question could be answered affirmatively, what might these differences mean for the study of interpersonal processes? Third, if systematic variations in the structure and dynamics of the interaction situation could be shown to have predictable effects upon the visual behavior of the interactants, could systematic variation of the visual behavior of one party to a social interaction predictably effect the response of others? Put another way, can visual behavior as a dependent variable be shown to be an indicator (Ekman, 1965) of mood, state, or orientation toward another? Can it, on the other hand, be an independent variable, driving or shaping the nature of the interaction process? It is to these questions that I will address myself in the remainder of this paper.

When reflecting upon the phenomena, we intuited that the phenomena, if capable of being reliably measured, would be related to questions of power and preference. These two themes would appear to run through the literature I mentioned earlier, but I do not claim that we were familiar with it at that time. We did have evidence that persons characterized by a high affiliation-to-achievement ratio did not raise group-decision issues as soon as did their opposites (Exline, 1962b), and also that the messages they wrote to coworkers in a group-decision task were less indicative of a desire to exert control over others than were those of their opposites (Exline, 1962a). These data may have influenced our thinking.

In any event, our first study was designed to check upon the hypotheses that those high in n-affiliation would be relatively more likely to engage in mutual glances with each other, and that such glances would be inhibited by a situation which required them to compete with one another. We assumed that as n-affiliation theoretically represents a preference for warm, close, intimate personal relations, while n-achievement represents a set of impersonal, task-oriented concerns, persons manifesting a relatively high ratio of affiliative-to-achievement concerns should engage in relatively more mutual glances than would persons characterized by a relatively low ratio of such needs. In addition we hypothesized that the incidence of mutual glances among the relatively more affiliative persons would be attenuated by the power issues inherent in a competitive situation.

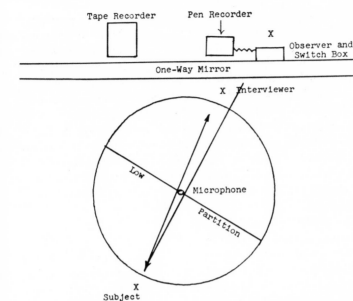

Fig. 4. Schematic representation of arrangements for the observation of visual orientation of subject to interviewer. (Reprinted by permission from R. V. Exline et al., "Visual behavior in a dyad as affected by interview content and sex of respondent," *Journal of Personality and Social Psychology*, 1965, **1**, 201–209. Copyright © 1965 by the American Psychological Association, Inc.)

I will touch only briefly upon this first study to show how we devised methods to answer the first question and to indicate how the results of our hypothesis testing led to more refined studies of the glances of power and preference.

Experimental Arrangements for the Observation and Recording of Eye-Contact Data

First let us address ourselves to some methodological considerations. Figure 4 constitutes a schematic representation of our usual arrangements for the observation and recording of eye contact. One person, usually a naive subject, sits more or less directly across a small table from another person. The second person is sometimes identified as an interviewer (as depicted in Figure 4), sometimes as an experimenter giving instructions, and sometimes as another student. In the latter case, the second person is sometimes a second naive subject, other times a student acting as a paid confederate of the experimenter. Observers, located almost directly behind the second person, are screened from the subject by a two-way-vision mirror and are positioned to give them almost the same view of the first subject's face as the person sitting in the interviewer's position. Whenever the observer judges that the subject has looked into the eyes of the interviewer, he depresses a noiseless button switch which activates an event recorder. In our early studies the switches were connected to pens of an Esterline-Angus Event Recorder. These pens inked out the patterns of looks and glances during speech and silence as a series of "on-off" events recorded on a moving paper tape, calibrated as to time. More recently we have used a specially constructed electronic apparatus to store and later print out the time units associated with the event patterns the system is instructed to record. Each system enables us to recapture the frequency of single events or combinations of events as well as the duration of each event or combination.

Figure 5 represents two 2-minute segments of actual records taken during one of the studies in which we used the Esterline-Angus Recorder. *S*'s visual behavior is depicted in the left pen tracing in each cluster of three tracings. The middle tracing represents the interviewer's speech behavior, while the right-hand line represents the speech of the subject. In this particular record each deflection of the "Subject look" pen represents a mutual glance because the interviewer was instructed to look steadily at the subject.

From this record we can obtain a great variety of information. For example, we can obtain: (a) the frequency of reciprocated (mutual) and nonreciprocated glances; (b) the duration of each event in the above two categories; (c) the number of times each persons speaks and the number of overlapping speeches; (d) the duration of each speech unit for each person, etc. By combining and recombining the various events we can obtain: (a) the total frequency of glances; (b) the total amount of time each person spends looking at and speaking to others; (c) the total amount of time spent in mutual and one-way glances; (d) the average duration of each

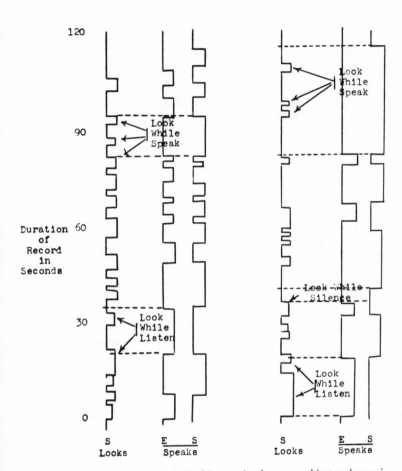

Fig. 5. Two-minute samples of visual interaction between subject and experimenter showing mutual glances during *S*'s speaking and listening behavior, and during mutual silence. (Reprinted by permission from R. V. Exline et al., "Visual behavior in a dyad as affected by interview content and sex of respondent," *Journal of Personality and Social Psychology*, 1965, **1**, 201–209. Copyright © 1965 by the American Psychological Association, Inc.)

speech or glance unit; and (e) the total amount of time and average duration of each time each person looks at the other while speaking, listening, or in total silence.

Data are generally reported either in terms of mean frequencies or mean percentages of visual behavior per unit of time; e.g., total time, listening time, speaking time, or silence.

Reliability and validity of eye-contact recordings. What is the evidence that the data I have shown you were reliably and validly recorded? Gibson and Pick (1963) have shown that individuals can report with a high degree of accuracy when they are and are not being looked at. We have found that well-trained observers, positioned as I described earlier, report almost identical patterns of eye contacts as does an observer seated across the table from the subject. Ten male and ten female students were interviewed by the author for periods of time ranging from 283 to 384 seconds. Eye contact of subject with interviewer was simultaneously recorded by the interviewer and by an out-of-the-room observer positioned as depicted in Figure 4. In order to investigate the effect on reliability of measurement of possible distractions associated with beginning and ending the interview, as well as to standardize the periods in which reliability was measured, interobserver reliability measures were

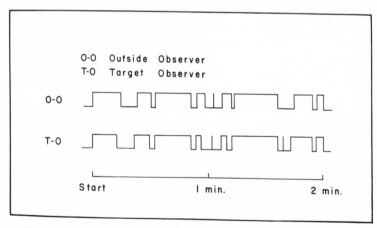

Fig. 6. A two-minute reproduction of two observers' recording *S*'s observed eye contact with a target observer (T-O).

derived from the following three time periods: (a) the first 15 seconds after the interviewer was signaled to start the interview, (b) the 250 seconds immediately following the first 15 seconds, and (c) the last 15 seconds of the interview. Figure 6 represents eye-contact profiles recorded by the two observers during 120 seconds taken from the middle 250 seconds of an actual interview. The measure of reliability was obtained by subtracting the number of seconds in which the two profiles did not overlap from the total number of seconds in the time period under consideration. The difference divided by total time (15 or 250 seconds) then gave the percent of interobserver agreement.

The mean percentage of profile agreement was .905, .942, and .916 in the three time periods respectively. The number of subjects for whom the obtained coefficients of agreement amounted to .900 or higher were 14, 18, and 18, in the three time periods respectively. The mean coefficient of agreement for men was not found to differ from that of women. It seems clear that, given the arrangements described in this paper, eye contact of one person with another can be very reliably recorded during the initial and final phases of the interaction as well as throughout the bulk of the interaction.[3]

Although we have relied on Gibson and Pick's study for evidence that eye contact can be validly measured, it is true that their study was not done in the context of a conversation. The reliability study just described above could easily be converted into a validity study by having both parties to the interaction take turn and turn about in recording (a) when they were actually looking the other in the eye and (b) when they thought the other was looking at them. Though we have not carried out such a study, we have data which suggest that individuals think they are being looked in the eye when in actual fact the looker is focused somewhere in a zone marked by the eyebrow and eye pouch above and below the eye, and by the eye corner nearest to the ear on either side of the head. Within this zone a look focused on the root of the nose between the eyes is often interpreted as an eye-to-eye look. It is my belief that the validity problem is not critical, for our observations indicate that

3. The author wishes to express his appreciation to Miss Bja Fehr, who was responsible for developing and carrying out the methodological study reported above.

most people turn their heads and faces slightly away from the other when they break contact. Even if one looks into a zone of regard rather than at the eye itself, the other reacts as if he were engaged in eye contact.

The arrangements in our first laboratory investigation differed somewhat from those shown in Figure 4, as we used three naive subjects and had three observers recording visual and speech behavior. Thirty-two groups of three like-sex subjects each were studied as they were processed through a discussion task in a $2 \times 2 \times 2$ factorial design. The independent variables were sex of group, affiliation-to-achievement ratio of group members, and the competitiveness of the task situation. The results of this study have been reported elsewhere in detail (Exline, 1963), and Figure 7 represents only the major findings.

These data demonstrate three interesting phenomena. First, mutual glances are relatively rare in task-oriented discussions, occurring, on the average, only during 3% of the total possible interaction time in male groups, and $7\frac{1}{2}$% of the time in female groups. Second, on all indices of visual behavior, mutual or nonreciprocal, women are more active than men. The percents of the total time that women looked at other women in this study averaged 37.3% as compared to 23.2% for men.[4] Third, there is a significant interaction of affiliation, competitiveness, and sex upon the tendency to engage in mutual glances. Finally, though not shown in this figure, Ss gave significantly more visual attention to another when listening to him than when speaking to him, and rarely engaged in mutual glances in silence. The last finding provides behavioral confirmation for the low comfort ratings given in the questionnaire study to an anticipated 100% look from another in silence.

Let us return for a moment to the interaction effect mentioned above. One possible interpretation of these data is that affiliative persons, especially if they are women, find the power struggle inherent in a competitive situation aversive. Thus a mutual glance in such situations takes on a different meaning from such a glance in less competitive situations. Perhaps the affiliative individual unconsciously indicates his or her desires not to interact with others

4. We have consistently observed this sex difference in visual attentiveness in all studies in which sex has been a variable.

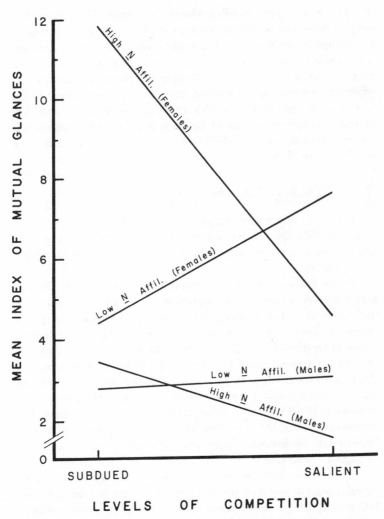

FIG. 7. Mean percentage of time each sex spends in mutual visual interaction for each of two levels of n-affiliation at two levels of competition. (Reprinted, by permission, from R. V. Exline, "Explorations in the process of person perception: Visual interaction in relation to competition, sex, and the need for affiliation," *Journal of Personality*, 1963, **31**, 1–20. Copyright © 1963 by the Duke University Press.)

in such situations by avoiding visual intercourse. Implicit in such an interpretation is the suggestion that those showing extremely low affiliative tendencies tend to orient themselves in more rivalrous ways toward others. One could argue that, in a competitive situation, the intimacy inherent in the mutual glance could be interpreted as the intimacy of combat, an intimacy less repellent to the nonaffiliative person than to his affiliative counterpart, and thus increase his motive to engage the other in a battle of eyeballs. We are reminded of Norman Mailer's description of his encounter with the American Nazi.

Studies of Attraction and Aversion

The next two figures suggest that, irrespective of one's own degree of affiliation motive, aversiveness and attractiveness of other persons are correlated with willingness to share a mutual glance with them.

Figure 8 demonstrates the effect of derogatory and complimentary feedback upon an *S*'s willingness to engage in eye contact with an interviewer. Eye contact was measured before and after the feedback session, and it is clear that only derisory feedback is followed by diminished eye contact in the second period. *S*s in the complimentary and control conditions were unaffected by feedback. All 12 *S*s in the derogatory condition reduced their eye contact with the interviewer, while there was a seven to three and a four to three increase-to-decrease ratio in complimentary and control conditions respectively. *S*s in the complimentary condition also evaluated the interviewer significantly more positively than did those in the derogatory condition.

Figure 9 depicts the results obtained when we measured the visual attention given to two interviewers of the *S*s' own sex, both before and after *S*s were removed from the presence of the interviewers and asked to state which one they found more attractive. It is clear that both sexes increased eye contact with the preferred interviewer and decreased it with the other. The slight crossover noted for females in the control group reflects the fact that control females developed a preference for one of the two interviewers whereas males would admit to no such preference.

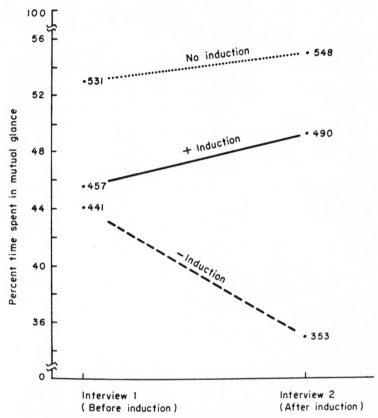

FIG. 8. Percent time spent in mutual glances by experimental and control *S*s in two interview periods (before and after affect induction). (Reprinted, by permission, from R. V. Exline and L. Winters, "Affective relations and mutual glances in dyads," in S. Tomkins and C. Izard [Eds.], *Affect, cognition, and personality.* Copyright © 1965 by the Springer Publishing Co.)

The studies mentioned to date provide rather good evidence that persons are more prone to engage in mutual glances when they find the relationship with another attractive rather than aversive. The relationship between considerations of interpersonal power and visual interaction, however, was only indirectly touched upon in the study of affiliation and competitiveness. I will now describe a

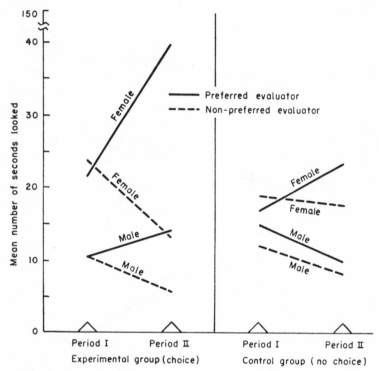

FIG. 9. Increments and decrements in the number of seconds *S*s looked at evaluators while speaking to them. (Reprinted, by permission, from R. V. Exline and L. Winters, "Affective relations and mutual glances in dyads," in S. Tomkins and C. Izard [Eds.], *Affect, cognition, and personality.* Copyright © 1965 by the Springer Publishing Co.)

study in which we measured the effect of power and influence on visual interaction by creating actual power differences between two persons.

Visual Interaction and Power Differences in Legitimate and Illegitimate Hierarchies[5]

Thibaut and Kelley (1959) define social power as the control one person has over another's outcomes. Assuming that individuals

5. Exline, R. V., and Long, B., unpublished MS, 1971.

are aware of the difference in power which defines their role relationship, we would expect that in a face-to-face interaction in which outcomes are in question, the person in the less powerful position would have a greater need to monitor the expressive behavior of the other. Such monitoring would serve two purposes: (a) it would provide the low power person (LP) with information concerning the reaction of the other to LP's efforts, information which LP could use to adjust his own behavior; (b) it enables the LP person to indicate that he is attentive to the higher power person (HP), thus serving as a signal that he accepts his role, or at least is behaving in a manner appropriate to his position.

Accordingly our first hypothesis was that *in a dyad marked by different power positions, the less powerful person would, everything else being equal, look more into the line of regard of the other.*

Implicit in the statement of the above hypothesis is the assumption that the LP person accepts the legitimacy of the power difference. If he does not, he should neither wish to obtain expressive feedback to adjust his behavior vis-à-vis HP's reactions, nor indicate acceptance of a subordinate role by giving the other his visual attention. Thus we proposed a second hypothesis as a qualification of our original hypothesis, namely that *the more legitimate the perception of the power hierarchy, the more will the less powerful person look into the line of regard of the other.*

Forty pairs of male *S*s were required, through discussion, to arrive at an agreed upon solution to each of three problems. None of the problems had an obviously correct solution, solutions being a question of opinion or judgment difficult to verify. The study was presented as an investigation into the processes of group decision making.

Upon arriving at the laboratory, *S*s were shown to separate rooms where they filled out a personality inventory, then were given the instructions designed to create differential power positions. Outcome control was established by instructing the person assigned the LP position that "the other person is going to divide the chips, giving you however much he wants to." On the other hand, the person assigned the HP position was instructed to divide a 10-chip reward for work on each task according to the following schedule: HP was to give LP 3 of the 10 chips after the first problem and 4 of

10 chips after each of the second and third problems. Thus the outcomes were controlled by the HP person, and the LP person always received a lower outcome. It was assumed that LP's lower reward would emphasize the power differences—especially after the 7-to-3 split following the first task. Both persons were told that chips would be exchanged for money at the end of the experiment.

The power induction was rationalized to both persons by pointing out that, in real-life groups, one person often had the power to determine the rewards and privileges of others. It should be noted that the HP person was to a degree a confederate of the experimenter. He was asked not to reveal that the division of chips was predetermined, and was assured that this aspect of the experiment would be explained to the other person upon completion of the experiment. After the instructions were completed, the LP person was taken to the work room where the HP person was already seated at a table facing the door.

The perception of the relative legitimacy of the power hierarchy was manipulated by selecting pairs in such fashion as to encourage the perception of legitimacy on the one hand and nonlegitimacy on the other. All 20 pairs in the legitimacy category were composed of one ROTC cadet officer and one ROTC basic (comparable to an enlisted man). Both men were in uniform and were taken from a drill class to participate in the study. Pairs in the illegitimate power condition were composed of two strangers released from a large gym class. Pairs of acquaintances were eliminated and replaced with strangers.

The problems consisted of one probability judgment, one human relations problem involving leadership in an industrial setting, and the development of a story from a TAT card. The problems were designed to provoke discussion and a certain amount of disagreement. In no case was there an obviously correct solution.

Subjects first read the problem and were allowed to take notes. After a specified time the experimenter collected the description of the problem and left the room. A buzzer signaled both the beginning and end of the discussion period. The problem period was terminated after 3 minutes, or after 10 seconds of silence following a quicker decision.

After completion of the third task the LP person was taken from the room and both *S*s filled out a questionnaire which enabled us to validate the effectiveness of the inductions and assess the degree of acquaintance.

In addition to the face validity of the power difference inherent in the assignment of control over the distribution of chips to one person, effectiveness of the power induction was inferred from the *S*'s preference for his own or the other's job. The HP person preferred his job to a significantly greater degree than did the LP person. The latter preferred the HP position to his own.

The effectiveness of the legitimacy induction was demonstrated by the following ratings: (a) the less powerful ROTC person reported that the HP person was within his rights in dividing the chips the way he did to a greater degree than did the LP gym person; (b) less powerful ROTC *S*s would like to work again with the HP person more than would LP gym *S*s; (c) less powerful ROTC more so than LP gym *S*s would like to have the HP position; (d) the ROTC pairs reported that they wanted to and tried to influence the other more than did the gym pairs. All of the above differences were significant beyond the .05 or .01 probability levels.

Figure 10 shows the effect of the power and legitimacy conditions upon the extent to which *S*s in the HP and LP positions visually monitored each other. It is clear that, over all periods and experimental conditions, the less powerful person looked more at the powerful person than vice versa. The trend was established in the first trial and reached significance in the second and third trials. This was the case for looking while listening and tended to be the case for looking while speaking.

One could argue that these results may merely reflect the tendency for visual monitoring to match the amount which the other spoke. Thus if the HP person spoke more, this would indicate that our induction influenced speech and that our results would be better explained in terms of a politeness convention which requires a listener to give visual attention to a speaker. Three pieces of evidence argue against this explanation, for the HP person did not consistently control the floor; speech increased in the second trial and decreased in the third, whereas the reverse was true for looking; and finally, a subsidiary analysis showed significant differences

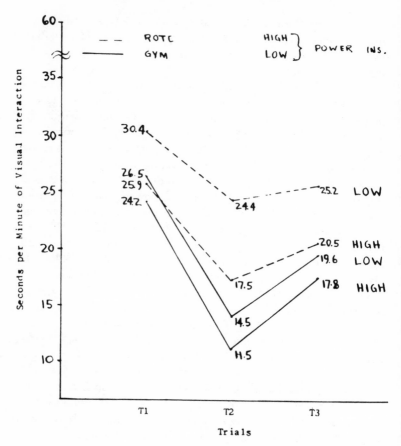

Fig. 10. Mean seconds per minute of visual interaction of high and low power members of gym and ROTC dyads during three decision-discussion trials ($N = 20$ per mean).

in the extent to which the looking behavior of HP and LP persons matched that of their opposites. HPs' looking while listening matched LPs' looking while speaking, but LPs' looking while listening overrode HPs' looking while speaking by some 10 seconds per minute on each trial.

What about the effect of the perceived legitimacy of the power hierarchy? Figure 10 shows that from the very first problem, the relative differences between HP and LP persons were greater in the legitimate than in the illegitimate condition; that the mean level of visual monitoring was significantly higher in the legitimate condition; and, bearing most directly upon our second hypothesis, that the LP person in the illegitimate (gym) as compared to the legitimate (ROTC) hierarchy tended to look less at HP in the first trial, and did look significantly less at him in the second and third.

While the data concerning the visual behavior of the LP person in a hierarchy would clearly seem to support the hypothesis that he who sees a power difference as illegitimate will be visually less attentive to the more powerful person, we cannot yet say that we have eliminated all alternative explanations for this phenomenon. We cannot yet say, that is, whether the reduced attentiveness was due to (a) negative affect felt toward one who would take advantage of his position to apparently violate a norm of fair play, (b) a desire to avoid any suggestion that one accepted a subordinate role felt to be illegitimate, or (c) a combination of both of the above explanations. A further study would seem to be required—one in which negative feeling toward the occupant of a power position perceived to be illegitimate is held constant.

Neither can we eliminate the possibility that the lower visual activity of the occupants of the HP position was due only to the power inherent in the position. It is possible that a feeling of guilt engendered by the power induction may have caused our HP subject to have avoided looking at the other. Ellsworth and Carlsmith (1968) have shown that we do not like those who watch us while they criticize us. We feel that they enjoy our discomfort. Perhaps an intuitive awareness of such feelings prevented the HP subjects from looking at those they felt they were required to take advantage of. Both of the above considerations can be eliminated by removing the inequities involved in the distribution of the rewards, and such a study is now underway. Until the results are in we can only say that the data of the study just described provide tentative but not definitive support for our theory concerning the effects of power considerations on visual interaction with another.

Perception of Another's Potency as a Function of the Personality of a Speaker and the Visual Behavior of a Listener[6]

We have also approached the study of power considerations in interpersonal visual behavior by identifying those persons who exhibit a need to exert control over their interpersonal environment. In the study which I will next describe, we identified such persons and then developed a situation in which visual behavior was manipulated as an independent variable.

Twenty male undergraduates of Oxford University were given Schutz FIRO B scale (1958), on the basis of which they were designated as being high or low in their orientation toward controlling others in their environment. Those assigned to the high-control category described themselves as wishing to control others more than they wanted others to control themselves, whereas the reverse was true of those assigned to the low-control category. A student confederate, seated across a table some 3 feet distant from S, then engaged each S in a 5-minute discussion of travel interests. During the conversation the confederate looked at all Ss approximately 50% of the time when he (the confederate) spoke, but systematically varied his visual attention when the S spoke. One half of the Ss in each control category received the undivided visual attention of the listening confederate (100% glance). When the remainder of the Ss spoke, the confederate never looked at them, but swept the air above their heads as he listened (zero glance).

The visual behavior of Ss was recorded as they spoke and listened to the confederate. Following the interview, Ss' impressions of the confederate were obtained by means of Osgood's semantic differential technique (Osgood, Suci, & Tannenbaum, 1957).

Since the visual behavior of the confederate was the major independent variable in this study, we were interested to learn whether or not Ss with the greater control orientation would respond more steadily to the steady glance of the listener. In view of the folklore which equates "outstaring" another with dominance, we speculated that control-oriented persons in the 100% look-listen condition would be more likely to look into the eyes of our con-

6. Exline, R. V., Fairweather, H., Hine, J., and Argyle, M., unpublished MS, 1971.

TABLE 2

Mean Percent Looking at Confederate by British *S*s,
Categorized as to Own Control Orientation and Speech Role,
and by Visual Attention of Confederate

Confederate's Visual Attention	*S*s' Speech Role	*S*s' Control Orientation					
		High Control		Low Control		Total	
		M	s	M	s	M	s
Zero	Speaker	47.4	17.9	63.4	16.8	55.4	17.1
	Listener	73.6	11.9	86.8	11.0	80.2	12.9
	Total	60.5	19.9	75.1	16.8	67.8	19.4
100%	Speaker	67.8	23.2	54.0	14.4	60.9	19.6
	Listener	76.4	18.1	63.4	16.8	69.9	17.8
	Total	72.1	20.1	58.7	15.6	65.4	18.8
Speech Role	Speak	57.6	22.3	58.7	13.9	58.2	18.1
	Listen	75.0	14.5	75.1	18.2	75.0	16.0
	Total	66.3	20.4	66.9	17.9		

federate both when speaking and listening to him than would the less control-oriented *S*s.

Data in Table 2 show that the high-control-oriented person does indeed look more at the confederate than does the low-control-oriented person when both speaking and listening to him. These differences approach, but do not reach, significance. When a separate analysis is carried out for looking while speaking and looking while listening, however, we find a significant interaction between the look received from the confederate and the control orientation of the subject, in its effect upon the visual attention a subject gives to the confederate while listening to him. The high-control-oriented *S* does not differ in the amount of visual attention he gives to the confederate, regardless of the amount of visual attention he receives from the confederate. However, the less controlling *S* gives significantly more visual attention to the confederate if the confederate has withheld his gaze from him. This is a complicated set of relationships, especially since the reverse of this interaction approached significance when the looking-while-speaking data were analyzed. The relationships are more clearly depicted in Figure 11.

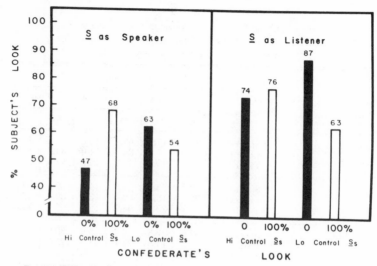

Fig. 11. Mean percent looking at confederate by British Ss categorized as to own control orientation and speech role, and by visual attention from confederate ($N = 5$ per mean).

What is most clear is that Ss, taken as a group, give a visually attentive confederate about the same amount of attention whether he speaks or listens to them, but give a visually inattentive speaker significantly more attention when listening than when talking to him. Previous research has shown that Ss generally look more when listening than when speaking (Kendon, 1967; Exline, Gray, & Schuette, 1965). Our data suggest that there may be something unsettling in receiving the 100% look of a listening other—especially for the less control-oriented Ss.

The visual behavior of the speaking Ss is reminiscent of the results I reported in a study with David Messick (1967). In that study we found that controlling and less controlling Ss showed very similar patterns of visual attention when they were speaking to a listener who provided them with very much or very little in the way of verbal social reinforcement. The control-oriented Ss, gave much more attention to the reinforcing listener, and the less controlling Ss to the nonreinforcing listener. The pattern was almost identical to that shown in Figure 11.

Some light may be thrown on the above findings by the ratings our subjects gave the confederate on the semantic differential. This consisted of 12 opposed adjective pairs, 4 pairs being very highly loaded on the potency factor, 4 on activity, and 4 on evaluation. Though the instrument was given as a heuristic device, we rather hoped that our two experimental looking conditions would each have a different impact upon our subjects. You will remember that in the questionnaire study described earlier, to receive no visual attention from a listener was rated as one of the two most uncomfortable interaction situations of those presented.

No differences between control types or across the confederate looking inductions were found for the evaluation factor, but there was an interesting and unexpected interaction between the independent variables with respect to the potency factor. As is indicated in Figure 12, control-oriented Ss rated the confederate who never looked while listening as being significantly more potent than those who received his undivided visual attention. Control-oriented Ss

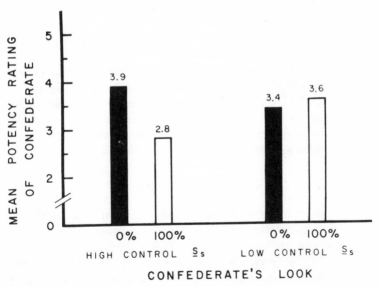

FIG. 12. Mean potency rating of confederate by British Ss categorized as to own control orientation and visual attention from confederate.

also rated the nonlooking confederate as more potent than did the less controlling subjects. Thus those who like to control others would seem to find those whose visual attention they cannot capture more powerful than those whose they can. Shades of Jean Paul Sartre—"I assimilate and seize the liberty of the other"—but only if I can capture his eyes.

Perhaps the potency impressions help to explain the rather complicated set of interactions shown in Figure 11. If one has control needs and wishes to retain the floor, it would behoove him not to look too much at one he feels has the capacity to wrest it from him, should he catch his eye. On the other hand, if the confederate looks steadily without attempting to speak, he may be seen as weak, which would enable one to look more steadily at him with impunity. The reverse could be true for the less controlling subject. The data show, though the interaction was not significant, that the the control-oriented subjects did look less steadily at the nonlooking than at the looking listener, while the reverse tended to be true for the less controlling subject. To look or not to look, that is the question. The answer, for those who need to control, may lie in the perceived force of the other.

Much of what I have reported in these studies of visual behavior and interpersonal power problems seems to be concerned with the avoidance of eye contact. Powerful people do not monitor less powerful people. Those who feel that another's power is illegitimate avoid potential eye contact with the usurper. Dominant men seem more impressed with the personal force of one who listens without looking and also seem more reluctant to look at those whom they perceive to be forceful. Why so much avoidance?

Eye Contact as a Sign between Man and Monkey

The literature on primates provides one compelling suggestion as to why men may be loath to look at one another. Over and over the ethologists have reported that the mutual glance between male primates initiates mutual threat displays which reaffirm or reorder one's place in the dominance hierarchy. The phenomenon has been reported for baboons (Hall & Devore, 1965), rhesus and bonnet macaques (Hinde & Rowell, 1962), langurs (Jay, 1965), and the mountain gorilla (Shaller, 1963). Van Lawick-Goodall (1967) did not specifically mention this phenomenon in her field studies of chimpanzees, but she did mention that they did not like to be "stared at." Many of these studies also identify the averted gaze as a sign of submission.

Diebold (1968) has suggested that such behaviors are part of a shared primate ethogram, and I would like to conclude my presentation of our empirical studies by briefly reporting some work in which we demonstrated that humans can elicit and inhibit threatening displays of rhesus macaques merely by initiating and breaking off mutual eye contact (Exline & Yellin, 1969).

Four male rhesus macaques, of Indian origin and approximately 18 months old, were stimulated in their cages by male experimenters who stood directly in front of each monkey's cage and stared fixedly at the eyes of the monkey. An observer, located out of the monkey's line of sight, recorded the reaction to each eye engagement.

Figure 13 shows the experimental arrangements.

The challenging look required the stimulator to stare without expression at the face of the monkey until he caught the monkey's full-faced visual attention. Once eye contact was achieved, the looker continued his stare until the monkey either moved or broke visual contact. Three blocks of 10 stimulus looks each were recorded on different days by each of the stimulators. All stimulus periods were scheduled during a period of generally high activity.

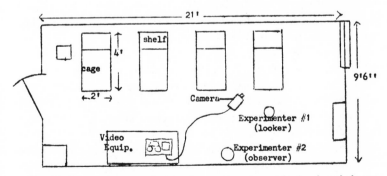

FIG. 13. Schematic representation of arrangements used to signal, and observe monkeys' responses to eye engagement.

In the deferent stimulus look condition, the experimenter first established eye contact with the monkey, then immediately lowered his gaze by dropping his head and eyes.

There was no difficulty in establishing that the looker had caught the monkey's attention. The monkey would suddenly pull himself together into a tight crouch, his head pulled down between his shoulders. For a second or two he would sit immobile, staring intently into the eyes of the looker. The look has been described as "hard" and certainly gives one the impression of menace, the brows generally being drawn into a V-shaped, frowning look. This concentrated look, which we used as the sign that eye engagement had been achieved, has been described (by Eimerl and DeVore, 1965) as the first and mildest stage of the macaque threat display.

Beginning with the "hard stare" (our sign of eye engagement), the macaque display progresses through a stare accompanied by an open mouth and bared teeth, to darting the head forward and pulling it back in a quick bobbing movement. If the opponent does not submit after the display reaches the third stage, the monkey will either attack or flee.

Preliminary observation showed that our caged monkeys manifested all of the above aggressive behaviors observed in field studies, plus such variations as pulling the head back but not darting it forward, or leaping in attack but falling short of the door of the cage. On the basis of these observations we developed an 8-point scale anchored by the avoidance of eye engagement at one extreme and by a direct leap at the face of the looker at the other. Summed over trials, readings of this scale enabled us to obtain an average aggressiveness response score for each monkey.

We also categorized the responses more simply under three headings: "avoidance" (breaking eye contact with no forward movement), "attack" (leaping at the experimenter), and "threat" (all intermediate responses, mouth open, head bob, etc.).

The next figure shows examples of avoidance, threat, and attack behaviors.

Table 3 shows the mean changes in aggressiveness of response to the challenging and deferent looks over the three trial blocks. A $4 \times 2 \times 2 \times 2 \times 3$ fixed effects analysis of variance showed significant effects for monkeys, looks, trial blocks, and monkeys by

Fig. 14. The "hard stare" of the rhesus macaque—first stage of the threat display.

Fig. 15. Three examples of *Macaca mulatta*'s response to eye engagement; left to right: avoidance, anger threat, and attack (leaping).

looks interactions. The Neuman-Keuls test demonstrated that the first monkey responded less aggressively and the third monkey more aggressively than the others. The Neuman-Keuls test also indicated that differences between trial blocks occurred between the first and second trials, and that two of the monkeys responded with significantly more aggression to the challenging as compared to the deferent look, while the other two only tended to do so.

TABLE 3

MEAN AGGRESSIVENESS RESPONSE (0–7) BY FOUR MONKEYS TO
DOMINANCE AND DEFERENCE SIGNS OVER THREE TRIAL BLOCKS OF
TEN BLOCKS EACH

Monkey No.	Trial Block	Stimulus Look		
		Direct Challenging Look	Downcast Deferent Look	Response per Monkey
		M	M	M
1	1	3.20	.75	1.58
	2	2.40	1.20	
	3	.75	1.20	
	Total	2.12	1.05	
2	1	3.60	2.80	2.39
	2	2.70	1.50	
	3	2.40	1.35	
	Total	2.90	1.88	
3	1	6.90	4.15	5.10
	2	6.85	3.60	
	3	6.05	3.05	
	Total	6.60	3.60	
4	1	3.65	2.10	2.39
	2	2.70	1.90	
	3	2.25	1.75	
	Total	2.87	1.91	
Stimulus Look × Trial Block				Response Per Trial Block
	1	4.33	2.45	3.39
	2	3.66	2.05	2.86
	3	2.86	1.83	2.34
Response per sign		3.62	2.11	

The analysis of the categorization of responses by avoidance, threat, and attack showed similar results. In fact, when χ^2 was computed for each monkey in regard to the frequency of response in each aggressiveness category over the two looks, the null hypothesis was rejected at better than the .01 level for each monkey. Examination of the data shows attack and threat behavior to be more frequently elicited by the challenging glance while nonaggressive responses are more likely to be elicited by the deferent downcast glance. These relationships are shown in Table 4.

We believe our data support the conclusion that maintenance of eye engagement (the mutual glance) serves as a dominance challenge to the rhesus macaque whether the contender is another rhesus as observed by the ethologists, or a human being, a member of another primate genus. Similarly, aversion of the gaze, once established, serves to inhibit the threat display of the rhesus regardless whether the looker is of the same or another primate genus.

We believe that eye engagement is a necessary feature of the stimulus complex which elicits the threat display, for when we assumed our stimulus posture with closed eyes our monkeys rarely

TABLE 4

PERCENT RESPONSES TO CHALLENGING (DIRECT) AND DEFERENT (DOWN) EYE ENGAGEMENTS, CODED AS ATTACKING, THREATENING, OR NONAGGRESSIVE ($n = 60$ per Stimulus Look per Monkey)

Monkey No.	Stimulus Look	Response Category		
		Attack	Threaten	Nonaggressive
1	Direct (Challenge)	35	15	50
	Down (Deferent)	18	4	78
2	Direct	25	48	27
	Down	22	20	58
3	Direct	97	0	3
	Down	54	0	46
4	Direct	23	55	22
	Down	25	25	50
Total Response × Look	Direct	47	29	24
	Down	28	12	60

if ever responded with a threat display. We do not claim it is a sufficient condition, however, for we attempted no variations such as smiling, grimacing, vocalizing, or moving the head while staring at the monkeys. Neither did we mask the face, leaving only the eyes active, nor did we provide an inanimate model, or picture of a human head with eyes open or closed.

Subsequent work has shown that posture is not a releaser, for the same intensity of response was elicited with both an erect and a stooped, crouching posture. Neither does movement alone serve to elicit aggressive displays, for though a darting human head will catch the monkey's attention, it is only when the eyes are in mutual contact that the threat or attack display is elicited. The features of a face do seem to play some part, however; for a while a head completely covered with a stocking mask elicits no response, adding eye holes and open eyes elicits only a small insignificant increase in threatening displays.

While more work remains before we can precisely characterize the context in which open eyes are sufficient to elicit threat, we do believe that an affirmative answer to Diebold's question is possible. We believe, that is, that eye engagement does serve an interpersonal-regulatory function in a shared primate ethogram. Perhaps men are generally predisposed to avoid visual engagement with another (especially in silence) to reduce the probability of getting caught up in disturbing dominance struggles.

DISCUSSION

The empirical studies just described have been based on the assumption that eye contact is one of the nonverbal processes we use to establish a relationship with another. We have focused mainly upon affiliative and dominance relationships, using what Mehrabian (1969) has called encoding and decoding methodologies to study the communication or indication of the relationships. Examples of the encoding method, in which the manipulation of the experimental situation is designed to elicit attitudes which can be inferred from postures, positions, or eye engagements concomitant to the induced attitude, are the studies of affiliation and competition, of preference and eye engagement, and of legitimate and illegitimate power hierarchies. Decoding methodology, in which subjects are presented with prepared stimuli and asked to infer feelings and attitudes of the stimulator, is represented by the study of the responses of British and American students to the visually attentive and avoidant listener.[7] In an unreported study, a speaker instructed to look was perceived as much more favorable and confident than when he delivered the identical message but avoided eye engagement (Exline & Eldridge, 1967). Thus both encoding and decoding methodologies can be used to study the role played by visual behavior in the establishment of affiliative or dominance relationships.

Other investigators provide valuable insights concerning relationships between eye engagements and affiliation or dominance. In regard to affiliation, Phoebe Ellsworth (Ellsworth & Carlsmith, 1968) has shown that those who look while telling us good things about ourselves are preferred to those who look when criticizing us; Efran and Broughton (1966) have shown that one looks more at a friendly familiar person than at one who is a stranger; Mehrabian (1968a, 1968b) has shown that eye contact shows an increasing but curvilinear relationship to liking for an addressee; and Rubin (1970) has found love to be significantly and positively related to mutual glances. Strongman and Champness (1968) have shown a positive relationship between dominance and "winning" a staring contest, as have Thayer (1969), and Edelman, Omark, and Freedman (1971, personal communication).

Argyle (1969) has pointed out that eye engagement serves an important function in processes other than those of establishing and defining the particular nature of the relationship. He suggests that it is also important in obtaining feedback about the reactions of others, in controlling the communication channel, and (through avoidance) in reducing the distracting effect of incoming information. With respect to channel control, Kendon (1967) has shown that patterned eye contact figures as a signal in turning over the floor to another during conversation. One looks away a few seconds before ceasing to speak and looks back at the listener just as he ceases speaking. Champness (personal communication) carried out

7. Exline, R. V., and Snadowski, A., unpublished MS, 1971.

an interesting study in which two people found themselves looking each other in the eyes as a curtain rose to signal the start of a conversation. Champness found that *dominant* Ss were the first to break the gaze. They looked away and immediately began speaking. Perhaps, as is suggested by Kendon's work, they realized that to sit looking at the other in silence was a cue for the other to speak, and what dominant person wants to cede the floor to another?

With respect to general gaze aversion, Exline and Winters (1965) demonstrated that systematic variation in the cognitive difficulty of a conversation topic decreased the amount of time a speaker looked at his listener in direct relation to the difficulty of the topic. Incidentally, personality variables served to moderate visual behavior in the above study. Personality considerations have also been shown to affect visual behavior by Lefcourt (Lefcourt & Wine, 1969), who categorized Ss by inner and outer locus of control, by Champness (personal communication), who grouped them by dominance-submission, and by our own group (Exline, Thibaut, Hickey, & Gumpert, 1970), which has made extensive use of Christie and Geis's Machiavellianism scale, Schutz's FIRO B (1958) and various measures of n-affiliation.

As was indicated earlier, it seems clear that eye engagement alone is not sufficient to indicate the nature of the relationship or the specific roles played by the interactants. Information relevant to the interaction context, facial displays, postural and spatial arrangements, and verbal themes are undoubtedly necessary to the specification of relationship and role. Eye engagement then is but one indicator variable, and the work of Wiener and Mehrabian (1968), Mehrabian (1968a, 1968b), Ekman and his colleagues (1965, 1967, 1969), Scheflen (1964), Birdwhistell (1970), Hall (1966), Duncan (1969), Sommer (1969), Argyle et al. (1970), and others, have thrown valuable light upon the operation of other nonverbal factors in the processes of interpersonal communication.

Notwithstanding the complex interrelations of gaze direction and other variables, we plan to continue our investigation of these phenomena. We are presently concerned with eye engagement, or the lack of it, as an indication of the authenticity of a spoken communication. We have data to suggest that, for women at least, eye contact is less when reporting false as opposed to true impressions of another person to the person in question.[8] The synchrony of eye engagements with other nonverbal expressive processes intrigues us. We have tentative evidence that the affect state of persons whose postural inclination toward or away from another matches the amount of their eye engagement with a listener can be judged more easily from silent films than can the affect states of those who lean forward and look little (or who lean back and look much).

We also wish to explore more thoroughly the implications of the specific planes or directions used by one who breaks or avoids eye contact with another. Would one who listens with downcast or sideways gaze impress a control-oriented speaker in the same fashion as did our upward-sweeping confederate? We doubt it, and suggest that specific affective impressions may be decoded from specific gaze directions.

Research concerning the development of eye engagement tendencies in children would seem to offer promise for understanding the development of affiliative and dominance tendencies. There are some suggestions that response to eye contact may be innate (Argyle, 1969) and that the orienting response leads to attending to the mother, especially if there is eye contact (Walters & Parke, 1965; Ambrose, 1961).

Hutt and Ounsted (1966) have observed that autistic children avoid looking at human faces and eyes. Rimland (1962) has reported that parents of autistic children are cold and withdrawn, while Singer and Wynne (1963) describe such parents as showing apathy about interaction and as manifesting an intellectualized distance from people. Taken together, the above reports suggest that the visual interaction of mother and child in the first year of life may be a critical factor in the healthy socialization of the child. Longitudinal studies in which the visual interaction of mother and child could be compared with other developmental indices, if possible to carry out, would be very interesting indeed. One wonders, also, if it would be possible to establish meaningful relationships with hostile and withdrawn children by using behavior modification techniques to shape mutual glance behavior with a therapist.

8. Exline, R. V., and Greenberg, E., unpublished MS, 1971; see also Exline, R. V., Thibaut, J., Hickey, C. B., and Gumpert, P., 1970.

Earlier, I mentioned that our studies of young adults showed women to be much more visually interactive than men. I recently learned of a Ph.D. dissertation carried out by Nancy Russo (personal communication). Russo found that sex differences in visual interaction did not appear until around the fourth grade. It would be interesting to explore the concomitants of this apparently age-related divergence. Is it due to social pressures toward the taking of sex-roles, roles which require different emphases on dependency and autonomy behaviors? Is it related to increasing concerns with dominance hierarchies and the threat displays which seem to be triggered by extended mutual glances between primate males? Is the mutual glance somehow cortically arousing (Wada, 1961), and are males "wired up" so that such arousal becomes more intense and disturbing as they physically develop than is the case for females?

I have no answers to the above questions, neither do I know if they are the best ones to pose. Nevertheless, systematic study of age-related sex differences in willingness to engage in mutual glances strikes me as worth pursuing.

Finally there is the question of cultural relativity of eye engagement. Our studies have been limited to British and American middle-class men and women. Russo studied only American children. There are undoubtedly cultural and subcultural norms concerning the appropriateness of the extent to which we engage in mutual and even one-way glances. No doubt there are also different codes concerning the inferences to be drawn from the adherence to, and violation of, such norms. We are presently moving to investigate black-white differences among college students in the use of the line of regard, but such a study merely scratches the surface of cultural comparisons.

We have found this work fascinating and stimulating, as well as occasionally perplexing. I hope I have managed to convey to you some of the excitement we have enjoyed in our research. If some of you, after reading this paper, are motivated to improve upon our efforts, what more can an investigator ask?

REFERENCES

Ambrose, J. A. The development of the smiling response in early infancy. In B. M. Foss (Ed.), *Determinants of infant behavior*. Vol. 1. London: Methuen, 1961.

Argyle, M. *Social interaction*. New York: Atherton Press, 1969.

Argyle, M., et al. The communication of inferior and superior attitudes by verbal and non-verbal signals. *British Journal of Social and Clinical Psychology*, 1970, **9**, 222–231.

Birdwhistell, R. L. *Kinesics and context*. Philadelphia: University of Pennsylvania Press, 1970.

Broch, H. *The Sleepwalkers: A Trilogy*. New York: Pantheon Books, 1964.

Diebold, A. R. Anthropology and the comparative psychology of communicative behavior. In T. A. Sebeok (Ed.), *Animal communication: Techniques of study and results of Research*. Bloomington: Indiana University Press, 1968. Pp. 525–571.

Duncan, S. Nonverbal communication. *Psychological Bulletin*, 1969, **72**, 118–137.

Edelman, M. S., Omark, D. R., & Freedman, D. G. Dominance hierarchies in children. Unpublished manuscript, *Committee on Human Development*, University of Chicago, 1971.

Efran, J. S., & Broughton, A. Effect of expectancies for social approval on visual behavior. *Journal of Personality and Social Psychology*, 1966, **4**, 103–107.

Eimerl, S., & Devore, I. *The primates*. New York: Time, Inc., 1965.

Ekman, P. Communication through nonverbal behavior: A source of information about an interpersonal relationship. In S. S. Tomkins and C. E. Izard, *Affect, cognition, and personality*. New York: Springer, 1965. Pp. 390–442.

Ekman, P., & Friesen, W. V. Head and body cues in the judgment of emotions: A reformulation. *Perceptual and Motor Skills*, 1967, **24**, 711–724.

Ekman, P., & Friesen, W. V. The repertoire of nonverbal behavior: Categories, origins, usage, and coding. *Semiotica*, 1969, **1**, (1), 49–98.

Ellsworth, P. C., & Carlsmith, J. M. Effects of eye contact and verbal content on affective response to a dyadic interaction. *Journal of Personality and Social Psychology*, 1968, **10**, 15–20.

Elworthy, F. T. *The evil eye: The origins and practices of superstition*. London: John Murray, 1895.

Exline, R. V. Effects of need for affiliation, sex, and the sight of others upon initial communications in problem-solving groups. *Journal of Personality*, 1962, **30**, 541–556. (a)

Exline, R. V. Need affiliation and initial communication behavior in task-oriented groups characterized by low interpersonal visibility. *Psychological Reports*, 1962, **10**, 78–89. (b)

Exline, R. V. Explorations in the process of person perception: Visual interaction in relation to competition, sex, and the need for affiliation. *Journal of Personality*, 1963, **31**, 1–20.

Exline, R. V., & Eldridge, C. Effects of two patterns of a speaker's visual behavior on the perception of the authenticity of his verbal message. Paper presented at the meeting of the Eastern Psychological Association, Boston, 1967.

Exline, R. V., Fairweather, H., Hine, J., & Argyle, M. Impressions of a listener as affected by his direction of gaze during conversation. Unpublished manuscript, University of Delaware, 1971.

Exline, R., Gray, D., & Schuette, D. Visual behavior in a dyad as affected by interview content and sex of respondent. *Journal of Personality and Social Psychology*, 1965, **1**, 201–209.

Exline, R. V., & Greenberg, E. Visual behavior in relation to the authenticity of a message in a dyad. Unpublished manuscript, University of Delaware, 1971.

Exline, R. V., & Long, B. Visual behavior in relation to power of position in legitimate and illegitimate power hierarchies. Unpublished manuscript, University of Delaware, 1971.

Exline, R. V., & Messick, D. The effects of dependency and social reinforcement upon visual behavior during an interview. *British Journal of Social and Clinical Psychology*, 1967, **6**, 256–266.

Exline, R. V., & Snadowsky, A. Anticipations of comfort with various age and sex partners according to visual behavior during speech and silence. Unpublished manuscript, University of Delaware, 1971.

Exline, R. V., Thibaut, J., Hickey, C. B., & Gumpert, P. Visual interaction in relation to Machiavellianism and an unethical act. In R. Christie & F. Geis. *Studies in Machiavellianism.* New York: Academic Press, 1970. Pp. 53–75.

Exline, R. V., & Winters, L. C. Affective relations and mutual glances in dyads. In S. S. Tomkins and C. E. Izard (Eds.), *Affect, cognition, and personality.* New York: Springer, 1965. (a)

Exline, R. V., & Winters, L. C. Effects of cognitive difficulty and cognitive style upon eye to eye contact in interviews. Paper read at Eastern Psychological Association Meetings, 1965. (b) Pp. 319–350.

Exline, R. V., & Yellin, A. Eye contact as a sign between man and monkey. Symposium on non-verbal communication, Nineteenth International Congress of Psychology, London, 1969.

Gibson, J. J., & Pick, A. D. Perception of another person's looking behavior. *American Journal of Psychology*, 1963, **76**, 86–94.

Hall, E. T. *The hidden dimension.* New York: Doubleday, 1966.

Hall, K. R. L., & Devore, I. Baboon social behavior. In I. Devore (Ed.), *Primate behavior: Field studies of monkeys and apes.* New York: Holt, Rinehart & Winston, 1965. Pp. 53–110.

Hinde, R. A., & Rowell, T. E. Communication by posture and facial expressions in the rhesus monkey (Macaca mulatta), *Proceedings of the Zoological Society of London*, 1962, **138**, 1–21.

Hutt, C., and Ounsted, C. The biological significance of gaze aversion with particular reference to the syndrome of infantile autism. *Behavioral Science.* 1966, **11**, 346–356.

Jay, Phyllis. Field studies. In A. Schrier, H. F. Harlow, & F. Stollnitz (Eds.), *Behavior of nonhuman primates: Modern research trends.* New York: Academic Press, 1965. Pp. 525–592.

Kendon, A. Some functions of gaze-direction in social interaction. *Acta Psychologica*, 1967, **26**, 22–63.

Lefcourt, H. M., & Wine, J. Internal versus external control of reinforcement and the deployment of attention in experimental situations. *Canadian Journal of Behavioral Science*, 1969, **1**, 167–181.

Magnus, H. *Die Sprache der Augen.* Wiesbaden: 1885.

Mailer, N. *The armies of the night.* New York: Signet Books, 1968.

Marsh, Nagio. *Spinsters in jeopardy.* Boston: Little, Brown, 1953.

Mehrabian, A. Inference of attitude from the posture, orientation, and distance of a communicator. *Journal of Consulting and Clinical Psychology*, 1968, **32**, 296–308. (a)

Mehrabian, A. Relationship of attitude to seat posture, orientation, and distance. *Journal of Personality and Social Psychology*, 1968, **10**, 26–33. (b)

Mehrabian, A. Significance of posture and position in the communication of attitude and status relationships. *Psychological Bulletin*, 1969, **71**, 359–372.

Ogden, A. Looks and glances. *Harper's Bazaar*, 1961, **84**, 109–110.

Osgood, C., Suci, G. J., & Tannenbaum, P. H. *The measurement of meaning.* Urbana: University of Illinois Press, 1957.

Rimland, B. *Infantile autism.* London: Methuen, 1962.

Rubin, Z. Measurement of romantic love. *Journal of Personality and Social Psychology*, 1970, **16**, 265–273.

Sartre, J. P. *Being and nothingness.* London: Methuen, 1957.

Schaller, G. *The mountain gorilla: Ecology and behavior.* Chicago: University of Chicago Press, 1963.

Scheflen, A. E. The significance of posture in communication systems. *Psychiatry*, 1964, **27**, 316–333.

Scheutze, A. Sartre's theory of the alter ego. *Philosophical and Phenomenological Research*, 1948, **9**, 181–199.

Schutz, W. C. *FIRO: A three-dimensional theory of interpersonal behavior.* New York: Holt, Rinehart & Winston, 1958.

Simmel, G. Sociology of the senses: Visual interaction. In R. E. Park & E. W. Burgess (Eds.), *Introduction to the science of sociology.* (Rev. ed.) Chicago: University of Chicago Press, 1969. Pp. 356–361.

Singer, M. T. & Wynne, L. C. Differential characteristics of childhood schizophrenics. *American Journal of Psychiatry*, 1963, **120**, 234–243.

Sommer, R. *Personal space: The behavioral basis of design.* Englewood Cliffs, N.J.: Prentice-Hall, 1969.

Strongman, K. T., & Champness, B. G. Dominance hierarchies and conflict in eye contact. *Acta Psychologica*, 1968, **28**, 376–386.

Thayer, S. The effect of interpersonal looking duration on dominance judgments. *Journal of Social Psychology*, 1969, **79**, 285–286.

Thibaut, J. W., & Kelley, H. H. *The social psychology of groups.* New York: Wiley, 1959.

Tomkins, S. S. *Affect, imagery, consciousness: The negative affects*, Vol. 2. New York: Springer, 1963.

Van Lawick–Goodall, J. *My friends the wild chimpanzees.* Washington, D.C.: National Geographic Society, 1967.

Wada, J. A. Modification of cortically induced responses in brain stem of shift of attention in monkeys. *Science*, 1961, **133**, 40–42.

Walters, R. H., & Parke, R. D. The role of the distance receptors in the development of social responsiveness. In L. P. Lipsitt & C. C. Spiker (Eds.), *Advances in child development and behavior*. New York: Academic Press, 1965. Pp. 59–96.

Wiener, M., & Mehrabian, A. *Language within language: Immediacy, a channel in verbal communication*. New York: Appleton-Century-Crofts, 1968.

Universals and Cultural Differences in Facial Expressions of Emotion[1]

PAUL EKMAN

University of California, San Francisco

Does a particular facial expression signify the same emotion for all peoples? Or does the meaning of any facial expression depend upon the culture of the expressor and the observer? Does an expression composed, for example, of a raised brow, widely opened eyes, and a dropped-open mouth always signify surprise, or only for Americans, or only for certain Americans? Might the same facial expression signify sadness for Japanese and anger for Chileans, and have no emotional connotations whatsoever in some other culture? A long-continuing dispute has been waged over the question of whether there are universal facial expressions of emotion or whether facial expression of emotion is specific to each culture.

The argument stems from differing theoretical explanations of how facial muscular movements become related to emotional states. Most universalists maintain that the same facial muscular movement is associated with the same emotion in all peoples through inheritance. Relativists view facial expression as in no way innate,

1. The research was supported by a grant from the Advanced Research Projects Agency, administered by the Air Force Office of Scientific Research, AF-AFOSR-1229-67; by a Research Scientist Development Award, 5-KO2-MHO6092; and by a research grant, MH 11976-06, from the National Institute of Mental Health. I am grateful to Wally Friesen for his contributions to the development of many parts of the theory, his collaboration in the conduct of all the research reported, and his useful comments on this article. I am also grateful to Allen Dittmann, Phoebe Ellsworth, Eleanor Heider, Jeremy Pool, and Silvan Tomkins for their comments on a draft of this article. I am also indebted to Patricia Garlan for her editorial help.

but akin to language and learned within each culture; therefore, only through a highly unlikely coincidence would a facial expression be found to have the same emotional meaning in two independent cultures.

Darwin (1872) proposed that universal facial expressions of emotion are inherited. He reasoned that at some early time in history certain facial movements were acquired to serve some biologically adaptive function, and that over countless generations their association with emotion became innate. They are now vestiges of once biologically useful movements which do communicate feelings, but which do not have as their primary purpose the "expression" of an inner state to another person. Floyd Allport (1924) agreed with Darwin's claim of universals but modified Darwin's theory as to their origin. Allport succinctly described his basic difference with Darwin as follows: "Instead of the biologically useful reaction being present in the ancestor and the expressive vestige in the descendant, we regard both these functions as present in the descendant, the former serving as a basis from which the latter develops" (p. 215).

Tomkins (1962, 1963), the most recent theorist to posit universals in facial expression, has developed the most complex and comprehensive theory to date of facial expressions of emotion. While Tomkins's main emphasis is upon the primary affects, which he considers innate, he also provides some discussion of the variables responsible for learned differences in facial expressions. Of the facial universalists, Tomkins is the least absolute; although he stresses universals, his formulation also suggests cultural variations in these innate facial expressions.

The culture-specific view received early support from Klineberg's (1938) descriptions of how the facial expressions described in Chinese literature differed from the facial behaviors associated with emotion in the Western world. Of the facial *relativists*, Klineberg is the least absolute; while stressing cultural differences, he did allow that there might be some few universal facial expressions of emotion (1940). Neither of the next two facial relativists has taken as moderate a view.

LaBarre (1947) claims that facial expressions have different meaning across cultures, provides a multitude of examples from exotic cultures, and concludes, "There is no 'natural' language of emotional gesture" (p. 55). A problem with this statement is LaBarre's failure to distinguish facial expressions of emotion from facial gestures. While some facial expressions of emotion can also be used as intentional communicative gestures to convey an explicit message (e.g., the smile), many facial gestures are independent of the facial behaviors usually considered as relevant to emotion. Such gestures as the head shake "no," raising one eyebrow, winking, etc., may well be culturally variable, while facial expressions of emotion are not. Darwin (1872) mentioned the need to distinguish between facial expressions of emotion, which are innate and universal, and facial gestures, which are learned and therefore culturally variable.

Perhaps the best known writer arguing today for the culture-specific view of facial expressions is Birdwhistell (1970). In describing the history of his own work, Birdwhistell wrote,

> When I first became interested in studying body motion ... I anticipated a research strategy which could first isolate universal signs of feeling that were species-specific. ... As research proceeded, and even before the development of kinesics, it became clear that this search for universals was culture bound. ... There are probably no universal symbols of emotional state. [1963, p. 126]

Birdwhistell cannot admit the possibility of universals in facial expressions and maintain his major central claim that facial and body behavior is a language, with the same types of units and levels of organization as spoken language, and is appropriately studied by linguistic methods.[2]

Until very recently there have been no data to resolve this dispute; each side has had to resort to anecdotes and/or systematic observations to buttress its view. The culture-specific or relativist view has been the most popular within psychology, perhaps because of antagonism toward theories which allow for innate determinants. Further, the relativist view was more congenial with the

2. Dittmann (1971), in a recent critical review of Birdwhistell's work, shows how current research on both facial expression and body movement contradicts Birdwhistell's hypothesis that this phenomenon is a language. In large part our research which will be reported in the "evidence" section of this article is a direct refutation of Birdwhistell.

impression that decades of psychological research had failed to show conclusively that facial expressions provide consistent information about emotion (cf. Hunt, 1941; Bruner & Tagiuri, 1954; Tagiuri, 1968). This interpretation of the literature has recently been substantially refuted by Ekman, Friesen, and Ellsworth (1971). The growing body of research in ethology and the increasing reputability of theories which allow for innate determinants have begun to challenge the relativist view, but the ethologists also have lacked systematic evidence of universals in facial expressions.

The purpose of this article is to provide a theoretical framework which reconciles the two sides of this controversy, and to present a series of studies from our laboratory which conclusively demonstrate the existence of universal facial expressions of emotion. First, however, we will give a short account of how we became interested in this problem.

THE DEVELOPMENT OF OUR VIEWPOINT

When we began to plan our cross-cultural research, we had done very little study of facial expressions even within any one culture. Our emphasis had been on the study of body movement in the United States. If we had a bias at the outset, it was against universals, for we were influenced by the predominant view within psychology.

Prior to planning our cross-cultural research, we had the good fortune to be loaned a large corpus of motion picture film taken by Carleton Gajdusek and Richard Sorenson of the National Institutes of Neurological Diseases and Blindness, showing the behavior of members of two different preliterate cultures in New Guinea, the South Fore and the Kukukuku (Gajdusek, 1963; Sorenson & Gajdusek, 1966). This film had been recorded over close to a 10-year period. The two cultures were very different and, at least in the early film records, few of the people shown had had much contact with Western cultures or with each other. We spent about six months inspecting the facial behavior shown in this film, utilizing slowed- and stop-motion procedures. We were struck by two "findings," which suggested that *both* the universal and relative views on facial expression might be correct. There were some facial behaviors which appeared to be very similar in both cultures, and which we felt we could correctly interpret as showing the same emotion as we had observed in U.S. subjects. There were also some facial behaviors which appeared in the films of one culture but not in the other, or which occurred in very different contexts, seemingly quite different from what we had observed in our own culture. Occasionally there was enough contextual information in the film records to suggest that our interpretations of the facial expressions of emotion were correct, and occasionally Gajdusek or Sorenson was able to provide information about what had happened before or after a given scene which corroborated our judgments of the facial expressions.

Near the end of this period of time, Silvan Tomkins visited our laboratory. We showed him some short samples of the facial behavior from each of the two cultures, providing him with no information about either of the cultures. Tomkins inferred many aspects of the differences between the two cultures in child rearing, marital practices, and adult-adult interaction, which we knew to be correct from information provided by Gajdusek and Sorenson. Tomkins showed us how he thought he made his inferences, based upon the frequency of occurrence of specific facial expressions of emotions, sequences of emotional expressions, the context in which facial expressions were shown, etc. Equally important, he pointed out some of the specific facial muscular movements upon which he based his interpretations.

These experiences convinced us that there must be both universal and culture-specific facial expressions. We set about developing a theoretical framework which could explain the occurrence of both, thus reconciling the differences in the past controversy over this issue. A briefer, less complete version of the theory to be described here was written prior to initiating any of our research, although the presentation which follows is informed by our own findings and those of others as well as by argument with colleagues about the phenomena. We owe a debt to the generosity of Gajdusek and Sorenson for lending us their films, and also for their cooperation in studies we later pursued among the South Fore of New Guinea. We are indebted to Tomkins also, not just for his wisdom, but for his interest in the research we were planning and his ability to show us some of the facial movements which distinguish among emotions.

A NEURO-CULTURAL THEORY OF FACIAL EXPRESSIONS OF EMOTION

We believe (Ekman, 1968; Ekman & Friesen, 1967, 1968, 1971) that universals occur through the operation of a facial affect program which specifies the relationship between distinctive movements of the facial muscles and particular emotions, such as happiness, sadness, anger, fear, etc. Cultural differences in facial expression occur (a) because most of the events which through learning become established as the elicitors of particular emotions will vary across cultures, (b) because the rules for controlling facial expressions in particular social settings will also vary across cultures, and (c) because some of the consequences of emotional arousal will also vary with culture.

We have called our theory *neuro-cultural* because it emphasizes two very different sets of determinants of facial expressions, one which is responsible for universals and the other for cultural differences. *Neuro* refers to the facial affect program—the relationships between particular emotions and the firing of a particular pattern of facial muscles. This program, as we will explain, is at least partly innate, and can sometimes be activated with relatively little prior cognitive processing or evaluation. *Cultural* refers to the other set of determinants—most of the events which elicit emotion, the rules about controlling the appearance of emotion, and most of the consequences of emotion. These, we hold, are learned and vary with culture. Some of the learning experiences which establish elicitors, rules about control, and consequences are constant within a culture. Others, however, vary within a culture, for in addition to the neural determinants of facial expressions of emotion (common to all humans) and the cultural determinants (common within a culture but responsible for differences across cultures) there are psychosocial determinants of facial expressions of emotion. These determinants are responsible for differences between subcultures, social classes, age groupings, sex roles, and families, and are necessary to explain how facial expressions of emotion vary with personality. We will not discuss psychosocial considerations, however, both because they are not fundamental to the question of universal facial expressions, and because both data and theory on these matters are less developed.

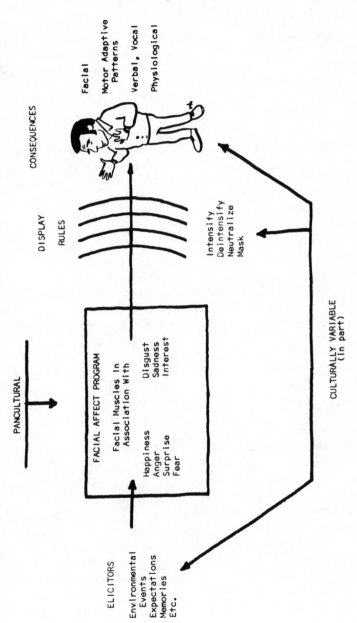

FIG. 1. Copyright © 1972 by Paul Ekman.

The term *neuro-cultural*, then, is meant to convey the two sets of determinants, and the interactions among them, which we will emphasize in explaining how universal and culture-specific facial expressions occur. Figure 1 illustrates the parts of our formulation we will discuss.

Elicitors

Emotional reactions to most events are learned, and learned in such a fashion that the elicitors will often vary with culture. All, or almost all, of the *interpersonal* elicitors of particular emotions are socially learned and therefore most will vary with culture. Some of the possible exceptions are the cry of distress in response to the mother's absence in the neonate and the fear face shown to strangers at a particular point in early infancy. More cross-cultural data on early infant facial responses to interpersonal events are needed to resolve this question.

There are certainly some *noninterpersonal* events which universally elicit a particular facial expression; e.g., tissue damage, a sudden loud noise, a bad smell, etc. For example, the nose and mouth movements in response to a bad smell or bad taste are universal. However, the disgust face is also elicited by interpersonal actions which do not involve taste or smell, and whether such a particular interpersonal action is disgusting depends upon social learning. Similarly, the startle-surprise face is elicited universally by a sudden loud sound, but which interpersonal actions are surprising depends upon social learning.

Our view of elicitors agrees with that of the relativists, and disagrees with that of some universalists. Darwin, Tomkins, and, most recently, Eibl-Eibesfeldt have claimed universal interpersonal elicitors of facial expressions. Eibl-Eibesfeldt (1970) writes of interpersonal "releasers" of facial expressions of emotion in humans. We are not as convinced as he that there is now conclusive evidence of this. Tomkins also argues for unlearned, interpersonal elicitors of facial expressions of emotion, but unlike Eibl-Eibesfeldt, he emphasizes that social learning introduces many more elicitors for each emotion. It is Tomkins's theory which led us to propose that most of the elicitors of facial expression are socially learned and may be expected to vary with culture and with social groupings within a culture; and, by late childhood, these socially learned elicitors will by sheer number overwhelm any possible unlearned elicitors. Presumably on this point relativists and most universalists would agree.

A common pitfall in cross-cultural observations of facial expressions of emotion is to forget or ignore this variability. All too often a common emotional state is inferred simply because the same event was compared. For example, at funerals Culture Y might show down-turned, partially open or trembling lips, inner corners of the brows drawn together and up, and tightened lower lids (the sad face), while Culture X might show up-turned, partially opened lips, deep nasolabial folds, wrinkling in the corners of the eyes, and bagging of the lower eyelid (the broad smiling face). Before declaring that the facial expression of sadness varies across these two cultures, it would be necessary to verify that the stimulus *funeral* normatively elicits the same emotion in the two cultures rather than being an occasion for sadness in one culture and happiness in another. It would also be necessary to ascertain whether the norms or habits regarding the control of facial expressions in this particular setting are the same or different in the two cultures being compared.

We believe that some of the relativists' observations of differences in facial expression across cultures are questionable because they did not sufficiently consider that the same event may have elicited different emotions across cultures. It would be a simpler world, not just for the relativist, but for the universalist as well, if all elicitors were pancultural. Our claim that most elicitors will vary with culture not only opens a loophole for the universalist to discount the observations of the relativist, but complicates the task for the universalist who attempts to substantiate his claim through observations of spontaneous facial expressions across cultures. Both universalist and relativist must obtain evidence, independent of facial expressions, that the events they are comparing elicit the same emotion across these cultures, or they will not obtain crucial data. If we are correct that most of the events which elicit emotion vary across cultures, this is no easy task. And, as we have mentioned, establishing that the same stimulus elicits the same emotion is not sufficient; attempts to control facial behavior and consequences must also be considered in the design of the research.

Facial Affect Program

An emotion elicited by some event, the nature of that event typically varying with culture, activates the facial affect program.[3] This program links each primary emotion to a distinctive patterned set of neural impulses to the facial muscles. When anger is elicited, one set of muscular movements will be triggered; when fear is elicited, a different set of muscle movements will be triggered, etc. It is this program which we claim is constant for all human beings. What is universal in facial expressions of emotion is the particular set of facial muscular movements triggered when a given emotion is elicited.

We refer to "triggering a set of muscular movements," or a "patterned set of neural impulses to the facial muscles," rather than "movement of facial muscles," or "changes in facial appearance," because we will presently postulate that learned habits about controlling the appearance of the face (display rules) can and often do intervene between the triggering of the facial muscles by the facial affect program and a visible change in facial appearance. It is beyond our expertise, and perhaps beyond current knowledge in neurophysiology, to speculate about where the facial affect program might be located in the brain. Our formulation does, however, depend upon certain minimal assumptions about brain functioning, and it might be well to make them explicit, so that those expert in neurophysiology can more readily determine if our assumptions are contradicted by current knowledge.

1. Cognitive processing of the eliciting stimulus may be more or

3. We have adopted the term *program* from Tomkins, although he included not only muscular facial behavior but also vascular responses, breathing, etc., within his description of the affect program. The term *program* is meant to describe a neurally coded set of instructions, or information, relating different sets of events. We hypothesize that these instructions specifying particular facial muscular movements for each emotion are genetically inherited, amplified, and elaborated by species-constant learning, and subject to suppression by species-variable social learning. The suppression, or overriding, of the affect program, on a habitual or occasional basis, will be discussed shortly under the rubric *display rules*.

less involved as a prerequisite for the activation of the facial affect program. It seems logical to expect that some of the noninterpersonal elicitors (in particular, those which are universal elicitors of facial expression) will activate the facial affect program with little or no prior cognitive processing, sorting, considering, etc. Affective responses to these elicitors may well be reflexes, or like reflexes. Interpersonal elicitors (in particular, those which are socially learned) probably involve at least some cognitive processing prior to the activation of the facial affect program. Presumably, the more complex or subtle the interpersonal event, or the more recent the social learning which established that elicitor, the more cognitive activity will precede the activation of the facial affect program. For example, a sudden loud noise may activate surprise in the affect program without much prior cognitive processing; but for the news of the day to be surprising, more cognitive processing of the input is required prior to the activation of the facial affect program. In both cases cognitive activity would occur, the difference being in its extent prior to the activation of the facial affect program.

2. Habits regarding the control of facial appearance (soon to be discussed as display rules) can interfere with the operation of the facial affect program, early or late in a sequence of internal events, in one of four ways: (a) they can prevent activation of the facial affect program with or without also preventing any other registration of emotion; or (b) if the facial affect program has been activated, they can prevent triggering of the facial muscles; or (c) if the facial muscles have been triggered, they can either interrupt the muscular contractions, making the appearance changes quite brief, or diminish the extent or scope of the muscular contractions, making the changes in appearance less pronounced; or (d) whether or not the facial muscles have been triggered by the facial affect program, these habits can override and thus mask with a different set of muscular contractions those directed by the affect program. We suggested earlier that the innate noninterpersonal elicitors, as well as those established by species-constant learning or very early learning experiences, would ordinarily activate the facial affect program with little or no prior cognitive processing of the eliciting stimuli. It would be logical to expect that when these elicitors are involved, habits to control facial appearance would tend not to

prevent activation of the affect program or block firing of the musculature, but more often the facial musculature would actually start to move before the control was accomplished by interruption or overriding. The same logic would suggest that for the culture-specific elicitors, where more cognitive activity precedes the activation of the facial affect program, there would be more opportunity for habitual controls of facial appearance to operate before there is any movement of the facial muscles, by preventing the activation of the facial affect program or by preventing the neural impulses, once triggered, from reaching the facial musculature. When the control of facial appearance results from well-learned habits rather than from deliberate consideration and decision, then it is more likely that the habits will operate to prevent activation of the affect program or block neural impulses from reaching the facial musculature rather than interrupting the facial muscular movement or overriding it with another facial movement.

3. Both voluntary decision and habits about the proper or expected display of affect can, without activation of the affect program, fire the facial muscles to produce visible changes closely resembling those occasioned by the facial affect program.

The facial affect program as we conceive of it links each emotion to a different pattern of neural impulses to the facial musculature. It is necessary to attempt to explain how the particular linkages came about. For example, why are the brows raised in surprise and lowered and drawn together in anger? Why does the program not contain just the reverse linkage? The relativists, who dispute the notion of a facial affect program, would not expect an invariant linkage; for them surprise might be shown with a lowered brow in one culture and with a raised brow in another. A plausible account of how a particular set of invariant linkages might have originated will make the postulation of an affect program more persuasive.

A number of theorists (Darwin, 1872; Allport, 1924; Huber, 1931; Andrew, 1963, 1965; Tomkins, 1962, 1963) have considered this question and have offered somewhat different explanations. We will distinguish four related and nonexclusive alternative accounts of the origin of the linkage between particular facial muscular movements and particular emotions.

1. The physiological-anatomical construction of the human organism requires certain movements of the facial musculature in response to certain stimuli in order to perform actions necessary for life. The facial movement is part or all of a specific adaptive pattern, and that pattern itself could be considered the emotion or its prototype. Let us take the example of the facial muscular movements anatomically required to regurgitate matter from the oral cavity. A specific event, some trouble with matter in the oral cavity, is followed by regurgitation and there is a facial muscular movement which is part of regurgitation. Some theorists would call that facial muscular movement during regurgitation the emotion of disgust. For others it is the prototype for disgust; it is the basis for the development of disgust. In the next step in the development of the emotion, some stimuli will become anticipatory cues for the total action pattern in question, and after a period of learning, these anticipatory events will regularly elicit all or part of the facial muscular action without performance of the total adaptive pattern. Returning to our example of disgust, bad tastes or bad smells or strange-looking food will, through learning, become elicitors of the disgust face, without any regurgitation occurring. All members of the species will have such anticipatory learning experiences, although the particular stimuli which become established as elicitors will vary depending upon the circumstances of the learner. The next step in the development of the emotion is that, through social learning, objects, ideas, persons, personal actions, etc., which are analogically or associatively related to the original elicitor or the anticipatory elicitors, will now call forth the facial muscular response. In terms of our example, an immoral idea may "smell fishy" and become through social learning an elicitor for the disgust face. Theorists have differed in terms of (a) whether the whole sequence or only the last step is called an emotion; (b) whether the whole sequence is innate, or only the first part, which requires the muscular movement for an adaptive action; and (c) whether the communicative value of the facial muscular movement in informing others about the inner state and probable action of the person is considered to play any role in this muscular pattern becoming innate.

2. This explanatory principle is quite similar to the preceding

one; it differs only in that the facial muscular action which is physiologically-anatomically required is part of a less specific adaptive sequence. Let us take the example of pressing the lips tightly together during great physical exertion. This movement is considered to be part of an adaptive sequence in which the tight pressure of the lips helps to force air back toward the lungs to prevent rupture of the capillaries during exertion. The facial muscular movement of closed-mouth lip pressure is not only the prototype of an emotion; while it will occur during attack and on that basis is seen in the anger facial expression, it will also occur when a person lifts a heavy object. In this sense, this facial action differs from the regurgitation facial action where the facial muscular movement is relevant only to the act of regurgitating; the lip closure occurs with attack but it also occurs with any physical exertion. It is part of a less specific adaptive action. All that is necessary to account for the presence of this facial movement in the anger facial expression is its physiological-anatomical necessity during attack. Through learning, this facial action will be elicited by events which anticipate the likelihood of attacking; and, again through social learning, other events, related analogically or associatively, will elicit this component of the anger face, when no attack subsequently occurs. As with the first principle, theorists disagree about how much of this is inherited, at what point to call the facial muscular movement an emotion, and whether the communicative value of the facial movement is relevant to its becoming innate.

3. Certain facial muscular movements are innately associated with emotions because of their survival value in signaling the intention of the organism. This principle differs from the first two in that the communicative value is primary in the association of a facial muscular movement with an emotion. However, like the first two, this principle postulates that the movement is not an arbitrary one, but part of an adaptive pattern, namely the early or preparatory part of the total action pattern; it serves to signal what is coming next, or the intention of the organism. The raised upper lip is part of the anger face in man and other animals because of its signal value, namely, the intention to bite.

It would be possible to develop this principle solely in terms of learning, assuming nothing more to be innate than that the lip is raised in biting, and prior to biting. Those who bite when they attack would learn through the response of others to raise the lip as a warning. But that is not how this principle has been explained by past theorists. Their assumption has been that over the course of evolution this action has become innate. When the organism is prone to attack, this facial muscular movement will occur, and through learning, other events will become established as elicitors of this response, much as we have outlined for the first two principles.

4. Certain facial muscular movements are programmed for a particular emotion because they are the opposite of other facial appearances (these other appearances having been programmed according to one of the first three principles). Two different explanations have been offered as to why an opposite movement would be made: (a) when an emotion is experienced which is opposite to another emotion, it is "natural" to assume an opposite facial appearance (Darwin's principle of antithesis); (b) a facial movement which stands in marked contrast to all other facial movements has a distinctive signal value. Some theorists explain the smile in happiness by this principle as being the appearance most unlike all of the negative emotion appearances; other theorists explain the smile according to one of the three other principles.

In integrating past speculations about the development of a facial affect program, we have outlined four alternative, nonexclusive views. Certainly much more information is needed about the early development of facial expressions in humans and in other animals. We have presented these speculations about the origins of a facial affect program only to indicate that there are plausible, if crude, explanations available. Later we will discuss in detail a body of evidence which consistently demonstrates the existence of universal facial expressions of emotion, thereby requiring the postulation of some such common facial affect program and raising the question of how invariant linkages between emotions and the triggering of particular facial muscles might originate.

In Figure 1 we have listed seven emotions within the facial affect program. This list (happiness, sadness, anger, disgust, fear, surprise, and interest) reflects both our theoretical orientation and our empirical results. The list is close to that of the emotion categories consistently found by all investigators within Western cultures who have, over a 30-year period, attempted to determine how many categories of emotion can be judged from the face (cf. Ekman, Friesen, & Ellsworth, 1971, Ch. 13).

It is not important whether there might be one or two more emotions than those listed, or one or two less. The central idea is that there are separate emotions (and not merely pleasant and unpleasant feeling states), which have distinguishable facial appearances. Later we shall describe the specific facial behaviors which distinguish among these emotions and present our evidence to suggest that these descriptions of the distinctive facial behaviors are correct.

The facial affect program links each of the emotions listed in Figure 1 with a distinctive pattern of neural impulses sent to the facial musculature which can result in a distinctive facial appearance. These emotions can be considered primary or basic states. It is necessary to distinguish them from what can be called secondary, blend, or multiple emotions. Without postulating the existence of blended expressions which present various mixtures of the primary emotions, we would not be able to account for the host of complex facial expressions of emotions and of emotion words, which far exceed the small list of primary emotions. For example, some mixture of happiness and anger (primary emotions) could account for the blend emotion of *smugness*.

Plutchik (1962) began research on the language of emotion to show that a limited number of primary emotion labels could account for a large number of complex blends, but that research was not completed. There is no definitive evidence on either the vocabulary or the facial expression of emotion to verify which are primary and which are blends. Nummenmaa (1964) and Ekman and Friesen (1970) did, however, obtain evidence to show that blends of facial expressions do occur, finding that still photographs of the face can convey information about two primary emotions to observers and verifying which parts of the face conveyed each of the primary emotions. Let us consider briefly how blends may be manifest in facial expressions, and then, relevant to our formulation here, whether blends are likely to be universal or culture-specific.

Blends may be manifest in four ways. (a) The very rapid succession of two primary facial expressions of emotion may for the observer appear as a blend. (b) There may be a division of labor across different muscle groups so that one emotion is shown in one area of the face while another emotion is shown in another facial area. (c) There may be a division of labor across the right and left sides of the face, so that one side shows one emotion, and the other side the other emotion. (d) Within each muscle group there may be a movement which is not the result of either of the primary emotions involved, but the product of the two sets of muscular movements which has an appearance dissimilar from each. The investigators who have studied this problem, including ourselves, have examined only the second type of blend; the other types are theoretically possible, but to our knowledge no one has demonstrated their occurrence.

It is likely that there is much more cultural variability in blend facial expressions than in facial expressions of primary emotions. Let us consider how each of three conceivable routes for the appearance of a blend suggests that blends are probably culture-specific.

1. An event may elicit two emotions, not one; winning the sweepstakes might commonly elicit both surprise and happiness rather than either separately or in time-separated sequence. We have argued that most elicitors of facial expression will vary with culture, though a few may be invariant and some may call forth the same emotion in any group of cultures being studied. The odds are against finding events which elicit the same primary emotion across two cultures, and the odds are even greater against finding events which will elicit the same blends across any two cultures.

2. Efforts to disguise a facial expression by overriding a felt emotion with the appearance of a presumably more acceptable facial expression may result in a blend. If we are trying to conceal our anger with a smile we may have an anger-happiness blend, and look smug. In order for blends due to masking to be the same across two cultures it is not only necessary that in both cultures an event elicit the same primary emotion, but that in both cultures the situation call forth the same display rule, specifying masking with the same overriding expression.

3. Feelings we have learned about our feelings may result in a blend. An event may elicit one emotion, and we may have a learned reaction about having that particular emotional response to that

particular elicitor; if the feeling about the feeling occurs quickly, the face may show the blend of both the original and the reactive feeling.[4] For example, a teacher becomes angry at an obstreperous child, immediately feels disgusted at himself for becoming angry, and shows the anger-disgust blend. In order for blends due to feelings about feelings to be the same across two cultures it is not only necessary that in both cultures an event elicit the same primary emotion, but that in both cultures habits associate the same feeling with the primary emotion.

While it may be difficult to ascertain in any given instance the basis of a particular blended facial expression, we must expect, then, that when facial expressions are compared across two or more cultures in a situation which elicits at least one common emotion for all the cultures being examined, it is probable that the blend will be more culturally variable than the expression of a single emotion. This is not to suggest that when the same blend occurs in two cultures it must look dissimilar; it could be the same, combined of the same muscular movements, or it could differ, reflecting a different anatomical combination. For example, the fear-surprise blend can occur with the muscular movements for surprise shown in the lower half of the face and eyes, and fear displayed in the brows, or with fear shown in the lower face and surprise in the eyes-lids and brow. It may be that there are particular blends which occur with a high frequency in one culture and have their own name, but which are rarely seen in another culture, are not named, and would not be readily interpreted.[5]

In the next two sections of our discussion (display rules and consequences) we will elaborate on the mechanisms which underlie the second and third explanations of blend faces. We will in those discussions emphasize that both depend on habits which are socially learned and will often vary across cultures as well as within cultures.

---

4. While some feelings about feelings may be shared within any one culture, presumably they also vary considerably among different members of a culture. The habitual feelings about feelings which characterize a particular individual are probably related to family background and early personal experience and are explicable in terms of personality.

5. It is our impression from our study of Gajdusek and Sorenson's films that the Kukukuku of New Guinea often show a happy-sad blend which is rarely seen in other cultures.

Display Rules[6]

Returning to Figure 1, an elicitor, which usually will be culturally variable, activates the facial affect program, which is universal;
but before we can deal with the observable facial appearance, we
must consider an interference system, which we have called a
system of display rules. The idea that man can and typically does
exercise some control over his facial expressions of emotion has been
frequently asserted by past writers, who suggest that this circumstance may obscure findings within as well as across cultures
(Murphy, Murphy, & Newcomb, 1937; Klineberg, 1940; Hebb,
1946; Asch, 1952; Honkavarra, 1961; Plutchik, 1962; Tomkins,
1962, 1963; Ekman, Friesen, & Ellsworth, 1971). Most investigations, however, have been conducted as if facial expression of
emotion were an involuntary output system. We (Ekman, 1968;
Ekman & Friesen, 1969a, 1969b) have described four *management
techniques* for controlling facial behavior: (a) intensifying a felt
emotion; (b) deintensifying a felt emotion; (c) neutralizing a
felt emotion; and (d) masking a felt emotion with the facial configuration associated with a different emotion. We have hypothesized that these management techniques for controlling facial
appearance are operative in most social situations. The concept of
display rules concerns what has been learned, presumably fairly early
in life, about which management techniques to be applied by
whom, to which emotions, under what circumstances. Display
rules may take account of four characteristics in specifying when
and by whom a management technique is to be applied: (a) static
personal characteristics (e.g., age, sex, and body size); (b) static
social characteristics (e.g., ecological factors; the social definition
of the situation, such as funeral, job interview, or a party; enduring
interpersonal relationships); (c) transient personal characteristics

6. Our use of the word *display* may be unfortunate since we do not have in
mind most of the connotations of that word as it is used by ethologists, and even
they seem to vary considerably in just what they mean by a display (cf. Hinde,
1966; Lorenz, 1970; Marler, 1959; Morris, 1970). Since we already have published
our ideas about the control of facial appearance under the rubric *display rules*, we
are reluctant to change phrases now. It should be clear, however, that in the use of
display we are referring only to appearance; display rules are rules about the appearance of the face.

(e.g., role, attitude); and (d) transient interaction regularities (e.g., entrances, exits; listening, talking; in play, out of play).

Display rules govern facial behavior on a habitual basis. Rarely will a person pause to consider what display rule to follow; such a pause would indicate that there is no display rule, or that something is ambiguous in the situation and the person does not know which display rule to follow. The operation of display rules is more noticeable when they are violated than when properly applied.

Some examples may help clarify and lend credence to this concept. Middle-class, white, adult, urban males in the United States follow the display rule of neutralizing or masking sadness and fear in almost all public places; their female counterparts, particularly those who are in the prematron age bracket, follow the display rule of neutralizing or masking anger. In a business setting where two executives have been competing for a job promotion, the display rule specifies that when they face each other, their peers, and their employer, the winner should deintensify expressions of happiness, while the loser should deintensify, neutralize, or mask with happiness the facial expression of sadness. At beauty contests the losers at the moment of announcement must mask sadness with happiness. These instances of display rules are probably much too simple, omitting necessary information about the static personal and social characteristics and the transient personal and interaction characteristics which would be necessary to specify exactly when they are and are not applied. But the examples should suffice to clarify what we mean by a display rule.[7]

We believe that the concept of display rules has considerable utility both in explicating past observations and in planning new research on facial expression. The varying operation of display

7. In emphasizing cultural differences in display rules, we do not mean to imply that display rules are necessarily the same within a culture. Presumably display rules are learned primarily within the family and are subject to idiosyncratic factors. Personality differences would be manifest in atypical application of display rules (e.g., by someone who can never show anger toward a member of the same sex); in the overextensive application of particular management techniques across situations (e.g., by a histrionic person who always intensifies facial expressions of emotion, or by a poker-faced person who always neutralizes facial expressions of emotion); and in the failure to follow a socially salient display rule (e.g., by a person whose behavior is considered immature or unmannerly, and perhaps by one who would be considered to be showing inappropriate affect).

rules may well explain why past observations have been so contra-dictory as to whether some facial expressions are universal. There should be many differences in display rules across and within cultures. The determination of such differences should be one of the most fruitful ways to explicate the nature of cultural variations in facial expression, and is also necessary for investigators seeking evidence of universals, if the universal element of facial expression is not to be obscured by differences in display rules.

In comparisons across cultures, investigators must be wary of interpreting evidence as showing a basic difference in the muscles involved in an emotional expression, when that difference could be due to the application of different display rules in the cultures being compared. Returning to the example of the funeral discussed in connection with elicitors, let us suppose that we are comparing two cultures in which this event actually elicits sadness, and yet we observe the sad face in one culture and the happy face in another. It is possible that in one culture the display rule calls for the manage-ment technique of intensifying the expression of sadness, while in the other culture the display rule calls for masking the sad expres-sion with a pleasant countenance. If we are not alert to the possibility of such different display rules, we can be misled into believing that sadness is a culturally variable facial expression, or that the smiling face has nothing to do with the emotion of happiness for that culture.

How can an investigator guard against drawing such mistaken conclusions? If the investigator is a relativist, how can he be certain that he has obtained evidence of cultural differences in facial expres-sion of emotion which rule out any claim to a universal element? If he accepts our general framework, and wishes to attack the problem of delineating cultural differences in facial expression, what should he do? There are two approaches. One is to derive information about display rules without directly studying facial behavior. The other is to infer or test hypotheses about display rules by measurement of spontaneous facial behavior.

In the first approach, information could be obtained from informants by asking direct questions, or by describing scenes or events and requesting the informant to state what a person would do or look like, or to choose among different facial expressions. In such studies display rules would be isolated by varying the information provided to the informant about various aspects of the situation in terms of the personal and social static characteristics, and of the personal and interactive transient characteristics, and asking him to determine what facial expression might be shown. For example, the informant could be told about a situation in which an employer is angry at his employee for arriving late to work; the sex of the employer and employee could be variously identified as both male, both female, or one male and the other female, and in each permutation the informant could be asked to choose from among a set of facial expressions the one most likely to occur. Literature is also a source of such information in some cultures, as Goffmann (1963) has shown. Etiquette books may list information about some of the rules of social interaction, and perhaps may also contain more specific information about display rules.

In the second approach, some measurement could be made of facial behavior in situations which vary in terms of the four characteristics listed earlier as relevant to display rules. Such measurement would be most useful if it revealed both the elicited emotion and the operation of the management technique for modifying that emotion, as dictated by the display rule. There are three possibilities for such measurement. (a) Facial micro-expressions (Haggard & Isaacs, 1966; Ekman & Friesen, 1969a) are facial movements which are so brief in duration that they are not easily seen. With slowed-motion film projection, however, they can be seen, and measurements taken. These micro-expressions are presumed to show feelings a person is attempting to conceal. (b) Aborted facial expressions, though brief like micro-expressions, do not show a full facial expression reduced in duration, but instead an interrupted movement of the facial muscles. In the aborted facial expression, slowed-motion inspection will not reveal what emotion has been interrupted; however, the occurrence of the interruptive process can be noted. (c) Our work in progress suggests that the control of the facial muscles affects the muscles in the lower face more than the muscles around the eyelids. We are currently testing our hypothesis that the appearance of the eyelids provides information about the actual felt emotion, while the lower face shows the expression dictated by a display rule.

All three of these measurement possibilities presume that the facial muscles have been fired by the facial affect program prior to interference by the display rule. In discussing the facial affect program, we suggested that a display rule could operate after the firing of the facial muscles, or before such firing occurred. In the former case, the display rule would manage facial appearance by interrupting or overriding the facial muscular movements dictated by the facial affect program; this type of control we suggested would be more likely when the elicitor is an unlearned, noninterpersonal event and the display rule was acquired late rather than early in life. In such instances, when the display rule operates by applying a management technique after the firing of the facial muscles has occurred, the measurement procedures we described should be useful. Display rules may also operate to control facial appearance before any firing of the facial muscles occurs, preventing activation of the affect program and/or firing of the facial muscles. In such instances the elicitors will tend to be socially learned, culture-specific events, and the display rules learned early rather than late in life. When the control of facial appearance is imposed prior to the movement of the facial muscles, the procedures for measuring the facial expressions we have described would not be of use.

Consequences

The last aspect of facial expression of emotion represented in Figure 1 is the consequence of emotional arousal. Some writers have considered the distinguishing characteristic of each emotion to be a single motor adaptive pattern, shown primarily in the body rather than the face; e.g., flight for fear, attack for anger, etc. This view is held by many of those studying facial behavior in nonhuman primates and is proposed also by some of those who study facial expression in man (e.g., Frijda, 1969). While we believe it is necessary to consider motor adaptive patterns for particular emotions, the view that they are either invariant for man, or the only or primary way to distinguish among emotions, or the only important consequence of emotional arousal is far too simple.

Let us distinguish six different consequences of emotional

arousal, some of which involve the face. First we have the facial behavior dictated by the facial affect program, which will occur if there is no interference by display rules. We have already described our view that these facial movements differ for each primary emotion, and are universal. They are a consequence of emotional arousal, but as we have just emphasized in our discussion of display rules, they are not a necessary consequence of emotional arousal. The second consequence is a substitute for the first; it is the masking facial behavior imposed by display rules to override and conceal the facial expression dictated by the affect program. The third consequence also involves facial expressions of emotion but it is a reactive feeling rather than an elicited feeling; it is the feeling about the feeling. For example, anger may be elicited in a given situation, and on an habitual basis the person may have a feeling of disgust about getting angry; anger is the elicited feeling, disgust the reactive feeling about the feeling. The fourth type of consequence is a motor adaptive pattern, which may involve the face and/or the body. This is an action pattern that copes with the aroused emotion or more generally is adaptive in regard to the elicitor. There are a number of facial responses which are best conceptualized as such coping or adaptive actions; they are not part of or specific to any single primary emotion expression. For example, biting the lip, sticking out the tongue, spitting, or blowing out air can occur as a consequence to several emotions. It is important to note that the repertoire of facial action far exceeds the particular muscular movements which are specific to the primary emotions; but we shall explain more about that later.

The fifth type of consequence is verbal or vocal behavior, which may consist of words or sounds describing internal states, or giving messages to another. The last consequence of emotion arousal is physiological change, in most cases presumably not observable. There has of course been considerable argument over whether physiological changes can distinguish among all of what we have called the primary emotions, and about the role of individual differences in determining which physiological variable is most reflective of emotion.

It is our view that emotions can be distinguished to a greater or lesser extent by all of these consequences. They are different aspects of emotion as it is experienced, or can be observed or measured. In a sense they are not consequences of emotion but part of what we mean by the term *emotion*. We would not limit emotion to these consequences, for it must also include the elicitors, the affect program and other neural events, display rules and other cognitive processes involving appraisal of the elicitor, imagery, memory, etc. All of these facets have at least some importance in a theory of emotion, in the measurement of emotion, and in the phenomenology of emotional experience.

We do not believe that motor adaptive patterns, whether shown in the face or the body, are more important, central, or distinctive for each emotion than the other consequences we have outlined. Neither do we believe that most of such motor adaptive patterns are innate or, through species-constant learning, universal. There may be a few universal motor adaptive patterns and these could be found through cross-cultural studies of early infant emotional behavior, but there is no conclusive evidence for this as yet. We would expect that any such linkages between motor adaptive patterns and emotions would not be firm, but instead readily modifiable or totally replaceable by socially learned coping mechanisms. These socially learned adaptive patterns should overwhelm by force and number any possible single, built-in adaptive pattern.

Our view then is that most of the immediate behavioral consequences of an emotion—the masking facial behavior, the reactive facial behavior, the verbal-vocal behavior, and the motor adaptive patterns—are socially learned ways of coping with emotion and emotion-eliciting events. They will vary across as well as within cultures. The physiological changes which accompany emotion may be less socially programmed, although some may be subject to interference by learned habits or instituted solely by learning. And the facial expressions of emotion, we have argued, distinguish among emotions and are universal, but they can be interfered with by display rules, and elicited by culturally variable events. Let us now consider how one type of consequence, the reactive facial expressions, may complicate study of the primary, elicited facial expression of emotion.

We agree with Tomkins (1962) that people learn emotional reactions to their own emotions; e.g., once angry, we may react *to* our anger with more anger, or with fear, or disgust, or happiness, etc. While these reactive emotions are reasonably stable within the behavior of a person, accountable in terms of personality, there may also be certain common feelings about feelings among members of sex, age, social class, ethnic, or cultural groups. If we draw upon our concept of display rules, we can complicate the matter by suggesting that in some instances the initial elicited emotion will not be observable in the face because of interference by display rules dictating neutralization of the appearance of that feeling, but the feeling *about* the feeling will not be affected by any management technique and will be quite apparent. Let us assume, for example, that anger is aroused by a particular elicitor and, on the basis of habit, the person feels afraid of feeling anger in the particular social setting. There may be a display rule operable to neutralize the facial expression of anger, but no display rule for the expression of fear. So he will *look* afraid, not angry. Of course all the other permutations are conceivably equally possible. The initial emotion may be shown and the reactive emotion not, or both may be shown, or both may be disguised or controlled. Tomkins (1971) did not specify these permutations, but agrees that they are consistent with his thinking.

Let us now consider how our view of consequences of emotional arousal complicates, but hopefully illuminates, cross-cultural observations of facial expression. First, the observation of different consequential behavior following or coincident with the same facial expression of emotion in two cultures should not be regarded as ipso facto evidence that the facial expression signifies different emotions. Instead such a finding would point to an important difference between the two cultures in what has been taught about how to cope with a particular emotion in a particular setting. Returning once again to our example of the funeral, let us presume the investigator to have established that the funeral is an elicitor for sadness in the two cultures he is observing, and that in both cultures there is no display rule to disguise the facial expression of sadness at funerals by the chief mourners. Now let us suppose that at the moment when the body of the deceased is buried, a very sad face is shown by the chief mourner in both cultures, but in Culture X he beats his body with his hands, while in Culture Y he reaches out to touch those around him. Careful observation would distinguish between the pancultural sad face and the culturally variable consequences of sadness in this particular setting. It would be documentation of our claim that within and across cultures very different consequences may be learned for the same emotional state.

Our discussion of consequences of emotion suggests another more subtle source of confusion in cross-cultural observations of facial expression. The cultures compared may differ in the typically learned emotional reaction to the first emotion aroused. In the example of the funeral, though it may be known that funerals elicit sadness in the two cultures being compared, in Culture X the learned reaction to sadness among mourners at funerals may be fear, and in Culture Y, anger. If neither culture had a display rule calling for neutralization or masking of the original or the reactive facial response, Culture X would show sadness-fear, and Culture Y would show sadness-anger. That could be confusing, if the reactive emotion response followed so quickly that it was blended with the original response, changing the overall facial configuration. But it could be even more confusing; as suggested earlier, the reaction may be visible in the face when the originally aroused emotion is not. Both cultures might have a display rule to neutralize the response of sadness. In that case our observer would see fear in Culture X and anger in Culture Y.

Summary

We have suggested that the pancultural element in the facial expression of emotion is the facial affect program, which triggers a different pattern of facial muscular movements for each of a number of emotions. The activation of this affect program *can* result in a characteristic facial appearance for fear, anger, sadness, disgust, surprise, happiness, and interest for all human beings. This part of our formulation completely contradicts the theoretical positions of such facial relativists as Birdwhistell, whose conceptualizations of the cultural determinants of facial expression have, in our opinion, obscured the role of the neural determinants of facial expression, namely, the universal facial affect program.

We do not propose that this facial affect program operates in a vacuum. On the contrary, the elicitors of the emotions, the display rules which govern facial appearance, and the behavioral consequences of emotion are all shaped by culture. We introduced the concept of display rules to describe a solely cultural mechanism which can override the affect program and control facial appearance. Our discussion of elicitors and consequences, while allowing for some universals (particular events always eliciting the same emotion and particular actions always following emotional arousal), emphasized how these would be overwhelmed by the culturally determined elicitors and consequences of emotion. Our emphasis on the enormous importance of social learning in facial expression of emotion distinguishes our theory from that of those universalists whose concept of the mechanisms responsible for pancultural expressions of emotion obscures the major sources of cultural differences in facial expression.

While the facial affect program provides the basic building blocks of facial expression, the sources of cultural variability are so many that it is exceedingly difficult to observe the common facial expressions of emotion across cultures. We have not denied these culturally variable aspects of the phenomenon, but have isolated them precisely as that and not as evidence against the existence of universal facial expressions. While our own research has been devoted to the study of universals, we regard the study of cultural differences as equally important. We believe, however, that if there are universals, the most sensible research strategy calls for their isolation first. Their description in a measurable form can then facilitate observation of how these universal expressions are modified in social life across cultures.

Admittedly, our theory goes far beyond the data which we will now present. Our findings do, however, provide very strong support for universal facial expressions, and that evidence requires *some* theoretical explanation. Our theory is such an explanation, which reconciles past contradictory theories and provides ample hypotheses to account for cultural differences. One basis for evaluating a theory is its utility in guiding research. We believe our theoretical framework to have been in large part responsible for our managing to obtain evidence of universal facial expressions. We were forewarned of the ways cultural determinants could obscure any sign of the operation of an affect program, as will become clear in the following pages. Let us now turn to the evidence.

RESEARCH EVIDENCE ON UNIVERSAL FACIAL EXPRESSIONS OF EMOTION

An Overview

We will present a number of separate experiments which we have conducted over the past five years. While some of the data have already been published, most have not. We will also for the first time integrate findings across a number of separate studies, relating our results to the theoretical framework we have outlined.

We will consider first a study on the recognition of spontaneous facial expressions across two literate cultures, those of Japan and the United States. Japanese and American observers were asked to interpret the spontaneous facial expressions of Japanese and American subjects, judging whether the facial expressions had occurred while the subject was watching a stressful or nonstressful film. The results show that the facial expressions of the Americans were interpreted in the same way by the Japanese and American observers, as were the facial expressions of the Japanese. While this experiment clearly supported our assertion of a universal facial affect program, it had three limitations. First, the data could not demonstrate that the Japanese and American subjects had actually shown similar facial expressions, but only that whatever facial expressions were shown were interpreted similarly by observers from the two cultures. Second, since the observers had been required to judge only whether the facial behavior had been shown during stress, the results could not establish that facial expressions were universally associated with *specific* emotions, but only that the *gross* distinction between pleasant and unpleasant emotions was comparably drawn across cultures. Third, because the members of these two cultures have had considerable visual contact with each other, the evidence could not rule out the possibility that members of the two cultures had learned how to recognize each other's unique facial expressions.

The second, third, and fourth experiments each address and resolve one or more of these limitations, consistently building evidence for universal facial expressions of emotion. The second experiment overcomes the first two limitations, demonstrating by actual measurement of the facial behavior of the American and Japanese subjects that very similar facial expressions were shown, and that these were specific emotional expressions, not a generalized unpleasant state. The third experiment addresses the second limitation, demonstrating that for happiness, sadness, anger, fear, surprise, and disgust the same facial expression is interpreted as showing the same emotion in Brazil, Argentina, Chile, the United States, and Japan. The last experiment addresses the third limitation, demonstrating that the same facial expressions are interpreted as showing the same emotions by members of two fairly isolated preliterate cultures.

Before turning to each of these experiments, we will first discuss two general methods which can be used in research on facial expression, both of which were employed in the series of experiments. One we have called a *components* approach and the other a *judgment* approach (cf. Ekman, Friesen, & Ellsworth, 1971, Ch. 6; also Ekman, 1965; and Ekman & Friesen, 1968, where these two methods were described for the study of body movement, utilizing the term *indicative* rather than *components*, and *communicative* rather than *judgment*).

In a components approach, facial behavior is treated as a response and is directly measured. There are two fundamental questions which can be answered through a components approach. Do the measurements of facial behavior differ depending upon *when* the behavior occurred, or *who* showed it? An example of the first type of question is whether the brow is more elevated when people watch stress films than pleasant films. An example of the second type of question is whether there is a difference between Japanese and American subjects in the frequency of brow elevations when watching stress films.

In a judgment approach, facial behavior is treated as a stimulus and observers are asked to judge emotion from viewing the facial behavior. There are three fundamental questions which can be answered through a judgment approach. Can observers make accurate judgments of facial behavior? Are some observers better than others? Are some subjects more accurately judged than others? An example of the first type of question is whether observers can correctly determine which facial expressions occurred while subjects watched a stress film and which occurred while subjects watched a pleasant film. An example of the second type of question is whether females are more accurate observers than males. An example of the third type of question is whether the facial expressions of American subjects are more accurately judged than the facial expressions of Japanese subjects, regardless of the culture of the observers.

Components studies of facial expression have been rare,[8] despite the fact that judgment studies, of which there have been many, are quite subject to confused results and error in interpretation. In fact, the judgment approach has been the bête noire of some investigators, primarily linguists and ethologists interested in the face, who have failed to understand what results from this method mean. The judgment approach can tell us much about the face, if the implications of positive results are clearly understood in relationship to facial components.

Let us take as an example the first experiment, shortly to be discussed in detail, in which observers in two cultures were asked to judge whether facial expressions of the subjects had been videotaped while they were watching a stress- or non-stress-inducing film. This study contains an accuracy question. Can observers determine the eliciting circumstance from samples of facial behavior? And it contains a question regarding universals. Can observers make accurate judgments only for their own countrymen?

Positive results would logically prove four propositions, two of which have nothing to do with the *judgment* of the face but pertain to the actual *expressions* shown by the face. If observers in one culture make accurate judgments, that is, if they can distinguish which facial behavior occurred during stress, then these two propositions would be proved: (a) *Facial expressions* are not random but at least some facial expressions are systematically related to an eliciting circumstance (in this case, watching stress films). If they were random, observers would make no better than chance judgment. (b) *Observers* have by some means learned prior to the experiment

8. Understandably so, because of the lack of any proven systematic method for measuring the face, and the enormous amount of time involved in taking facial measurements.

what at least some facial behaviors mean, and they share this knowledge. If they did not, their judgments would disagree.

If observers in two cultures make accurate judgments regardless of the culture of the person they judge, and if their judgments are highly intercorrelated, then two more propositions are demonstrated: (a) *Facial expressions* in both cultures are not random, but in both cultures are systematically related to the same eliciting circumstance. (As we shall see later, this is not proof that the same facial behavior necessarily occurs in both cultures.) (b) *Observers* in both cultures have by some means learned prior to the experiment what some facial behaviors mean, and must utilize the same set of interpretive rules.[9]

Let us now compare the judgment method with the components method, for findings from the two are not necessarily redundant. It is possible to obtain positive results with one method and negative results with the other, because each method has its own shortcomings. The facial behavior of members of two cultures might through measurement be shown to be highly similar, yet observers from each culture might make different judgments between the facial behavior of their own and another culture. This could occur if (a) the observers themselves (in either or both cultures) have some stereotype, not based on fact, about what facial behavior signifies when it is shown by members of the other culture; then, even though they saw the same facial behavior in the other culture as in their own, they would interpret it differently; (b) the observers (in either or both cultures) do not base their judgments on the same behaviors as those scored in the measurement procedure, but either do not know what facial behavior to look for, or respond to some other set of cues, e.g., physiognomic variations.

It is also possible for the judgment approach to provide positive findings and the components approach, negative findings. In a judgment approach, it could be shown that observers in each

9. Phoebe Ellsworth has questioned this logical inference, since it would be possible for observers in one culture to regard only the eyes or forehead and those in the other culture to regard only the lower face. If this were to occur, then it would be possible for observers in both cultures to make accurate judgments without having any shared interpretive rules, since they essentially were obtaining or selecting different parts of the face as input. We consider this possible but extremely unlikely.

culture are able to judge accurately members of both their own and the other culture, yet the measurement approach might fail to show similarities across cultures. That would occur for one of two reasons: (a) The observers were recognizing behaviors which the measurement system failed to score, perhaps because its units were too small, too large, or just irrelevant. (b) Different emotional reactions were elicited in the two cultures and were accurately interpreted by the observers as being stress reactions, but the measurement of the facial behavior permitted finer distinctions which correctly reflected those different facial expressions. For example, if the stress film elicits fear in one culture and sadness in another culture, observers might still accurately interpret both the fear faces and the sad faces as having occurred during stress, but facial measurement would reflect the differences between the fear and the sad response. It is of course possible to obtain positive results from both methods, and this is most useful not only because consistency is reassuring, but because, as will become evident when we discuss the first two experiments, somewhat different questions are asked in each.

The Recognition of Spontaneous Facial Expressions in Two Literate Cultures[10]

The basic question asked from the research materials gathered for this and the next experiment is whether there is similarity in the facial expression of emotion of Japanese and Americans. In this first experiment, the ability to recognize emotion from facial expressions of members of one's own culture is compared with the ability to recognize emotion from facial expressions of members of another culture. The accuracy of Japanese observers in judging fellow Japanese is compared with their accuracy in judging the facial expressions of Americans; and the accuracy of American observers in judging their fellow Americans is compared with their

10. This and the next experiment were collaborative studies carried out in cooperation by three research groups: my own (Ekman, W. V. Friesen, and E. J. Malmstrom), Richard Lazarus's group at the University of California, Berkeley (R. C. Lazarus, J. R. Averill, and E. M. Opton, Jr.), and Masatoshi Tomita's group at Waseda University, Tokyo (M. Tomita and M. Kodama).

accuracy in judging the facial expressions of Japanese. The second related question asked in this experiment is whether the interpretive rules for judging facial expressions can be inferred to be the same regardless of the culture of the observer. Are the judgments of the Japanese and Americans positively correlated, or is a facial expression which is accurately judged by one culture inaccurately judged by another, or judged at chance?

The relativist, who holds that all facial expressions are culture-specific, would expect a different facial "language" in each culture, and would consider it unlikely that a Japanese would know or understand American facial language, or vice versa (unless he had learned it from observation, a consideration we will discuss later). Thus, the relativist would predict: (a) observers of one culture may accurately judge the facial expressions shown by members of their own culture, but not those shown by members of another culture; and (b) a comparison of the judgments made by observers from the two cultures will yield no correlation or a negative correlation. We made the opposite predictions: (a') observers will be *no* more accurate in judging the facial expressions of members of their own than of another culture; and (b') the judgments made by observers from the two cultures will be highly positively correlated.

The sample of facial expressions of emotion to be shown to the observers in each culture was crucial. Our theoretical framework suggested that it would be difficult to obtain evidence of the universal aspects of facial expression unless the facial expressions were drawn from a situation which met three criteria: by and large, the same emotions must be elicited in both cultures; display rules to disguise the facial behavior must be inoperative or similar in their operation in the two cultures; and behavioral consequences which might obscure the facial expressions of emotion must be unlikely. A set of stress-inducing films, shown to both Japanese and American subjects, was the elicitor selected. This elicitor was chosen because Lazarus (Lazarus, Opton, Tomita, & Kodama, 1966) had obtained evidence that these films elicited a comparable verbal report of emotional arousal from Japanese and American subjects, and although there was some ambiguity in the psychophysiological measures of arousal, those data were interpreted (Averill, Opton,

& Lazarus, 1969) as allowing the inference that the stress films have common eliciting properties in these two cultures.

We were also attracted to the idea of studying Japanese subjects because of the popular belief in the inscrutability of the Japanese and the difficulty that Westerners have in seeing beneath a presumed mask. It seemed particularly interesting to attempt to obtain evidence of universals for this sample. The popular idea that the Japanese masks with politeness his facial expressions of emotion emphasized the need to try to sample facial behavior when display rules would not be operative. We attempted to accomplish this by recording the facial expressions of the subjects, in both the United States and Japan, while they were seated alone in a room rather than in the presence of others; though aware that psychophysiological measures (GSR and heart rate) were being taken, they did not know that a continuous video recording of their facial expression was being taped. Showing a film to a person while he sat by himself also seemed to be the type of elicitor unlikely to call forth behavioral consequences which would obscure the facial expressions of emotion. The main coping response we expected was for some subjects to turn away from the source of the stress, the movie screen.

One more aspect of this experiment should be emphasized at the outset, for while it is a source of strength it also is a weakness of the study. The facial expression of emotion shown to the observers in these two cultures was *spontaneous* behavior, i.e., facial behavior which occurs without prompting or request by the investigators. The virtue of utilizing spontaneous behavior rather than, for example, poses of emotion is that the behavior judged is behavior which is intrinsic to each culture. There is no need to worry about whether the results are limited to some strange set of faces "cooked up" by the investigator. What is sacrificed by this use of a spontaneous situation is specificity of emotional information. While we know which behaviors occurred during the stress film and which during a neutral film, we have no way of specifying when the subject might have felt disgusted or angry or sad or afraid, etc. This is the usual shortcoming of spontaneous eliciting circumstances; by contrast, with posing it is possible to specify exactly what face represents what emotion, but this is at the cost of having to contend with the question of whether the faces are artificial or atypical.

Twenty-five subjects were recruited from Waseda University in Japan and 25 from the University of California. An investigator from their own culture explained the experiment and attached the GSR and heart rate leads. The subjects viewed a 23-minute film containing both neutral material (a travelogue) and a series of Lazarus's stress-inducing films. The videotape records of their behavior were too long to show in their entirety to observers in each culture. Instead, we selected 1 minute from the record taped during the neutral film and 1 minute from the record taped during the stress series for each subject; the same sampling points were selected for all subjects.

Two kinescopes were made for each culture of these 1-minute samples of facial expression shown during stress and neutral film watching. Each kinescope contained a 1-minute sample of each of the 25 subjects from that culture, but it showed a given person in only one of the two conditions, neutral or stress. Four separate groups of observers in each culture (about 40 in each group) viewed the kinescopes. Two groups in Japan saw the two kinescopes of Japanese facial expressions and two other groups in Japan saw the two kinescopes of American facial expressions. The same procedure was followed in the United States. All observers were told the nature of the film-watching situation and asked to judge whether each person they saw had been watching the stress or neutral film.

Both Japanese and American observers achieved a significant but low level of accuracy in judging the facial expressions of both Japanese and American subjects. The proportion of correct judgments ranged from a low of .57 to a high of .62 (where chance would be .50); these proportions of accurate judgments for each group of observers were found by a binomial test to be significant beyond the .01 level of confidence. In looking for differences attributable to some interaction between the culture of the expresser (the person shown in the kinescope) and the culture of the observer, it is possible to make two types of comparisons. Were the observers better able to judge members of their own culture than members of the other culture? Were the American observers more accurate than the Japanese observers when judging American facial expression, and less accurate when judging Japanese facial expression? As might be expected by the limited range of accuracy scores reported earlier, none of these four comparisons yielded a significant difference (*t* tests between proportions).[11]

Since only about 60% of the judgments by the observers in either culture were correct, the possibility remained that the observers from the two cultures were correctly judging different stimulus persons. That is, most of the correct judgments of the Japanese subjects by the Japanese observers might have been for persons who were not accurately judged by the American observers. The test of this culture-specific hypothesis was to correlate the proportion of correct responses by the Japanese and the American observers on each subject. This correlation, which is also the best statistical test of our hypothesis of universal facial expressions, was made to determine if those who were judged correctly by one culture were also judged correctly by the other culture (a positive coefficient), if those judged correctly by one culture were judged incorrectly by the other (a negative coefficient), or if there was no relationship between the cultures in their judgments (a zero-order coefficient).

The correlations were both positive and high. The correlation (Pearson product-moment) between Japanese and American observers' judgments of the United States subjects' facial expressions was .86, and between their judgments of Japanese subjects' facial expressions was .79.

These findings were completely replicated in a second experiment, with different samples of facial expressions (20 additional persons from Japan and 20 from the United States) and new groups of observers in both the United States and Japan. The proportion

11. This was tested not only by calculating the proportion of correct judgments across the entire sample of facial expressions observed, but also by calculating the proportion of correct responses to each 1-minute sample of facial expression for the Japanese observers and for the American observers. A Wilcoxin matched-pairs signed-ranks test was performed, comparing Japanese with American observers in their judgment of the Japanese neutral facial expression samples, the Japanese stress facial expressions, the American neutral facial expressions, and the American stress facial expressions. Only the last comparison was statistically significant. We have relegated this result to a footnote because this evidence of a culture difference is not consistent with the findings from seven of the eight comparisons made. Further, the correlations to be reported next offer additional strong evidence that the observers from the two cultures responded similarly to the facial expressions they judged. And in a replication to be reported below, no differences between American and Japanese observers were found.

of correct judgments was about the same, from .56 to .64; and these levels of accuracy were again statistically significant. None of the comparisons within or between cultures was significant. The correlations were positive and high. The correlation (Spearman rank order) between Japanese and American observers' judgments of the facial expressions of the United States subjects was .77, and of the Japanese subjects, .79.

Discussion. These findings provide strong evidence in support of our position that there are universal facial expressions of emotion. There was no evidence to support the contention that facial expressions are so specific to each culture that only members of that culture can accurately recognize them; quite the contrary was found. Neither the culture of the observer nor the culture of the facial expresser mattered in the accurate judgment of whether facial expressions had occurred during the stress or neutral film. Facial expressions shown by Americans must have had the same meaning to Japanese observers as they had to American observers, and the same was true for the interpretation of the facial expressions of Japanese subjects. The high correlations between the judgments of the Japanese and American observers could only occur if both groups of observers similarly interpreted the behavior they viewed. When they saw a facial response in both cultures, the observers must have interpreted it as being the type of facial behavior which would occur while watching a stress film. It is reasonable to expect that they would make that decision by a reasoning process in which they judged facial behavior as showing a particular emotion, for example, disgust, and disgust as being an emotion which would be more likely to occur during a stress than a neutral film. It is true that we have no data on how they made their judgments, and thus we cannot be certain that they made such emotion-specific inferences, but the observers were told in their instructions to expect to see unpleasant reactions of various kinds for stress film–watching, and neutral, disinterested, or mildly pleasant reactions for the neutral film–watching facial expressions.

It could well be that facial response X was interpreted as showing disgust by the Japanese and anger by the American observers; then, though they differed in their interpretation of specific emotions, they would have made the same general inference, unpleasant emotion, and thus the same judgment, stress film–watching. This is a limitation of this experiment. It does not provide evidence that the two cultures necessarily interpret the same facial expressions as the same *specific* emotions, only that they interpret the same facial expressions as representing unpleasant and pleasant emotions, a more *global* distinction. In introducing the experiment, we pointed out this limitation in the use of spontaneous facial behavior. With most, if not all, elicitors of spontaneous expression there is no way to determine what specific emotion will occur. In our study, no accuracy criterion was available other than the gross distinction of whether the stress or neutral film was watched, and therefore we could not ask the observers to judge specific emotion in order to measure accuracy of judgment. The third set of experiments we will discuss overcomes this limitation by showing that observers across five literate cultures associate the same facial expressions with the same *specific* emotions.

There are further limitations on the conclusions that can be drawn from this study, both intrinsic to its design, which also allow the relativist to argue that this experiment does not disprove his claim that there are no universal facial expressions of emotion.[12] These problems stem from the visual contact between the cultures. The actual facial expressions might have been quite different, as would be expected if such behavior is a culture-specific, languagelike phenomenon. Japanese and Americans might simply have learned how to judge each others' facial language through visual contact across cultures. The response to this counterargument is actually to measure the facial behavior shown by the American and Japanese subjects and determine whether it is similar or different. The next experiment we will discuss accomplished just that.

Even if measurement establishes that the facial behavior shown by the Japanese and American subjects was quite similar, the relativist can advance another argument, again based on visual

12. While raising the counterarguments of the facial relativist is a heuristic device to facilitate discussion of the implications of our evidence, it is not merely that. In most instances, the arguments raised in the name of the relativist are based on actual discussions of each experiment with experts on facial expression who maintain the relativist point of view. We have not had the opportunity before to present first our theoretical framework and then the entire series of experiments, answering the counterarguments with data from all of the studies conducted.

contact between the cultures. He could argue that even if the same facial behavior did occur, it was because the facial language acquired in Japan and the United States is based on the same visual source. Perhaps people in both cultures learn their facial expressions by observing the same models on television; John Wayne's look of anger, not evolution or serviceable habits, may have established the facial configuration associated with that emotion. Similar facial behavior in cultures which share visual contact would therefore not prove the existence of universal facial expressions. While this claim seems farfetched in the light of all of the impressionistic observations about the differences in facial behavior between Japan and the United States, the objection has been seriously made by some, and it can only be decisively answered by data. The fourth series of experiments we will discuss was conducted to answer this objection, by studying peoples who were more visually isolated, with methods of investigation appropriate for working within preliterate cultures.

The Measurement of Spontaneous Facial Expressions in Two Literate Cultures

This experiment, like the first, was designed to determine whether facial expressions of emotion shown by members of two different cultures in a particular eliciting circumstance are the same or different. However, rather than a judgment approach, a components approach was used. The facial behavior of the Japanese and American subjects was measured directly to eliminate the possibility that the high correlations found in the first experiment were achieved because observers could interpret culturally differing facial behavior correctly, and to establish that the facial behavior (and not only the judgments) was similar across cultures. We hypothesized that the repertoire of specific facial expressions of emotion shown during the stress film would be similar between the Japanese and American subjects, and less so during the neutral film. Lazarus's prior research showed that the stress film aroused emotion and that the neutral film did not. Our predictions pertained to emotional expressions in the face, and these could be expected when the subjects watched the stress film. There would be less likelihood of any emotional reactions to the neutral film, the only possibilities being anticipations of seeing the stress film or mild happiness about the content of the neutral film. The lack of any strong emotion-arousing properties in the neutral film would increase the likelihood of idiosyncratic responses within each culture and thus reduce the chances of similarities between cultures.

In introducing the first experiment, we mentioned the potential problems which could prevent our obtaining similar facial behavior. We shall briefly review these now, because some of the sources of potential difficulty are not relevant to the use of a measurement approach but pertain only to judgment studies, and some are obviated by the positive results of the first study. We need no longer worry about whether the observers in either or both cultures might not know how to interpret facial behavior, or whether either set of observers might apply some stereotype which would cause them to interpret facial behavior differently when shown by members of their own or another culture. Nor need we worry about whether the elicitor, the stress film, aroused any distinguishable facial behavior, for if it had not, the observers would not have been able to make significantly accurate judgments and the high correlations would not have been possible. But three potential sources of difficulty remain, two of which were problematic for the first study also, and one of which is new.

1. The stress film may have elicited different emotions in the two cultures; perhaps seeing someone undergo surgery arouses negative emotions, but different negative emotions for Japanese than for American subjects. In that case, the positive findings from the judgment study would not be supported by the measurement study, which instead would indicate that the Japanese and American subjects showed different facial behavior.

2. Even if the stress film elicited the same emotion(s) in the two cultures, differences in facial behavior could occur because of differences between cultures in display rules. The judgment study could have succeeded even with some differences in display rules, but not the measurement study. For example, if the Japanese utilized the management technique of masking and the Americans did not, observers might have detected, at least in some subjects, that negative emotion was present, though masked. The measure-

ment study would reflect these differences between the cultures in facial behavior.

3. The last potential problem, unique to the use of a measurement procedure, is that the measurements themselves might not score the relevant units of facial behavior.

If we failed to support our hypothesis, if the facial behavior shown by the American and Japanese subjects was different, we would have these bases or excuses for arguing with the relativist as to whether our results support his viewpoint. However, the measurements themselves were expected to provide data relevant to whether or not different emotions were elicited and whether display rules were operable. If we proved our hypothesis by finding similarity in the facial behavior, we would succeed in forcing the relativist to modify, if not abandon, his claim. He would have to admit that the same facial "language" is employed, and while he might argue about the origin of that similar facial behavior, other data from other experiments with less visually contaminated subjects could resolve the issue. The relativist would have to acknowledge that we have shown comparable facial behavior, but he might argue about how we can be certain that our measurements actually differentiate among specific emotions. We will introduce evidence on this point and also later present another set of experiments to confirm our evidence on that point.

The sample of facial behavior of the Japanese and American subjects was larger than that shown to the observers in the previous experiments. It consisted of the last 3 minutes of each subject's facial behavior (rather than 1 minute) videotaped during the neutral film, and the entire 3 minutes recorded during the last stress film. Measurement utilized a new procedure developed by Ekman, Friesen, and Tomkins, the Facial Affect Scoring Technique (FAST). We can here provide only a brief description of this scoring procedure. Details about its derivation, use, and reliability are reported elsewhere (Ekman, Friesen, and Tomkins, 1971).

There are two separate steps in FAST measurement, location and classification. In location, scorers determine the beginning and end (and thereby the duration) of each observable movement of the face. In classification, each of these located facial events is compared with a list of items and assigned the score which represents the item it most closely resembles. Location and classification are done separately for the brows-forehead, the eyes-lids, and the lower face. When one of these facial areas is scored, the other two areas are blocked from the view of the FAST scorer. Location requires slowed- and stop-motion viewing. Classification requires consulting a list of facial items for each of the three facial areas. There are 8 items for the brows-forehead, 17 for the eyes-lids, and 59 for the lower face. Each item represents a distinctive appearance of the face. The items do not include or mention emotion, but instead describe a behavioral appearance, for example, a lip press. Most of the items are depicted visually by photographic examples; a few of the items for the lower face are instead described in words. Figure 2 shows the photographic definitions of the FAST brow-forehead items for surprise, fear, and anger.

Most of the items were based on theory, although some were empirically derived. Ekman, Friesen, and Tomkins constructed their scoring system on a priori grounds, including as facial items only behavior which they thought would distinguish among six primary emotions.

Chart 1 describes the general appearance which characterizes each of these six primary emotions, giving only enough detail to convey to the reader what we mean by a distinctive facial appearance.

These descriptions of the distinctive appearance of these emotions are of necessity oversimplified, sketching only the most obvious characteristics of the prototypical facial expression of each emotion. FAST measurement uses a more elaborate description, too lengthy and too awkward to present in words here. FAST items for each emotion include not only these elaborations but also items for measuring differences in intensity and variations associated with physiognomy. The eyes-lids and the lower face are represented by more than one item for each emotion; e.g., there are three mouth and two eye items for fear. The brows-forehead is represented by only one item for each emotion except sadness, for which there are four.

In devising FAST no attempt was made to include all facial behavior, but only that which was thought to distinguish among specific emotions. For the brows-forehead and the eyes-lids, the set

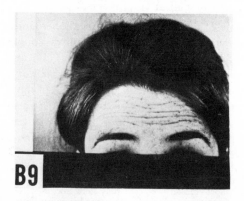

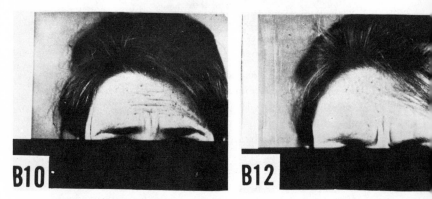

Fɪɢ. 2. Examples of the Facial Affect Scoring Technique (FAST) scoring definitions: the brows-forehead items for surprise (B9), fear (B10), and anger (B12). Copyright © 1972 by Paul Ekman.

CHART 1

APPEARANCE OF THE FACE FOR SIX EMOTIONS

	Brows-Forehead	Eyes-Lids	Lower Face
Surprise	Raised curved eyebrows; long horizontal forehead wrinkles	Wide opened eyes with schlera showing above and often below the iris; signs of skin stretched above the eyelids and to a lesser extent below	Dropped-open mouth; no stretch or tension in the corners of the lips, but lips parted; opening of the mouth may vary
Fear	Raised and drawn together brows; flattened raised appearance rather than curved; short horizontal and/or short vertical forehead wrinkles	Eyes opened, tension apparent in lower lids, which are raised more than in surprise; schlera may show above but not below iris; hard stare quality	Mouth corners drawn back, but not up or down; lips stretched; mouth may or may not be open
Anger	Brows pulled down and inward, appear to thrust forward; strong vertical, sometimes curved forehead wrinkles centered above the eyes	No schlera shows in eyes; upper lids appear lowered, tense and squared; lower lids also tensed and raised, may produce an arched appearance under eye; lid tightening may be sufficient to appear squinting	Either the lips tightly pressed together or an open, squared mouth with lips raised and/or forward; teeth may or may not show
Disgust	Brows drawn down but not together; short vertical creases may be shown in forehead and nose; horizontal and/or vertical wrinkles on bridge of nose and sides of upper nose	Lower eyelids pushed up and raised, but not tensed	Deep nasolabial fold and raising of cheeks; mouth either open with upper lip raised and lower lip forward and/or out, or closed with upper lip pushed up by raised lower lip; tongue may be visible forward in mouth near the lips, or closed with outer corners pulled slightly down

CHART 1 *(Continued)*

	Brows-Forehead	Eyes-Lids	Lower Face
Sadness	Brows drawn together with inner corners raised and outer corners lowered or level, or brows drawn down in the middle and slightly raised at inner corners; forehead shows small horizontal or lateral curved and short vertical wrinkles in center area, or shows bulge of muscular contraction above center of brow area	Eyes either glazed, with drooping upper lids and lax lower lids, or upper lids are tense and pulled up at inner corner, down at outer corner with or without lower lids tensed; eyes may be looking downward or eyes may show tears	Mouth either open with partially stretched, trembling lips, or closed with outer corners pulled slightly down
Happiness	No distinctive brow-forehead appearance	Eyes may be relaxed or neutral in appearance, or lower lids may be pushed up by lower face action, bagging the lower lids and causing eyes to be narrowed; with the latter, crow feet apparent, reaching from outer corner of eyes toward the hairline	Outer corners of lips raised, usually also drawn back; may or may not have pronounced nasolabial fold; may or may not have opening of lips and appearance of teeth

of theory-based items almost completely exhausts the anatomically possible facial appearances. For the lower face, a number of facial appearances were excluded from the list of FAST items because they were not considered to be distinctive for a particular emotion (e.g., lip bite). Since we intended in this experiment to measure all facial behavior, not just facial behavior which theoretically is relevant to emotion, we expanded the list for the lower face by empirically deriving additional items for any facial appearance which was found to occur frequently in these videotape records. There were 15 of these non-FAST items in addition to the 44 FAST items utilized in scoring the lower face. Location and classification of all facial movements which could be reliably observed was separately performed for each of the three facial areas. Three scorers independently located and classified all observable movements in each area of the face. Approximately 3 hours of scoring time were required for each minute of facial behavior; the largest fraction of this time was consumed in obtaining exact locations of events.

The most direct way to test our hypothesis was to correlate the facial measurements of the American and Japanese subjects to determine whether their facial behavior was similar during the stress film. Table 1 reports a number of different correlations (Spearman rank order). All of the correlations reported in Table 1 are based on frequency rather than duration measures; the number of times a given type of facial behavior occurred across the 25 subjects in each culture was the measure employed rather than the duration for a given type of facial behavior. Correlations were separately calculated with the duration measures, and the findings were the same as those reported in Table 1.

Results are given for facial behavior in the neutral and stress conditions for each of the three separate facial areas. Within each of these conditions the correlations were calculated on the measurements both of items and of emotions. The item correlations were based on the actual scoring items utilized in the classification of facial behavior. The emotion correlations were based on combining particular items which our theory specified as variants of the same emotion. Let us take as an example the item and emotion correla-

TABLE 1

RANK ORDER CORRELATIONS BETWEEN JAPANESE AND AMERICAN SUBJECTS OF FACIAL BEHAVIOR FREQUENCY MEASUREMENTS

	Neutral		Stress	
	Item	Emotion	Item	Emotion
Brows-Forehead	.69[a]	.97[b]	.92[b]	.86[a]
Eyes-Lids	.39	.86[a]	.72[b]	.95[a]
Lower Face	.68[b]	.75[a]	.78[b]	.96[b]

[a] $p < .05$
[b] $p < .01$

tions for the eyes-lids. There were 17 eyes-lids items. The frequency of occurrence of each of these 17 items across all Japanese subjects was correlated with that for the American subjects, separately for the neutral and stress conditions. When the correlation was calculated for emotions, the 2 eyes-lids items which our theory specifies are variants of anger were combined to yield a single anger frequency, the 3 items for happiness were combined to yield a single frequency for happiness, etc. Thus, combined item frequency scores for each emotion were obtained, and these emotion frequencies were correlated. Items, then, describe actual behavior, all of the observable facial behavior. Emotions are groups of items categorized in accordance with our theory.

With one exception, the emotion correlations are higher than the item correlations. This is because differences between cultures on specific items were eliminated or reduced when the items were grouped according to emotion. The largest such difference was in the eyes-lids-area correlations during the neutral condition. The Japanese and American subjects differed in the frequency of occurrence of those eyes-lids items which by our theory are variants on sadness. When the items were grouped into emotions, this difference in frequency was eliminated and the correlation increased from .39 on an item level to .86.

Except for this instance, the correlations on facial behavior in the three separate areas of the face for both items and emotions were high. As we had expected (and explained in introducing this experiment), these correlations were higher for the facial behavior during the stress than the neutral condition, but even for the latter the correlations were substantial.

Let us now turn from the measurement of separate facial areas to consideration of behavior where the whole face was involved. Whole faces were defined as those actions when two or three areas of the face were simultaneously in movement. When we considered these whole-face incidents on an item level, examining the particular combinations of facial items from different areas of the face, the results were idiosyncratic. In the neutral condition there were no whole-face item combinations which occurred more than twice; in the stress condition there were few (less than 5%) whole-face item combinations which were shown by more than two persons in either culture. When items were grouped into the emotion categories, however, clear results emerged for the whole faces.

The items for each area of the face were converted into emotion scores and these emotion scores were summed for a particular whole-face incident in order to classify it as either a single-emotion facial expression or a blend expression. It was classified *single emotion* if one emotion predominated in the scores for the whole face, and *blend* if two emotions had similar scores. (The formulae employed for distinguishing single from blend whole-face expressions are reported in Ekman, Friesen, and Tomkins, 1971). As had been expected, and as found for the separate areas of the face, the whole-face, single-emotion correlations were higher for the stress condition (.88) than for the neutral condition (.59). The latter correlation was not significant, the former reached the 1% level of confidence.

It was not possible to calculate a correlation coefficient for the whole-face blends in the neutral condition since there were very few blend facial expressions (five in each culture). The correlation for blend faces in the stress condition was, as predicted, quite low (.25).

When we consider the results in terms of emotion rather than of behavioral description (items), we have considerably more confidence in the whole-face data than the partial-face data. It is probably safer to say an emotional expression occurred on the face if more than one area was involved; it is less likely that the movement was a twitch or an event unrelated to emotion, and particularly if the movements, when separately and independently measured, were classified in terms of items which represent the same emotion. Table 2 reports the frequency of occurrence of whole-face, single-emotion expressions for both cultures and both conditions. (These are the figures which were utilized for calculating the whole-face, single-emotion correlations of .59 and .88.)

Table 2 shows the similarity in the relative frequency of particular emotional expressions in the two cultures; the correlations show the similarity was quite pronounced in the stress condition, and less so in the neutral condition. Table 2 provides information concerning which emotions occurred most frequently for each culture in each condition, and the opportunity to examine whether the change in emotional expressions from neutral to stress was the

TABLE 2

FREQUENCY OF TYPE OF EMOTIONAL BEHAVIOR
SHOWN IN WHOLE FACES

	Nonstress		Stress	
	U.S.	Japan	U.S.	Japan
Anger	18	5	29	28
Disgust	2	2	61	48
Fear	0	3	2	1
Happiness	7	0	8	14
Sadness	12	14	59	126
Surprise	22	6	76	50
Blends	4	5	37	52
Unclassifiable	5	5	29	24
Total Whole-face Events	70	40	301	343

same in both cultures. There was a marked increase in the total number of facial expressions shown in the stress as compared to the neutral condition *in both cultures*. This was not simply an increase in all facial expressions, but the shift in activity was related to the specific emotion involved. There was little change in the absolute number of fear expressions or happiness expressions; the largest increase was in the number of disgust expressions *in both cultures*. This is true even if the shift in total number of facial expressions is removed by converting the entries in Table 2 into percentages of the total activity shown by a culture in a condition. The largest increase from neutral to stress was in disgust faces *in both cultures*. Figure 3 shows some video frames of whole-face behavior of both Japanese and American subjects which was measured by FAST as disgust.

The last comparison between cultures also utilized the data on single-emotion, whole-face expressions. Here, the type of expressions shown by each *person* within each culture was considered. The correlations in Table 2 do not indicate whether, for example, in Japan the subjects who showed disgust also showed sadness, while in the United States those who showed disgust never showed sadness. When tallies for each emotion are made across all subjects (as in Tables 1 and 2) within a culture, such a possibility is obscured.

We assigned subjects to one of six categories on the basis of the

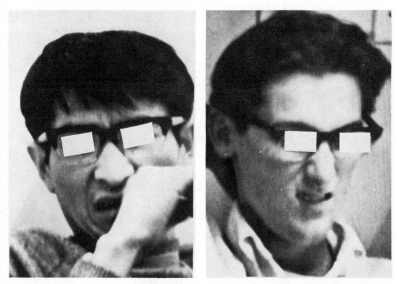

FIG. 3. Video frames of facial behavior scored by FAST as showing disgust; a Japanese subject on the left and a U.S. subject on the right. Copyright © 1972 by Paul Ekman.

different whole-face expressions shown during stress. One category was for those who showed no facial expressions of emotion. Another was for those who showed only happiness, and another for those who showed only surprise. The next three categories were based on interview material that we have been gathering on other subjects in the United States, examining their reactions to stress films which show surgical scenes of a person suffering. The interviews suggest three major emotional reactions to witnessing such stressful material: an empathetic reaction in which the person feels sadness or fear, both signs of concern for the sufferer; a disgust response, which we interpret as a lack of empathy and the product of viewing the sufferer as an object, or anger, reflecting irritation with having to see the material; and some alternation between the two. On the basis of these impressions we established three more categories: (a) disgust and/or anger but neither sadness nor fear; (b) sadness and/or fear but neither disgust nor anger; and (c) both sadness and/or fear, and disgust and/or anger. Table 3 shows the number of subjects in each culture who showed each of these six emotional reactions during the stress condition. Clearly the stress film did not elicit

TABLE 3

NUMBER OF SUBJECTS WITHIN EACH CULTURE WHO SHOWED PARTICULAR TYPES OF FACIAL EXPRESSION OF EMOTION IN THE STRESS CONDITION BASED ON WHOLE-FACE SINGLE-EMOTION DATA

	Japan	U.S.
No Whole-face Emotion Expressions	5	6
Happiness Only	2	1
Surprise Only	2	0
Disgust and/or Anger but neither Sadness nor Fear	3	4
Sadness and/or Fear but neither Disgust nor Anger	3	5
Sadness and/or Fear plus Disgust and/or Anger	10	9
Rank Order Correlation = .97		

just one type of emotional reaction, but the crucial point for our purposes here is that the same types of facial expressions of emotion were shown by about the same number of people in both cultures. The correlation between cultures calculated on these figures is extraordinarily high (.97).

Discussion. This experiment, like the first, provides strong evidence in support of our contention that there are universal facial expressions of emotion. Both experiments dealt with the same records of facial expression in the same eliciting circumstance, but different research methods were applied to address related but different questions about universal facial expressions of emotion. The first experiment disproved the notion that facial expressions are culture-specific in the sense that members of each culture can only accurately recognize the reactions of members of their own culture. Instead, the first experiment showed that the facial expressions of Japanese and Americans have a similar meaning to Japanese and American observers. But that experiment studied only the judgment of facial expression and could not tell us if the actual facial expressions shown by the Japanese and American subjects were similar. This experiment has answered that question. We have found great similarity in the facial expressions shown during the stress films in both these cultures. Whether measurements of separate facial areas or of combined activity of the total face were considered, and whether the measurements were considered on the level of specific behavioral description or integrated into emotion categories on the basis of theory, the results were the same: strikingly similar facial responses in the two cultures.

The question might be raised as to whether we have actually shown that the emotional expressions were the same in the two cultures, or only that the facial behavior was the same. How do we know that the behavior we called fear, for example, is not actually behavior unrelated to emotion, or behavior relevant to anger? Before answering this question, it is important to emphasize that even if we had only measurements which could be interpreted on the level of behavioral descriptions of the face, we have in this experiment supported our theoretical formulation of universals in facial expressions of emotion. We have shown that in a situation described by subjects as calling forth emotion, the same facial behaviors occurred in these two quite different cultures. But let us turn to the question of whether we have been able to show that specific emotions were compared, or whether the behavioral similarities we have found were again evidence only of a comparable *global* negative emotional state.

We have no direct evidence to show that the items we call fear correlate with either a subject's immediate self-report, or with the elicitation of that one emotion. (We are in the process of obtaining such validation data.) But we do have data which show that the emotion represented by each FAST item does correspond with independent judgments of emotional expressions. We utilized our scoring system to measure still photographs of the face, and converted the item measurements into our emotion categories. The FAST emotion scores correctly predicted the emotion term assigned by untrained observers to these photographs in 88% of the cases (Ekman, Friesen, & Tomkins, 1971). What FAST measures as emotion is at least valid in accounting for how people respond to facial expression when they interpret how someone feels.

While we believe this is convincing evidence in support of our claim that FAST measures specific emotions, we wanted further evidence to support our claim that there are facial expressions which are universal for specific emotions. The next experiment was designed to accomplish just that, with a very different procedure which allowed clear specification of particular emotions.

The Recognition of Facial Expressions of Emotion in Five Literate Cultures[13]

The main ambiguity in the results from the first two experiments was whether the evidence of universality was for *specific* emotional expressions or more *global* states. In the first experiment the observers' judgments of facial expression were global distinctions between negative and positive or neutral affect and no conclusion could be drawn as to whether specific facial expressions were interpreted as showing the same specific emotions in both of the cultures studied.

13. Dr. Carlos Sluzki, Centro de Investigaciones Psiquiatricas, Lanus Province of Buenos Aires, collected the data on the Argentinian and Chilean observers; we collected the data on the Brazilian and Japanese subjects with the aid of Professor Robert Berryman of the National University of Brazil and Professor Tomita of Waseda University, Japan.

In the second study it could be argued that the Facial Affect Scoring Technique is an a priori system which has not yet completely established that it validly measures specific emotions. We could only be certain that the same specific facial behaviors were shown in both cultures, not necessarily the same specific *emotional* expressions.

The purpose of this next experiment was to prove that the universality of facial expressions of emotion extends to specific emotions. This experiment was designed to show that across literate cultures people recognize the same facial expressions for happiness, anger, sadness, fear, disgust, and surprise. The relativist, of course, would expect negative results.

The most crucial aspect of the design of this experiment is how the sample of faces to be shown to observers across cultures was selected. The typical procedures utilized by other investigators were not appropriate for our purposes. Sampling pictures on the basis of the actor's intended pose (i.e., Triandis & Lambert, 1958), or showing poses which had elicited high agreement within one culture to members of another culture (i.e., Izard, 1968) would be vulnerable to the inclusion of facial expressions which were culture-specific. If an actor tried to pose fear, he might not show the presumed universal fear expression, but a reaction to trying to pose the emotion which might be recognized by members of his own culture as a fear attempt. If the reaction were culture-specific, then the recognition that he is "looking afraid" might also be culture-specific.

Another problem is that the actor when trying to pose fear might also by accident or habit show components of surprise, and the resulting face might be a fear-surprise blend. In one culture a fear-surprise face might be judged as showing fear; but in another culture the surprise element might be more salient, or the combination simply confusing.

If we were to keep emotion-related, but nonemotional, facial responses out of the set of faces to be shown across cultures, and if only faces showing a single emotion were to be included, then we could not trust either the intent of a poser or the agreement reached by observers within any one culture as the basis for selection. We needed some other means for deciding whether a face showed emotion at all, and if it showed one emotion only.

We selected faces on the basis of descriptions of the facial configurations which distinguish among emotions, concurrently being developed by Ekman, Friesen, and Tomkins for their Facial Affect Scoring Technique. The scoring procedure itself was not complete at the time, so selection could not be based on precise scoring techniques. Instead we used the cruder procedure of examining the descriptive lists of distinctive facial features while we inspected over 3,000 pictures of facial expressions, both posed (Engen, Levy, & Schlosberg, 1957; Frois-Wittmann, 1930; Tomkins & McCarter, 1964) and spontaneous (Ekman & Friesen, 1968).

Selection, then, was done by applying to each face a *theoretically* based set of criteria, which specified the presumed appearance of each emotion. No consideration was given to poser's intent or observer's judgment of emotion. An attempt was made to include faces which varied in intensity. This seemed possible for happiness, anger, and sadness, but there was little apparent variation in the intensity of the other emotions shown in the pool of photographs.

Thirty photographs met the criteria for showing a single particular emotion. These included faces of both male and female Caucasians, adults and children, with most expressions posed and a few spontaneous. Figure 4 shows some of these photographs.[14]

The pictures were shown one at a time (usually for 10 seconds each) to observers in five cultures. The observers were asked to choose from among six emotion categories the one which best described each photograph. Each category was defined by a single word in the language of the culture, except the disgust category, which contained both the word for *disgust* and the word for *contempt*. The observers were also asked to judge the intensity of the emotion on a 7-point scale.

The primary question is whether or not the same emotion was judged for the same faces by observers from the five cultures; and the secondary question is whether judgments of intensity varied with culture. Let us consider first the primary question. Table 4 lists as percentages the most frequent (modal) judgment for each of the 30

14. We selected some of Tomkins's photographs for this figure since all of the other photographs except those of Ekman and Friesen have already been published. The Ekman and Friesen photographs could not be published since they were of mental patients.

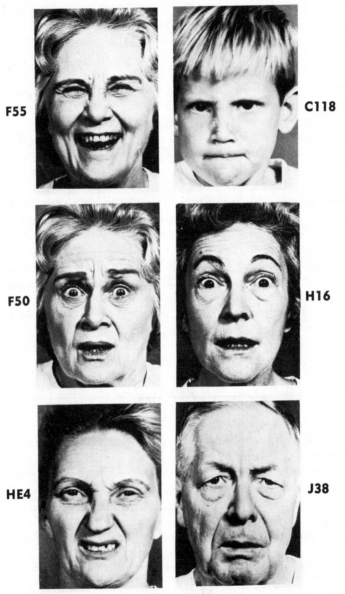

FIG. 4. Photographs from Tomkins's series utilized in cross-cultural research; observer norms on these faces reported in Table 4. Copyright © 1972 by Paul Ekman.

TABLE 4

JUDGMENTS OF EMOTION IN FIVE LITERATE CULTURES

Emotion Represented	Investigator Who Originally Obtained the Face Photograph	Identification Number of the Face	U.S. (N = 99)	Brazil (N = 40)	Chile (N = 119)	Argentina (N = 168)	Japan (N = 29)
Happiness	Ekman	26F8	100	97	93	96	97
	Ekman	26F2	92	90	76	78	44 disgust 41 happy
	Schlosberg	LF32	97	85	88	96	83
	Schlosberg	LF14	96	87	84	93	83
	Tomkins	F55	100	92	94	96	100
	Tomkins	E15	99	92	97	97	100
	Tomkins	HE32	97	95	95	98	100
	Tomkins	I18	96	95	95	98	90
Fear	Schlosberg	LF6	91	87	88	82	76
	Tomkins	F50	85	67	68	54	66
Disgust	Frois-Wittmann	15	58	72	66	59	83
	Frois-Wittmann	51	75	80	91	78	83
	Tomkins	HE4	93	90	95	92	69
	Tomkins	I57	89	95	90	87	97
	Tomkins	D10	94	82	76	68	69
	Tomkins	H53	92	97	92	92	90

Anger	Frois-Wittmann	FW39	64	90	87	75	45
	Frois-Wittmann	FW36	95	97	75	81	90
	Tomkins	H2	49	52	62	47	48 disgust / 31 anger
	Tomkins	C118	67	90	94	90	90
	Schlosberg	LF11	67	82	62	65	59
Surprise	Frois-Wittmann	27	95	87	93	95	100
	Tomkins	E34	90	77	83	89	76
	Tomkins	H16	88	80	89	95	86
Sadness	Ekman	4A2	97	87	94	84	97
	Ekman	5A15	74	82	88	79	83
	Ekman	19A1	77	67	84	88	69
	Ekman	19A5	93	88	92	95	97
	Schlosberg	LF20	87	87	94	86	45
	Schlosberg	LF49	90	95	94	96	93
	Tomkins	J38	84	59	88	78	62
	Tomkins	H47	93	88	93	95	97

faces for each of the five cultures. When the modal judgment for a face was not the emotion term which we had expected on the basis of our selection procedures, both the expected and obtained percentages are listed.

The relativist prediction would be that the 30 faces will yield different emotion judgments across the five cultures. Simply reading the entries in the table shows this did not happen. An analysis of variance utilizing the entries in Table 4 was performed to test the relativists' hypothesis that there is a difference between cultures and/or an interaction between culture and emotion judged. Neither was significant. Another contention of the relativist might be that even though the most typical (first mode) emotional meaning of the faces did not differ across the five cultures, the next most typical judgment (second mode) might. Another analysis of variance was performed utilizing the second modes rather than the first modes. Again there was no significant effect for culture nor any interaction between culture and emotion judged. For almost all of the faces, the second mode was the same across the five cultures. Since there has been some theoretical interest (Boucher & Ekman, 1965; Schlosberg, 1954) in second-mode responses as a basis for establishing relationships between emotions, we have listed those results in Table 5.

Our hypothesis, of course, was that a particular facial expression would be judged as showing the same emotion regardless of culture. Table 4 shows that this occurred for 28 of the 30 pictures; for one

TABLE 5

The Second Most Frequent Emotion Judged for Each Expression across All Five Literate Cultures

When the majority of the observers judged this emotion:	The minority of the observers judged this emotion:
Surprise	Fear
Fear	Surprise
Disgust	Sadness
Sadness	Disgust
Anger	Disgust
Happiness	Sadness: Argentina & Chile
	Disgust: U.S.A., Japan, & Brazil

TABLE 6

KAPPA COEFFICIENTS ON THE JUDGMENTS OF EMOTION FROM
FIVE LITERATE CULTURES

U.S.	.82
Brazil	.81
Chile	.80
Argentina	.82
Japan	.73

happy face and one anger face the Japanese observers differed from the other four cultures in their judgment. Chi-squares were calculated for each entry in Table 4; all but these same two were significant ($p < .01$), showing not only that the modes were the same across the cultures but that they represented a significant level of agreement within each culture. A Kappa correlation was also calculated to test our hypothesis. Within each culture the judgments obtained were compared with those expected for each set (emotion category) of photographs. The correlations, shown in Table 6, were all significant ($p < .01$), and show that within each culture the faces were judged as we had expected.

The second question asked in this experiment is whether the intensity judgments varied with the culture of the observers. The relativist would expect such differences, and our theory might suggest them also. Display rule differences between cultures *could* be such that in one culture there is typically a more overt level of emotional expression than in another, perhaps across all emotions. If so, then when observers from different cultures looked at the same expression, they might differ in their judgment of its intensity. For example, if we believe the folklore about Latin cultures, we might expect that what United States observers will judge as intense anger would be judged as only moderate anger by Brazilians or Argentinians, etc. This expectation depends upon the folklore being true and applicable to most or all emotions, and upon our showing a sufficient sampling of intensity variations. The statistical tests failed to show any difference in intensity. An analysis of variance on the mean intensity scores for the 30 photographs showed no main effect for culture and no interaction between culture and emotion judged. Further, the correlations between cultures in intensity

TABLE 7

CORRELATIONS BETWEEN MEAN INTENSITY AND
BETWEEN STANDARD DEVIATIONS ON INTENSITY JUDGMENTS

	U.S.A.	Brazil	Chile	Argentina
U.S.A.	—	78	72	82
Brazil	96	—	68	83
Chile	93	95	—	77
Argentina	96	97	97	—

judgments were extraordinarily high. Table 7 shows two sets of correlations (Pearson product-moment), the bottom set based on the mean intensity score for each face within each culture, and the top set based on the standard deviation intensity score for each face within each culture. These correlations show that the facial expressions of emotions we have studied had the same intensity value across the five literate cultures.

Discussion. These results provide very strong evidence that facial expressions are universally associated with the same specific emotions. With two exceptions, the same facial expressions were interpreted as showing happiness, fear, disgust, anger, surprise, and sadness, regardless of the language or culture of the observer. Comparable results were also obtained by Izard (1971) with his own set of facial expressions and observers from seven cultures.

For these results to be obtained, the observers in each culture must have been already familiar with these facial expressions. They must have had experiences which would cause them to associate each facial expression with a particular emotion. Furthermore, those experiences must have been quite similar across these cultures, or how can we explain that what is judged fear in one culture is not judged anger in another?

Our explanation, of course, rests on our postulated facial affect program. It is this neurally based affect program linking particular facial muscular movements with particular emotions which is responsible for the associations in all cultures between these particular facial expressions and emotions. Even though the specific elicitor for an emotion can and often will vary from culture to culture, when an emotion is aroused the same set of facial muscular movements will be fired by the affect program. It is the affect program, then, which acquaints observers in all cultures with this particular set of facial expressions; it is because of this program that observers relate these distinctive facial expressions to particular contexts described by one or another emotion term. Unfortunately there is one loophole which could be used to totally discount the evidence from this experiment and from the first two as well—visual contact among the cultures.

The relativist could argue (and has) that these findings do not prove the existence of universal facial expressions of emotion, or of any facial affect program. They only show that in cultures which have an important shared visual source (television, motion picture films, magazines, etc.), people can and do learn their facial expressions from the same mass media models, and will therefore have learned the same facial expressions. To close this loophole, we undertook an extensive study of two groups of people who have had little or no exposure to the mass media, to Caucasians, or to each other. Let us turn now to that final and crucial experiment.

The Recognition and Expression of Emotion in Two Preliterate Cultures[15]

The purpose of this experiment was to establish that the same facial expressions are associated with the same emotions in preliterate as in literate cultures. Our intent was to minimize the possibility of contamination from a common visual source. Because the subjects in the first three experiments shared exposure to the same mass media models and to members of each others' cultures, they could conceivably have learned to recognize each others' facial expressions; or perhaps they all learned their facial expressions from imitating the same mass media models. By studying subjects from remote, visually isolated, preliterate cultures, we hoped to

15. The study of the Fore which is reported here developed out of a previous study of these people in which Richard Sorenson was a coinvestigator (Ekman, Sorenson, & Friesen, 1969). We are grateful to Sorenson and to Neville Hoffman (University of Western Australia) for their help in gathering and interpreting the data reported here. Part of the Fore data has been reported on (Ekman & Freisen, 1971). The study of the Dani was pursued in cooperation with Eleanor and Karl Heider (Brown University). Ekman, Friesen, and E. Heider planned the design of that study; the Heiders collected the data, made some design decisions, and shared in the data analysis.

substantiate our earlier findings and thereby our theory that commonalities in facial expression are not an artifact of visual contact across certain cultures, but are truly universal due to the operation of a facial affect program.

Two different experiments were performed in two very different preliterate cultures in New Guinea. In the first experiment the recognition of emotion was studied, and in the second experiment the expression of emotion was studied. We will briefly describe the two cultures and then each experiment.

The first culture studied, in 1967/68, was the Fore linguistic-cultural group of the South East Highlands of New Guinea. Until 12 years ago this was an isolated, Neolithic, material culture (Gajdusek, 1963; Sorenson & Gajdusek, 1966). By the time our research began, many of these people had had extensive contact with missionaries, government workers, traders, and United States scientists; some, however, had not. We were most interested in the latter persons, and adopted the following selection criteria for participation in our research: they had seen no movies, neither spoke nor understood English or Pidgin, had not lived in any of the Western settlement or government towns, and had never worked for a Caucasian. These criteria made it unlikely that subjects would have so completely learned some foreign set of facial expressions of emotion that their judgments and expressions of emotion would be no different from those of members of literate cultures.

The second culture studied, in 1970, was the Grand Valley Dani, who live in the Central Highlands of New Guinea and speak a Papuan language which perhaps is remotely related to the language of the Fore (Heider, 1970). They live some 500 miles to the west of the Fore, in West Irian, the Indonesian half of New Guinea. Only during the 1960s did they give up intertribal warfare and stone axes. Although all of the individuals tested had seen a few Caucasians, these contacts were casual and incidental to their own way of life. They are most remarkable for their isolation and continued disinterest in European and Indonesian influences. The adolescents studied were attending school, but none had had Caucasians as teachers.

A different judgment procedure was required for working with people who did not read or write, because of the problem of appropriately describing emotion concepts in their languages. Instead of showing one facial expression at a time and asking the observer to choose a word from a list of emotion terms, as in the literate cultures, two or three faces were shown simultaneously, an emotion story was told, and the subjects were requested to point to the face which showed the emotion described in the story. (This procedure was first used by Dashiell, 1927, with young children.) Simple stories were developed within each culture to be relevant to that culture and to connote only one emotion, not a blend (details about the judgment procedure and the stories are described in Ekman & Friesen, 1971; and in Ekman, Heider, Friesen, & Heider, in preparation).

Forty photographs of 24 different persons were used in the Fore experiment, and 53 photographs of 26 different persons were used in the Dani. These photographs had been scored with the Facial Affect Scoring Technique as showing one specific emotion. Furthermore, judgment studies had found that these faces conveyed a single specific emotion to observers within at least one literate culture.

Three photographs were shown with each story to male and female adults in the Fore ($N = 189$); two photographs were shown with each story to male and female children in the Fore ($N = 130$), and to male adults ($N = 10$), male and female children ($N = 20$), and male adolescents ($N = 34$) in the Dani. To facilitate comparisons between the two cultures, we have reported in Table 8 only data derived from subjects to which two faces had been shown in the judgment task: the Fore children and the largest group of Dani, the adolescents. These results well represent the findings for the other age groups in each culture.

Each row in Table 8 is organized to show how often the observers in these preliterate cultures chose the same facial expression for a particular emotion as had members of literate cultures. For example, in the first row the figure of 92% for the Fore signifies that when the Fore were read a happiness story ("His friends have come and he is happy") and were shown a facial expression judged as happy by persons in literate cultures, and either a surprise, anger, sadness, or disgust face (as judged by literate-culture observers), 92% of their choices were of the happiness face.

TABLE 8

PERCENT OF THE JUDGMENTS BY MEMBERS OF TWO PRELITERATE
CULTURES WHERE THE FACIAL EXPRESSION OF EMOTION AGREES
WITH LITERATE CULTURE RESULTS

Emotion Described In the Story	Fore 130 Observers	Dani 34 Observers	Discriminated from:
Happiness	92	98	Surprise, Anger, Sadness, Disgust
Sadness	81	77	Anger, Fear, Disgust Dani Only: Surprise Fore Only: Happiness
Disgust	85	91	Sadness Dani Only: Happiness, Surprise, Anger
Surprise	98	89	Happiness, Fear, Disgust
Fear	88 92 100 —	80 81 — 56	Anger Sadness Disgust Surprise
Anger	— 90 — —	94 61 76 48[a]	Happiness Sadness Fear Disgust

[a] Not significant; all other figures $p < .01$.
Copyright © 1972 by Paul Ekman.

The results are very clear for both the Fore and the Dani, on happiness, sadness, disgust, and surprise. We have reported the fear and anger results in more detail because not all of these emotion discriminations were as clear. When the fear stories were read, the fear face was chosen over the anger, sadness, and disgust faces. While fear was also chosen over the surprise face by the Dani adolescents, and at a significant level, the percentage was low. The discrimination of fear from surprise was low but statistically significant in the other two Dani age groups also (59% for the adults, 63% for the young children). Unfortunately, through an oversight the fear from surprise discrimination was not tried with the Fore children; but the Fore adults were unable to make this discrimination; fear was chosen in only 43% of the trials.

When the anger stories were read, angry facial expressions were chosen instead of happy, sad, and fearful ones; but anger was not chosen more often than disgust by the Dani adolescents. The failure to choose the anger face rather than the disgust face when the anger stories were read was also evident with the adults (41%) and the young children (33%) in the Dani. This choice was not given to the Fore children, but when the Fore adults were read the anger stories they chose the angry expression (87%) rather than disgust.

The judgment studies with the Fore and the Dani provide very strong evidence of universal facial expressions. All but one of the discriminations of facial expressions of emotion made in literate cultures were also made in both of these preliterate cultures. We are presently investigating whether the failure of the Fore to discriminate fear from surprise, and of the Dani to discriminate anger from disgust, represents some facet of their culture or is instead an artifact of the research procedure.

In the second study of the expression of emotion, other members of these two cultures, who had not seen the photographs of facial expressions, were the subjects. Each subject was asked to show how his face would appear if he was the person described in one of the emotion stories. Videotape recordings were made of the attempts to show emotions in the face. Only the records of the Fore have been analyzed to date.

Unedited videotapes of nine members of the Fore were shown to 34 college students in the United States, who were asked to judge what emotion was being expressed. Figure 5 shows some frames from the videotapes of these poses.

Table 9 shows that these American college students, who had never seen any New Guineans, were able to accurately judge the emotion intended by the Fore for four of the six emotions. Happiness, anger, disgust, and sadness were correctly judged, while fear and surprise were not judged accurately. The fear poses were just as often judged surprise as fear, and similarly, the surprise poses were just as often called fear as surprise. Interestingly, as Table 8 showed, fear and surprise were the emotions which the Fore had difficulty in discriminating.

While the level of accuracy achieved in the judgments of happiness, anger, disgust, and sadness was not very high, it was far better than chance. It should be noted that the Fore were not a select

HAPPY   **SAD**

ANGER   **DISGUST**

FIG. 5. Video frames of attempts to pose emotion by subjects from the Fore of New Guinea. Copyright © 1972 by Paul Ekman.

TABLE 9
PERCENT CORRECT JUDGMENTS
BY U.S. OBSERVERS
OF FORE FACIAL EXPRESSIONS

Emotion Intended by the Fore	
Happiness	73[a]
Anger	51[a]
Disgust	46[a]
Sadness	68[a]
Surprise	27 not significant
Fear	18 not significant

[a] $p < .01$, binomial test assuming chance to be one-in-six.

Copyright © 1972 by Paul Ekman.

sample of experienced actors, and that the unedited videotapes showed not just the attempts to express each emotion (which we selected to show in Figure 5) but the embarrassment, confusion, frustration, or nervousness of the subjects in reaction to the task and the comments on their performance by their friends who were looking on.

Discussion. We interpret these findings on both the recognition and expression of emotion as clear evidence of universal facial expressions of emotion. The data disprove the argument that our findings from the first three experiments are attributable solely to visual contact among the literate cultures. We have now shown the same facial expressions of emotion in these visually isolated, pre-literate cultures, where the people did not have the opportunity to learn some foreign set of facial expressions from the mass media.

The only way to dismiss this evidence would be to claim that even though these New Guineans· were quite isolated they still had seen some Caucasians, sufficient for them to learn to recognize and express uniquely Western facial expressions. This argument seems highly implausible for two reasons. (a) The criteria for selecting subjects in the Fore and the isolation of the Dani make it highly unlikely that they could have learned a "foreign" set of facial expressions so well that they could not only recognize them, but also express them as well as those to whom such facial expressions were native. (b) Contact with Caucasians did not have much influence on the judgment of emotion. The Fore women, who have had even less contact with Caucasians than the men, did as well in recognizing emotion; in the Fore, a control group of persons who were most Westernized (had been to mission schools, had seen movies, and spoke English) did no better than the least Westernized Fore and, like the latter, failed to distinguish fear from surprise; and the Dani, who have had much less contact with Caucasians than the Fore, did no worse.

A last point which could be raised to discredit the results is the possibility that the investigators might have unwittingly influenced the subjects or the translators to give the preferred response. Precautions were taken in the conduct of these studies to guard against experimenter bias, but the best protection is to have investigators with a different bias or no bias. While the Fore data were gathered by investigators who by that point did believe there are universal facial expressions (Ekman and Friesen), the Dani data were gathered by investigators who had no such commitment and were at least mildly skeptical about universal facial expressions at the time (Eleanor and Karl Heider).

Conclusion

The evidence is remarkably consistent from the four experiments and, in our evaluation, conclusively proves that there are universal facial expressions of emotion. We have reported data on five literate cultures, four Western and one Eastern, and on two preliterate cultures from New Guinea. The samples were drawn from six different language groups: Dani, English, Fore, Japanese, Portuguese, and Spanish. The first experiment studied judgment of spontaneous facial expressions in Japan and the United States, showing that these facial expressions were judged the same way by members of both cultures. In the second experiment we then showed through measurement that the same facial behaviors (and, perhaps we can also say, the same specific emotional expressions) characterized the Japanese and American reactions to a stress film. Further evidence of the universality of facial expressions of emotion was obtained in the third experiment, which showed that the same facial expression was interpreted as showing the same emotion in five literate cultures.

The possibility that these findings might not reflect the operation of a facial affect program, but that facial expressions are pancultural only among people who have had sufficient visual contact to learn each others' facial expressions or learn common expressions from mass media models, was eliminated in studies of two visually isolated, preliterate cultures. The same facial expressions were found for the same emotions among these people who had no opportunity to learn Western or Eastern facial expressions from the mass media and who had seen so few Caucasians that it was unlikely that they could have learned a foreign facial language.

We believe, then, that we have isolated and demonstrated the basic set of universal facial expressions of emotion. They are not a language which varies from one place to another; one need not be taught a totally new set of muscular movements and a totally new set of rules for interpreting facial behavior if one travels from one culture to another. While facial expressions of emotion will often be culture-specific because of differences in elicitors, display rules, and consequences, there is also a pancultural set of facial expressions of emotion.

Let us briefly mention evidence gathered by other investigators which is consistent with our data and our neuro-cultural theory of facial expressions. Two investigators have conducted studies similar to our third experiment. Dickey and Knower (1941) found that Mexicans and Americans interpreted facial expressions as showing the same emotions. Izard (1971) also found this among observers from the United States, England, Germany, Spain, France, Switzerland, Greece, and Japan.

Some investigators have compared blind with sighted children to determine if similar facial expressions occur when there is no opportunity for imitative learning (Eibl-Eibesfeldt, 1970; Fulcher, 1942; Goodenough, 1932; Thompson, 1941). While the absence of vision does not rule out opportunities for the child's facial behavior to be influenced by sighted adults, the evidence of similar facial expressions in blind children does contribute to a formulation which emphasizes that facial expressions are not entirely based on imitative learning.

A last source of complementary findings is the field studies of Eibl-Eibesfeldt (1970). While we consider his evidence on facial expressions of emotion in humans as more illustrative than definitive, he has obtained impressive examples of similar facial expressions of emotion in many different preliterate cultures. Working from an ethological perspective, utilizing very different methods and rules of evidence, and with no knowledge of our work until recently, Eibl-Eibesfeldt has also concluded that there are universal facial expressions of emotion.

Our findings, supported by those of others, now provide the basis for settling the old dispute as to whether facial expressions are completely specific to each culture or totally universal. Our neuro-cultural theory maintains there are both universal and culture-specific expressions. The evidence now proves the existence of universal facial expressions. These findings require the postulation of some mechanism to explain why the same facial behavior is associated with the same emotion for all peoples. Why are observers in all these cultures familiar with a particular set of facial expressions (a set which is only a fraction of the anatomically possible facial muscular configurations)? But they are not merely familiar with these facial expressions. Regardless of the language, of whether the culture is Western or Eastern, industrialized or preliterate, these facial expressions are labeled with the same emotion terms: happiness, sadness, anger, fear, disgust, and surprise. And it is not simply the recognition of emotion that is universal, but the expression of emotion as well. How do we explain that the same facial muscular movements occur in Japanese and Americans in response to a stress film, or that the same facial muscular movements occur whether a New Guinean or an American is asked to show what his face would look like if his child had died, or if he were angry and about to fight, etc.?

We must abandon the notion that facial expressions are a language, where arbitrary facial muscular movements have a different meaning in each culture; but we must also attempt to explain the basis for the demonstrated pancultural facial expressions of emotion. Our neuro-cultural theory postulates a facial affect program, located within the nervous system of all human beings, linking particular facial muscular movements with particular emotions. It offers alternative nonexclusive explanations of the possible origin of the linkages in the affect program between the felt emotion and the movement of the facial muscles. Our theory holds that the elicitors, the particular events which activate the affect program, are in largest part socially learned and culturally variable, and that many of the consequences of an aroused emotion also are culturally variable, but that the facial muscular movement which will occur for a particular emotion (if not interfered with by display rules) is dictated by this affect program and is universal.

While most of the elicitors and many of the consequences are socially learned and vary with culture, there is some uniformity in both within a culture, and even more within smaller social groupings in a culture. Thus all human beings grow up learning that one facial expression is most often elicited by one set of events while another facial expression is elicited by a different set of events. Further, they learn that a facial expression is typically seen with one set of motor adaptive actions, with particular verbal and vocal behavior, and perhaps with certain psychophysiological changes.

These sets of elicitors and consequences are, then, included with memories, images, and cognitions as part of the experience of happiness, anger, sadness, etc. It is their more or less systematic cooccurrence with facial expressions which leads people to describe these facial behaviors as expressions of emotion. While we claim that most of the elicitors and consequences of each emotion vary with culture, there must be some similarity across cultures as well. Perhaps on an abstract or general level there are commonalities across cultures in some of the elicitors of each emotion, or in some of the consequences, or in both. Or perhaps this is so only at a very early period in life, where similarities across cultures are due to a possible few innate relationships between an elicitor or a consequence and an emotion. These are questions for which there are no conclusive data as yet.

In closing we want again to emphasize that our theory postulates culture differences in facial expression as well as universals, provides a number of explanations as to the source of cultural differences, and describes how these differences may be manifest. It was designed to distinguish cultural differences from universals so that each could be more readily studied. With the establishment of pancultural facial expressions and the availability of a procedure for measuring facial expressions (FAST), it is now feasible to study systematically the differences in facial expression across cultures. In our laboratory we are at present studying cultural differences in display rules and investigating how expression and recognition of emotion in the face vary with individual differences in mood and personality within our own culture.

REFERENCES

Allport, F. H. *Social psychology*. Boston: Houghton Mifflin, 1924.

Andrew, R. J. Evolution of facial expression. *Science*, 1963, **142**, 1034–1041.

Andrew, R. J. The origins of facial expressions. *Scientific American*, 1965, **213**, 88–94.

Asch, S. E. *Social psychology*. Englewood Cliffs, N.J.: Prentice-Hall, 1952.

Averill, J. R., Opton, E. M., Jr., & Lazarus, R. S. Cross-cultural studies of psychophysiological responses during stress and emotion. *International Journal of Psychology*, 1969, **4**, 88–102.

Birdwhistell, R. L. The kinesic level in the investigation of emotions. In P. H. Knapp (Ed.), *Expression of the emotions in man*. New York: International Universities Press, 1963. Pp. 123–139.

Birdwhistell, R. L. *Kinesics and context*. Philadelphia: University of Pennsylvania Press, 1970.

Boucher, J. D., & Ekman, P. A replication of Schlosberg's evaluation of Woodworth's scale of emotion. Paper presented at the meeting of the Western Psychological Association, 1965.

Bruner, J. S., & Tagiuri, R. The perception of people. In G. Lindzey (Ed.), *Handbook of social psychology*. Vol. 2. Cambridge: Addison-Esley, 1954. Pp. 634–654.

Darwin, C. *The Expression of the emotions in man and animals*. London: John Murray, 1872.

Dashiell, J. F. A new method of measuring reactions to facial expression of emotion. *Psychology Bulletin*, 1927, **24**, 174–175.

Dickey, E. C., & Knower, F. H. A note on some ethnological differences in recognition of simulated expressions of the emotions. *American Journal of Sociology*, 1941, **47**, 190–193.

Dittmann, A. T. Review of Ray L. Birdwhistell, Kinesics and context. *Psychiatry*, 1971, **34** (3).

Eibl-Eibesfeldt, I. *Ethology: The biology of behavior*. New York: Holt, Rinehart & Winston, 1970.

Ekman, P. Communication through nonverbal behavior: A source of information about an interpersonal relationship. In S. S. Tomkins & C. E. Izard (Eds.), *Affect, cognition, and personality*. New York: Springer Press, 1965. Pp. 390–442.

Ekman, P. The recognition and display of facial behavior in literate and non-literate cultures. Paper presented at the symposium "Universality of the Emotions" of the American Psychological Association, 1968.

Ekman, P., & Friesen, W. V. Origin, usage, and coding: The basis for five categories of nonverbal behavior. Paper presented at the Symposium on Communication Theory and Linguistic Models, Buenos Aires, 1967. In Veron, E., and others, *Lenguaje y comunicacion social*. Buenos Aires: Nueva Vision, 1969.

Ekman, P., & Friesen, W. V. Nonverbal behavior in psychotherapy research. In J. M. Shlien (Ed.), *Research in psychotherapy*. Vol. 3. Washington: American Psychological Association, 1968. Pp. 179–216.

Ekman, P., & Friesen, W. V. Nonverbal leakage and clues to deception. *Psychiatry*, 1969, **32** (1), 88–106. (a)

Ekman, P., & Friesen, W. V. The repertoire of nonverbal behavior. *Semiotica*, 1969, **1** (1), 49–98. (b)

Ekman, P., & Friesen, W. V. Progress report, 1970, Grant No. MH 11976–05, National Institute of Mental Health.

Ekman, P., & Friesen, W. V. Constants across cultures in the face and emotion. *Journal of Personality and Social Psychology*, 1971, **17** (2), 124–129.

Ekman, P., Friesen, W. V., & Ellsworth, P. *Emotion in the human face: Guidelines for research and an integration of findings*. New York: Pergamon Press, 1971.

Ekman, P., Friesen, W. V., & Tomkins, S. S. Facial Affect Scoring Technique (FAST): A first validity study. *Semiotica*, 1971, **3** (1), 37–58.

Ekman, P., Heider, E., Friesen, W. V., & Heider, K. Facial expression in a preliterate culture: Further evidence of universals. In preparation.

Ekman, P., Sorenson, E. R., & Friesen, W. V. Pan-cultural elements in facial displays of emotions. *Science*, 1969, **164** (3875), 86–88.

Engen, T., Levy, N., & Schlosberg, H. A new series of facial expressions. *American Psychologist*, 1957, **12**, 264–266.

Frijda, N. H. Recognition of emotion. In L. Berkowitz (Ed.), *Advances in experimental social psychology*. Vol. 4. New York: Academic Press, 1969. Pp. 169–223.

Frois-Wittmann, J. The judgment of facial expression. *Journal of Experimental Psychology*, 1930, **13**, 113–151.

Fulcher, J. S. "Voluntary" facial expression in blind and seeing children. *Archives of Psychology*, 1942, **38** (272), 1–49.

Gajdusek, D. C. Kuru. *Transactions of the Royal Society of Tropical Medicine and Hygiene*, 1963, **57** (3), 151–169.

Goffman, E. *Behavior in public places*. New York: Free Press, 1963.

Goodenough, F. L. Expression of the emotions in a blind-deaf child. *Journal of Abonormal and Social Psychology*, 1932–33, **27**, 328–333.

Haggard, E. A., & Isaacs, K. S. Micro-momentary facial expressions as indicators of ego mechanisms in psychotherapy. In L. A. Gottschalk & A. H. Auerbach (Eds.), *Methods of research in psychotherapy*. New York: Appleton-Century-Crofts, 1966. Pp. 154–165.

Hebb, D. O. Emotion in man and animal: An analysis of the intuitive processes of recognition. *Psychological Review*, 1946, **53**, 88–106.

Heider, K. G. *The Dugum Dani: A Pupuan culture in the highlands of west New Guinea.* Chicago: Aldine, 1970.

Hinde, R. A. *Animal behaviour.* New York: McGraw-Hill, 1966.

Honkavarra, S. The psychology of expression. *British Journal of Psychology,* 1961, **32,** 1–96.

Huber, E. *Evolution of facial musculature and facial expression.* Baltimore: Johns Hopkins University Press, 1931.

Hunt, W. A. Recent developments in the field of emotion. *Psychological Bulletin,* 1941, **38** (5), 249–276.

Izard, C. E. Cross-cultural research findings on development and recognition of facial behavior. Paper presented at the symposium "Universality of the Emotions" of the American Psychological Association, 1968.

Izard, C. E. *Face of emotion.* New York: Appleton-Century-Crofts, 1971.

Klineberg, O. Emotional expression in Chinese literature. *Journal of Abnormal and Social Psychology,* 1938, **33,** 517–520.

Klineberg, O. *Social psychology.* New York: Henry Holt, 1940.

LaBarre, W. The cultural basis of emotions and gestures. *Journal of Personality,* 1947, **16,** 49–68.

Lazarus, R. S., Opton, E., Jr., Tomita, M., & Kodama, M. A cross-cultural study of stress-reaction patterns in Japan. *Journal of Personality and Social Psychology,* 1966, **4** (6) 622–633.

Lorenz, K. *Studies in animal and human behavior.* Vol. I. Cambridge: Harvard University Press, 1970.

Marler, P. Developments in the study of animal communication. In P. R. Bell (Ed.), *Darwin's biological work.* New York: John Wiley, 1959. Pp. 150–206.

Morris, D. *Patterns of reproductive behavior.* New York: McGraw-Hill, 1970.

Murphy, G., Murphy, L. B., & Newcomb, T. M. *Experimental social psychology.* (Rev. ed.) New York: Harper Brothers, 1937.

Nummenmaa, T. *The Language of the face.* (Jyvaskyla Studies in Education, Psychology and Social Research 9) Jyvaskyla, Finland: Jyvaskylan Yliopistoyhdistys, 1964.

Plutchik, R. *The emotions: Facts, theories, and a new model.* New York: Random House, 1962.

Schlosberg, H. Three dimensions of emotion. *Psychological Review,* 1954, **61,** 81–88.

Sorenson, E. R., & Gajdusek, D. C. The study of child behavior and development in primitive cultures. A research archive for ethnopediatric film investigations of styles in the patterning of the nervous system. *Pediatrics,* 1966, **37** (1, Pt. 2), 149–243.

Tagiuri, R. Person perception. In G. Lindzey & E. Aronson (Eds.), *The handbook of social psychology.* (2d ed.) Reading, Mass.: Addison-Wesley, 1968. Pp. 395–449.

Thompson, J. Development of facial expression of emotion in blind and seeing children. *Archives of Psychology,* 1941, **37** (264), 1–47.

Tomkins, S. S. *Affect, imagery, consciousness.* Vol. 1. *The positive affects.* New York: Springer, 1962.

Tomkins, S. S. *Affect, imagery, consciousness.* Vol. 2. *The negative affects.* New York: Springer, 1963.

Tomkins, S. S. Personal communication, 1971.

Tomkins, S. S., & McCarter, R. What and where are the primary affects? Some evidence for a theory. *Perceptual and Motor Skills*, 1964, **18**, 119–158.

Triandis, H. C., & Lambert, W. W. A restatement and test of Schlosberg's theory of emotion with two kinds of subjects from Greece. *Journal of Abnormal and Social Psychology*, 1958, **56** (3), 321–328.

Chronological List
of Contents of the Nebraska
Symposia on Motivation

1953 (Vol. 1)

Brown, J. S. Problems presented by the concept of acquired drive, pp. 1–21.

Harlow, H. F. Motivation as a factor in new responses, pp. 24–49.

Postman, L. J. The experimental analysis of motivational factors in perception, pp. 59–108.

Nowlis, V. The development and modification of motivational systems in personality, pp. 114–138.

Newcomb, T. M. Motivation in social behavior, pp. 139–161.

Mowrer, O. H. Motivation and neurosis, pp. 162–185.

1954 (Vol. 2)

Farber, I. E. Anxiety as a drive state, pp. 1–46.

Atkinson, J. W. Exploration using imaginative thought to assess the strength of human motives, pp. 56–112.

Ritchie, B. F. A logical and experimental analysis of the laws of motivation, pp. 121–176.

Festinger, L. Motivation leading to social behavior, pp. 191–219.

Klein, G. S. Need and regulation, pp. 224–274.

Nissen, H. W. The nature of the drive as innate determinant of behavioral organization, pp. 281–321.

1955 (Vol. 3)

Maslow, A. Deficiency motivation and growth motivation, pp. 1–30.

McClelland, D. C. Some social consequences of achievement motivation, pp. 41–65.

Olds, J. Physiological mechanisms of reward, pp. 73–139.

Peak, H. Attitude and motivation, pp. 149–189.

Young, P. T. The role of hedonic processes in motivation, pp. 193–238.

Rotter, J. B. The role of the psychological situation in determining the direction of human behavior, pp. 245–269.

1956 (Vol. 4)

Beach, F. A. Characteristics of masculine "sex drive," pp. 1–32.
Koch, S. Behavior as "intrinsically" regulated: Work notes towards a pre-theory of phenomena called "motivational," pp. 42–87.
Marx, M. H. Some relations between frustration and drive, pp. 92–130.
Miller, D. R., & Swanson, G. E. The study of conflict, pp. 137–174.
Seward, J. P. A neurological approach to motivation, pp. 180–208.
Solomon, R. L., & Brush, E. S. Experimentally derived conceptions of anxiety and aversion, pp. 212–305.

1957 (Vol. 5)

Morgan, C. T. Physiological mechanisms of motivation, pp. 1–35.
Lindsley, D. B. Psychophysiology and motivation, pp. 44–105.
Rodnick, E. H., & Garmezy, N. An experimental approach to the study of motivation in schizophrenia, pp. 109–184.
Wittenborn, J. R. Inferring the strength of drive, pp. 191–259.
Sears, P. S. Problems in the investigation of achievement and self-esteem motivation, pp. 265–339.
Osgood, C. E. Motivational dynamics of language behavior, pp. 348–424.

1958 (Vol. 6)

Bolles, R. C. The usefulness of the drive concept, pp. 1–33.
Estes, W. K. Stimulus-response theory of drive, pp. 35–69.
Spence, K. W. Behavior theory and selective learning, pp. 73–107.
Littman, R. A. Motives, history and causes, pp. 114–168.
Eriksen, C. W. Unconscious processes, pp. 169–227.
Malmo, R. B. Measurement of drive: An unsolved problem in psychology, pp. 229–265.

1959 (Vol. 7)

Schneirla, T. C. An evolutionary and developmental theory of biphasic processes underlying approach and withdrawal, pp. 1–42.
Hess, E. The relationship between imprinting and motivation, pp. 44–77.
Cattell, R. B. The dynamic calculus: Concepts and crucial experiments, pp. 84–134.
Levin, H., & Baldwin, A. L. Pride and shame in children, pp. 138–174.
Whiting, J. W. M. Sorcery, sin, and the superego. A cross-cultural study of some mechanisms of social control, pp. 174–195.
Janis, I. L. Motivational factors in the resolution of decisional conflicts, pp. 198–231.

Logan, F. A. The free behavior situation, pp. 99–128.
Edwards, A. L. The assessment of human motives by means of personality scales, pp. 135–162.
Mandler, G. The interruption of behavior, pp. 163–219.
Schachter, S., & Latané, B. Crime, cognition, and the autonomic nervous system, pp. 221–273.

1965 (Vol. 13)

Kendler, H. H. Motivation and behavior, pp. 1–23.
Leeper, R. W. Some needed developments in the motivational theory of emotions, pp. 25–122.
Premack, D. Reinforcement theory, pp. 123–180.
Hunt, J. McV. Intrinsic motivation and its role in psychological development, pp. 189–282.
Campbell, D. T. Ethnocentric and other altruistic motives, pp. 283–311.
Guilford, J. P. Motivation in an informational psychology, pp. 313–332.

1966 (Vol. 14)

Holt, R. R. Measuring libidinal and aggressive motives and their controls by means of the Rorschach test, pp. 1–47.
Burke, C. J. Linear models for Pavlovian conditioning, pp. 49–66.
Masling, J. Role-related behavior of the subject and psychologist and its effects upon psychological data, pp. 67–103.
Dethier, V. G. Insects and the concept of motivation, pp. 105–136.
Helson, H. Some problems in motivation from the point of view of the theory of adaptation level, pp. 137–182.
Malamud, W. The concept of motivation in psychiatric practice, pp. 183–200.

1967 (Vol. 15)

Berlyne, D. E. Arousal and reinforcement, pp. 1–110.
Scott, J. P. The development of social motivation, pp. 111–132.
Katz, I. The socialization of academic motivation in minority group children, pp. 133–191.
Kelley, H. H. Attribution theory in social psychology, pp. 192–238.
Pettigrew, T. F. Social evaluation theory: Convergences and applications, pp. 241–311.

1968 (Vol. 16)

Grossmann, S. P. The physiological basis of specific and nonspecific motivational processes, pp. 1–46.
McClearn, G. E. Genetics and motivation of the mouse, pp. 47–83.

Alphabetical List
of Contents of the Nebraska
Symposia on Motivation
by Author

Aronfreed, J. Aversive control of socialization. 1968, **16**, 271–320.

Aronson, E. Some antecedents of interpersonal attraction. 1969, **17**, 143–173.

Atkinson, J. W. Exploration using imaginative thought to assess the strength of human motives. 1954, **2**, 56–112.

Bandura, A. Social learning through imitation. 1962, **10**, 211–269.

Barker, R. G. Ecology and motivation. 1960, **8**, 1–49.

Beach, F. A. Characteristics of masculine "sex drive." 1956, **4**, 1–32.

Berkowitz, L. The contagion of violence: An S-R mediational analysis of some effects of observed aggression. 1970, **18**, 95–135.

Berlyne, D. E. Arousal and reinforcement. 1967, **15**, 1–110.

Bindra, D. The interrelated mechanisms of reinforcement and motivation, and the nature of their influence on response. 1969, **17**, 1–33.

Birch, D. A motivational interpretation of extinction. 1961, **9**, 179–197.

Black, R. W. Incentive motivation and the parameters of reward in instrumental conditioning. 1969, **17**, 85–137.

Bolles, R. C. The usefulness of the drive concept. 1958, **6**, 1–33.

Brehm, J. W. Motivational effects of cognitive dissonance. 1962, **10**, 51–77.

Brown, J. S. Problems presented by the concept of acquired drive. 1953, **1**, 1–21.

Burke, C. J. Linear models for Pavlovian conditioning. 1966, **14**, 49–66.

Campbell, D. T. Ethnocentric and other altruistic motives. 1965, **13**, 283–311.

Cattell, R. B. The dynamic calculus: Concepts and crucial experiments. 1959, **7**, 84–134.

Cook, S. W. Motives in a conceptual analysis of attitude-related behavior. 1969, **17**, 179–231.

Denenberg, V. H. The mother as a motivator. 1970, **18**, 69–93.

Dethier, V. G. Insects and the concept of motivation. 1966, **14**, 105–136.

Deutsch, M. Cooperation and trust: Some theoretical notes. 1962, **10**, 275–319.

Donaldson, M. Preconditions of inference. 1971, **19**, 81–106.

Edwards, A. L. The assessment of human motives by means of personality scales. 1964, **12**, 135–162.

Ekman, P. Universals and cultural differences in facial expressions of emotion. 1971, **19**, 207–284.

Elkind, D. Cognitive growth cycles in mental development. 1971, **19**, 1–32.

Epstein, S. The measurement of drive and conflict in humans: Theory and experiment. 1962, **10**, 127–206.

Eriksen, C. W. Unconscious processes. 1958, **6**, 169–227.

Estes, W. K. Stimulus-response theory of drive. 1958, **6**, 35–69.

Exline, R. Visual interaction: The glances of power and preference. 1971, **19**, 163–206.

Falk, J. L. The behavioral regulation of water-electrolyte balance. 1961, **9**, 1–33.

Farber, I. E. Anxiety as a drive state. 1954, **2**, 1–46.

Festinger, L. Motivation leading to social behavior. 1954, **2**, 191–219.

Grossman, S. P. The physiological basis of specific and non-specific motivational processes. 1968, **16**, 1–46.

Guilford, J. P. Motivation in an informational psychology. 1965, **13**, 313–332.

Harlow, H. F. Motivation as a factor in new responses. 1953, **1**, 24–49.

Heckhausen, H. Achievement motive research: Current problems and some contributions towards a general theory of motivation. 1968, **16**, 103–174.

Heider, F. The Gestalt theory of motivation. 1960, **8**, 145–172.

Helson, H. Some problems in motivation from the point of view of the theory of adaptation level. 1966, **14**, 137–182.

Hess, E. The relationship between imprinting and motivation. 1959, **7**, 44–77.

Hilgard, E. R. The motivational relevance of hypnosis. 1964, **12**, 1–44.

Holt, R. R. Measuring libidinal and aggressive motives and their controls by means of the Rorschach test. 1966, **14**, 1–47.

Hunt, J. McV. Intrinsic motivation and its role in psychological development. 1965, **13**, 189–282.

Janis, I. L. Motivational factors in the resolution of decisional conflicts. 1959, **7**, 198–231.

Katz, I. The socialization of academic motivation in minority group children. 1967, **15**, 133–191.

Kelley, H. H. Attribution theory in social psychology. 1967, **15**, 192–238.

Kelly, G. A. Europe's matrix of decision. 1962, **10**, 83–123.

Kendler, H. H. Motivation and behavior. 1965, **13**, 1–23.

King, J. A. Ecological psychology: An approach to motivation. 1970, **18**, 1–33.

Klein, G. S. Need and regulation. 1954. **2**, 224–274.

Koch, S. Behavior as "intrinsically" regulated: Work notes towards a pre-theory of phenomena called "motivational." 1956, **4**, 42–87.

Lazarus, R. S. Emotions and adaptation: Conceptual and empirical relations. 1968, **16**, 175–266.

Leeper, R. W. Some needed developments in the motivational theory of emotions. 1965, **13**, 25–122.

Levin, H., & Baldwin, A. L. Pride and shame in children. 1959, **7**, 138–173.

Levine, S. Hormones and conditioning. 1968, **16**, 85–101.

Lindsley, D. B. Psychophysiology and motivation. 1957, **5**, 44–105.

Rapaport, D. On the psychoanalytic theory of motivation. 1960, **8**, 173–247.

Ritchie, B. F. A logical and experimental analysis of the laws of motivation. 1954, **2**, 121–176.

Rodnick, E. H., & Garmezy, N. An experimental approach to the study of motivation in schizophrenia. 1957, **5**, 109–184.

Rogers, C. R. Actualizing tendency in relation to "motives" and to consciousness. 1963, **11**, 1–24.

Rotter, J. B. The role of the psychological situation in determining the direction of human behavior. 1955, **3**, 245–269.

Sarason, S. B. The contents of human problem solving. 1961, **9**, 147–174.

Schachter, S., & Latané, B. Crime, cognition, and the autonomic nervous system. 1964, **12**, 221–273.

Schneirla, T. C. An evolutionary and developmental theory of biphasic processes underlying approach and withdrawal. 1959, **7**, 1–42.

Scott, J. P. The development of social motivation. 1967, **15**, 111–132.

Sears, P. S. Problems in the investigation of achievement and self-esteem motivation. 1957, **5**, 265–339.

Sears, R. R. Dependency motivation. 1963, **11**, 25–64.

Seward, J. P. A neurological approach to motivation. 1956, **4**, 180–208.

Solomon, R. L., & Brush, E. S. Experimentally derived conceptions of anxiety and aversion. 1956, **4**, 212–305.

Spence, K. W. Behavior theory and selective learning. 1958, **6**, 73–107.

Taylor, D. W. Toward an informational processing theory of motivation. 1960, **8**, 51–79.

Teitelbaum, P. Disturbances in feeding and drinking behavior after hypothalamic lesions. 1961, **9**, 39–65.

Toman, W. On the periodicity of motivation. 1960, **8**, 80–95.

Vinacke, W. E. Motivation as a complex problem. 1962, **10**, 1–46.

Walker, E. L. Psychological complexity as a basis for a theory of motivation and choice. 1964, **12**, 47–95.

White, R. W. Competence and the psychosexual stages of development. 1960, **8**, 97–141.

Whiting, J. W. M. Sorcery, sin, and the superego. A cross-cultural study of some mechanisms of social control. 1959, **7**, 174–195.

Wike, E. L. Secondary reinforcement: Some research and theoretical issues. 1969, **17**, 39–82.

Wittenborn, J. R. Inferring the strength of drive. 1957, **5**, 191–259.

Young, P. T. The role of hedonic processes in motivation. 1955, **3**, 193–238.

Zimbardo, P. H. The human choice: Individuation, reason, and order versus deindividuation, impulse, and chaos. 1969, **17**, 237–307.

Subject Index

Accelerating mental growth, 21–25
  in children, 23–25
Alethic concepts in inference making, 86–87
Applications of findings of imperfect communication, 148–153
  advertising, 150
  nonverbal versus verbal behaviors, 148–150
  psychopathology of communication, 153
  social reinforcement learning, 150–151
Arbitrary errors in inferential responses, 87–88
Argentina. *See* Literate cultures
Attainment of mastery in mental growth, 3

Brazil. *See* Literate cultures

Chile. *See* Literate cultures
Circumstantial restraints in verbal responses, 85
Cognitive growth cycles in mental development, 1–30
  anecdotal evidence, 7–8
  competence versus performance, 27
  conclusions, 28–30
  corollary hypotheses, 6
  critical periods, 18–21
  final (play) stage, 9
  language, 10–14
  mental acceleration, 21–25

  motivation, intrinsic and extrinsic, 25–28
  overreliance on intrinsic motivation, 28
  perception, 6–10
  realization cycles, 1–4
  reasoning, 14–18
  research evidence, 8
  rote memory, 4–6
Critical periods in cognitive growth, 18–21

Dani. *See* Preliterate cultures
Deferred imitation in rote memory, 5
Developmental sequence in response making, 92

Epistemic concepts in inference making, 86
Esterline-Angus Event Recorder, 174

Facial affect program, 216–224
  assumptions regarding brain functioning, 216–218
  blends of emotions, 222–224
  linkage between movements and emotions, 218–221
  seven emotions, 213, 221–222
Facial Affect Scoring Technique (FAST), xii, 256, 257, 260–262
  in measurement of facial expressions, 248–253
Facial expressions of emotion, 108–109, 207–280

295

Author Index

300